A Practical Approach to Merchandising Mathematics

A Practical Approach to Merchandising Mathematics

$\leqq \; \Sigma \; \sqrt{\;} \; \pm \; \neq \; / \; \times \; \} \; \div \; \approx \; =$

LINDA M. CUSHMAN
SYRACUSE UNIVERSITY

Fairchild Books
NEW YORK

Executive Editor: Olga T. Kontzias
Acquisitions Editor: Joseph Miranda
Editorial Development Director: Jennifer Crane
Associate Art Director: Erin Fitzsimmons
Production Director: Ginger Hillman
Production Editor: Jessica Rozler
Project Management: GEX Publishing Services
Cover Design: Erin Fitzsimmons
Text Design: Rachel Reiss
Page Composition: GEX Publishing Services

Library of Congress Catalog Card Number: 2007928028
ISBN: 978-1-56367-624-6
GST R 133004424

Printed in The United States of America
TP13

To Jack, Chelsie, and Jordan

Contents

Extended Contents

4. Reductions   83

Preface

Retailing today encompasses every business function necessary to procure goods from a manufacturer and facilitate the sale of these goods to the end user or consumer. These functions may include product development, store operations, visual merchandising, marketing/promotions, human resource management, electronic or website sales, and buying and planning. This textbook is devoted to mastering the mathematical concepts, techniques, and analysis utilized in the buying and planning process.

Chapter 1 provides a brief review of basic mathematical concepts. Although retail buyers use calculators and computerized spreadsheet programs daily, it is important to recognize that the answer can only be as good as the information entered. Included in every chapter are three chapter review assessments. Although you may be rusty, the mathematical concepts in the chapter should be familiar to you. Your instructor may assign one or more chapter review assessments for Chapter 1 **before** you begin in order to determine any areas of weakness that will require additional focus.

Each chapter begins with definitions and mathematical formulas that will be useful in mastering the concepts in that particular chapter. Although the glossary at the end of the text provides a thorough, alphabetical list of terms, this format gives you fast access to those terms and formulas that will assist you in the chapter as you work.

New concepts introduced in each chapter are followed by a practice section entitled "Practicing What You Have Learned." The answers to these problems are located in the back of the text, providing a quick way for you to ensure proficiency and confidence in each concept. Your instructor may assign these pr oblems for homework and ask that you show each step of your work.

Chapter review assessments are provided at the end of every chapter and may be assigned by your instructor as homework to determine specific areas of weakness that should be targeted for additional study or as a quiz for learning assessment. Unlike the problems in "Practicing What You Have Learned," many of the chapter review questions ask you to apply several concepts to the same problem. These pages are perforated and can be removed and given directly to the instructor.

Following the chapter review problems in each chapter is a review of basic Excel spreadsheet concepts in an Excel Spreadsheet Concepts Tutorial. The Tutorial in Chapter 1 is a fairly comprehensive description of how to use many of the basic Excel functions. Depending on your familiarity with the Excel software, you may need to refer to this Tutorial often when completing the practical application problems assigned by your instructor. The tutorials at the end of Chapters 2 through 9 provide a basic guideline for analyzing the concepts included in that chapter using Excel. Each textbook includes a CD-ROM that contains a set of pre-programmed worksheets to be used with each of the tutorials and some of the practice problems. You will be instructed at the beginning of each exercise which file will need to be opened. Although you will not be able to save files to the CD provided, instructions will also be given for saving your work on the hard drive of your computer or on a separate travel drive.

Each chapter concludes with a set of practical application problems that reinforce the concepts covered in the text. The Excel review problems themselves are comprehensive in nature. Each of the questions is a mini case study requiring the application of multiple concepts in a real-world situation. Unlike in the tutorials, these problems begin with a blank spreadsheet and require a great deal of analysis and creativity on the part of each student to effectively and professionally present the information and results.

Computerized spreadsheets are only as accurate as the information and formulas that are entered. However, the presentation of material in spreadsheet format can be a useful tool in communicating information and performance results. Buyers and merchandisers manipulate data every day with the assistance of computerized spreadsheets in order to reduce the time spent making mathematical calculations, organizing data, and communicating results to the organization.

Acknowledgments

I am very grateful to the reviewers, industry executives, and educators who offered their expertise and suggestions for improvement. Many thanks are due to the following reviewers for their helpful comments and insight:

Special thanks and heartfelt gratitude goes to Myrna Jacobs, who spent many hours providing direction that resulted in a decidedly more professional and much less verbose presentation of this text.

Finally, I thank my husband, Jack, and children, Chelsie and Jordan, for encouraging me throughout this process. This book is the result of many hours spent away from them and would not have been possible without their understanding and willingness to help.

CHAPTER 1

Basic Math Concepts

When most people think about retail buying, the first thing that comes to mind is probably beautiful merchandise, designer goods, or maybe even the merchandise display in the retail store. Often one of the last things that comes to mind is math. The reality is that simple arithmetic concepts are at work in nearly every decision a buyer makes.

Buyers utilize percentages, fractions, and decimals every day. Buyers use percentages to plan promotional strategies and determine inventory composition. They use decimals in currency calculations and profit planning. Although a buyer does not often work in fractions, the conversion of fractions to decimals and percentages is an important and often-utilized skill.

This chapter provides a brief review of these basic mathematical concepts. Although retail buyers usually use calculators and spreadsheet programs, it is important to recognize that the answer can only be as good as the information put in.

Working with Decimals

Decimal form is the form used in monetary expressions. Decimals can be used to indicate fractions of dollars. For example, if Paul has $1.75, Paul would have 1 dollar plus 75 one-hundredths of a dollar.

The format of a decimal is represented as follows:

Example: 1.750

                ↑   ↑   ↑
             Tenths Hundredths Thousandths

You can add any number of zeros to the end of a decimal or whole number without changing the value. For example, 1.75 is equivalent to 1.7500000. Similarly, 75 is equivalent to 75.00:

$$175.00 + 25.50 + 430 \text{ should be thought of as:}$$

$$
\begin{array}{r}
175.00 \\
25.50 \\
+430.00 \\
\hline
630.50
\end{array}
$$

You multiply decimals in the same way you multiply whole numbers except you must correctly position the decimal. In order to locate the proper position of the decimal, you add the number of decimal places in each of the numbers to be multiplied. For example:

$$
\begin{array}{r}
4.30 \\
2150 \\
\underline{1260} \\
14.750 \\
\uparrow
\end{array}
$$

There are a total of three decimal places in the numbers to be multiplied so you move the decimal three places from the right in the answer.

Dividing decimals is also similar to dividing whole numbers as long as the divisor is a whole number.

$$\downarrow \text{ Divisor}$$
$$12.00 \div 3.00 = 4.00 \leftarrow \text{Quotient}$$
$$\uparrow \text{ Dividend}$$

Just remember that the quotient or answer must have as many decimal places as the dividend.

When the divisor is a decimal, you must first make it into a whole number. Move the decimal to the right until no numbers remain after the decimal. Then, move the decimal the same number of places to the right in the dividend:

$$12.00 \div 3.05 \text{ should be thought of as } 1200 \div 305$$

In merchandising mathematics, we often need to round the decimal to the nearest hundredth, as in monetary expressions, but sometimes it will be appropriate to round to a whole number. For example, if you are calculating how many $12.00 T-shirts can be purchased with $100.00, you would answer 8 T-shirts, not 8.33 T-shirts. You cannot purchase 1/3 of a T-shirt!

Practicing What You Have Learned

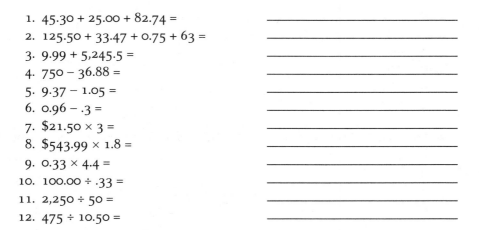

1. 45.30 + 25.00 + 82.74 = _____
2. 125.50 + 33.47 + 0.75 + 63 = _____
3. 9.99 + 5,245.5 = _____
4. 750 − 36.88 = _____
5. 9.37 − 1.05 = _____
6. 0.96 − .3 = _____
7. $21.50 × 3 = _____
8. $543.99 × 1.8 = _____
9. 0.33 × 4.4 = _____
10. 100.00 ÷ .33 = _____
11. 2,250 ÷ 50 = _____
12. 475 ÷ 10.50 = _____

Converting Percentages, Fractions, and Decimals

Merchandising concepts often involve both dollars and percents. Percents, like decimals, are parts of a whole. We express percentages in hundredths, for example:

50% is 50 ÷ 100 or .50

To convert a fraction to a percent, divide the denominator into the numerator. The result will be a decimal that you can easily convert to a percentage by moving the decimal two places to the right. For example, 4/6 = .67, and when you move the decimal two places to the right the result is 67%.

In the same way, we sometimes need to convert a percentage to decimal form. In this case, you will need to place the percentage in decimal format by moving the decimal two places to the right. Percentages are merely parts of 100. For example, 40% is the equivalent of 40/100. To create a decimal, divide 40 by 100 to get .4 and then move the decimal two places to the right to get 40%.

Practicing What You Have Learned

13. For each of the percentages listed below, convert the percentage to decimal form:
    a. 0.5% _____
    b. 25% _____
    c. 100% _____
    d. 33 1/3% _____
    e. 125% _____
    f. 75% _____
    g. 60% _____

14. For each of the decimals listed below, convert the decimal to percentage form:
    a. 0.25   _____
    b. 125.5   _____
    c. 6.345   _____
    d. .076   _____
    e. 9.9   _____
    f. 10.75   _____
    g. 0.108   _____

15. For each of the fractions listed below, convert the fraction to percentage form:
    a. 1/2   _____
    b. 1 1/2   _____
    c. 3/4   _____
    d. 33 1/2   _____
    e. 1/10   _____
    f. 2/3   _____
    g. 4/5   _____

16. A buyer purchases 3 gross (1 gross = 12 dozen) of white crew socks and 5 gross of white ankle socks. If the buyer sold every pair for $2.00 in August, how much in total revenues was earned?

17. A buyer for a local department store bought 600 pink T-shirts in 4 women's sizes for the upcoming summer season. If 15% were size small, 30% were size medium, 40% were size large, and the remaining 15% were size x-large, how many shirts were purchased in each size?

18. If a salesperson earns a monthly commission of 5% on every sale after the first $200, how much commission would be earned on monthly sales of $3,500?

19. The visual merchandising team for a specialty store borrowed 30 pairs of shoes for its back-to-school displays. Management found that the new displays resulted in an 11% increase in sales over last year's sales figure of $223,780 for the same time period. What were the sales for this year?

20. What would be the cost of 8 3/4 yards of fabric if the fabric cost $10.99 per yard?

21. Due to a recent decline in new home sales, a real estate development team plans to reduce its sales force of 300 people by 12%. How many employees will remain after the downsizing?

22. If a sale on ice cream offered 2 cones for $3.50, how much would 5 cones cost?

23. Jill's average sales during the 3 summer months she spent working at her hometown shoe salon were $860. If her sales for June were $975 and her sales for July were $543, what were her sales for August?

24. If a manufacturer has 32 dozen ruby buttons and each shirt it manufacturers requires 8 buttons, how many shirts can it manufacture?

25. The following order was placed by the accessories buyer; what is the total cost including an 8.25% sales tax?

    3 dozen belts (50% black, 50% brown) costing $3.50 each
    200 pairs of earrings costing $9.95 per pair
    24 pairs of gloves at $5.67 each

Chapter 1 Review Exercise A

Add each of the following:

1. 12.98 + 3.04 + 208 =   _____

2. $654.00 + $35.86 + $10,735.23=   _____

3. 0.978 + 0.2549 + 0.33 =   _____

Subtract each of the following:

4. $47.99 − $33.05 =   _____

5. $8,640 − $1,906.75 =   _____

6. $0.49 − $0.05 =   _____

Multiply each of the following:

7. $500 × 3.67 =   _____

8. $1,308.00 × 0.78 =   _____

9. 0.9564 × .01 =   _____

Divide each of the following:

10. $37.99 ÷ 3.3 =   _____

11. $1,047.00 ÷ 231 =   _____

12. 0.896 ÷ 0.12 =   _____

Convert each of the following as indicated:

13. 8 1/3 dozen = _____ pieces

14. 4 gross = _____ dozen

15. $260.00 ÷ 5% = _____

16. $650,000 × 52% = _____

17. 1/4 = _____ %

18. 37/100 = _____ %

19. 1 = _____ %

20. 6 2/5 = _____ %

21. The denim buyer purchased 350 pairs of juniors' jeans. If 30% were low-rise, how many pairs did she order?

22. Bondine's department store received a special shipment of 220 T-shirts for the Fourth of July. If 30% were red, 45% were white, and 25% were blue, how many of each color did the store receive?

23. Justin earned $430 in commission this week. His commission represents 17% of the total commissions earned in the shoe department this week. What is the total amount of commission for the shoe department?

Chapter 1 Review Exercise B

1. If the sweater sales for this year are $109,500 compared to sales last year of $98,000, what is the percentage increase in sweater sales?

2. A large department stored hired 75 new employees in the executive trainee program this year, of which 40% are male. How many males joined the program?

3. Jessica recently visited the local stationery store and purchased the following:

   2 dozen envelopes at 39 cents apiece
   4 boxes of monogrammed stationery at $25.99 per box
   6 colored writing pens at $3.49 each

   What was the total amount of the purchase?

4. If Percy sold 68 pairs of shoes in the first week of August and went on to sell 102 pairs, 59 pairs, and 87 pairs in the following 3 weeks, what were his average sales for August?

5. A local fabric store offers a 15% discount on all purchases of 10 or more yards of fabric. What would be the total amount of Julie's bill if she purchases 12 yards of corduroy at $9.99 per yard?

6. Wilson's Toys received 2 1/3 gross of wooden puzzles for the holiday season. How many wooden puzzles did it receive?

7. What would be the final cost of a blazer priced at $199 on sale for 40% off?

Convert each of the following as indicated:

8. 32% of $135,800 = _____

9. $1,250 × .85 = _____

10. 2/9 = _____ %

11. 11/16 = _____ %

12. 3 1/2 = _____ %

13. 54 units = _____ dozen

14. 6.82 of 10 = _____ %

15. 3.75 of 100 = _____ %

Chapter 1 Review Exercise C

1. What is the total cost of the following order?

   3 dozen pairs of socks at $2.49 per pair
   115 ties at $13.50 each
   2 1/2 dozen silver money clips at $12.80 each

2. Eric sells houses for a local realty office. His average home sales for the 3-month summer selling season were 14 sales. If he sold 18 houses in August and only 9 houses in July, how many houses did he sell in June?

3. Fresh food sales in a convenience store chain are calculated at 44% of total store sales. What would fresh food sales be if the total store sales were $1,249,500?

4. Paula purchased 6 1/3 yards of material at a price of $14.99 per yard. If sales tax on the purchase was 8%, what was the total cost of the purchase?

5. A candy store has a sale on lollipops offering 5 for $1.00. How much do 8 lollipops cost?

6. In the latest shipment of 6 dozen picture frames, Kelly found that 4% were broken. How many picture frames arrived broken?

7. Doug earns 12% commission on all sales after the first $250. If Doug sells $1,700 in merchandise during the period, how much commission will he earn?

Convert each of the following as indicated:

8. 43% of $65,400 = _____

9. $2,575 × 4.3 = _____

10. 6/10 = _____ %

11. 23/25 = _____ %

12. 8 1/4 dozen = _____ units

13. 99 units = _____ dozen

14. 79 of 100 = _____ %

15. $5,600 ÷ 38% = _____

Basic Spreadsheet Concepts
Excel Tutorial 1

Throughout this textbook you will be using Excel (or a similar spreadsheet application) to perform the mathematical calculations associated with merchandising. In this Tutorial, you will have a chance to practice many basic spreadsheet operations as well as entering formulas that will be used in subsequent Tutorials. As you work your way through the rest of this textbook, you will often be reminded to refer to the instructions in this Tutorial if you have forgotten how to perform the operations required in the lesson.

Opening a File

1. Open Excel (usually located on your desktop as an icon or can be accessed from the Start menu at the bottom left-hand corner of your screen).

2. Place the CD that comes with your textbook into the CD drive. Locate the file named Lesson1.1.xls and from the **File** Menu and choose **Open>Lesson1.1.xls**. Your screen should resemble **Figure 1.1**.

Fig. 1.1:

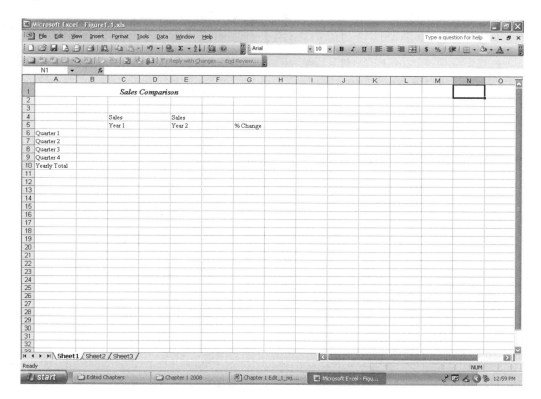

Entering Data

3. To enter data in a cell, click on the cell and enter the data, then press **Enter** or click on the green check mark (✓) in the formula bar. Now, enter the following data in the appropriate cells:

Under the column **Sales for Year 1**:　　　　Under the column **Sales for Year 2**:
Quarter 1, enter **40,000**　　　　　　　　　Quarter 1, enter **43,000**
Quarter 2, enter **38,000**　　　　　　　　　Quarter 2, enter **41,000**
Quarter 3, enter **41,000**　　　　　　　　　Quarter 3, enter **44,000**
Quarter 4, enter **48,000**　　　　　　　　　Quarter 4, enter **53,000**

Formatting Numbers

4. The sales figures you have just entered need to be represented as dollar amounts. Each cell in Excel defaults to a "general" format. The figures you just entered need to be represented as dollar sales figures, so you will need to format the data as currency.

5. Place your cursor in cell **C6**. Click on the cell. Holding the left mouse button down, drag your cursor down to cell **C9** and then release the button. The highlighted area can now be formatted. Click on **Format>Cells**, select **Number** from the box that appears, and then click on **Currency**. In the **Sample** box, you can see how your formatting will look. You should format the currency with 0 decimals and a $ (e.g., $40,000). Press **Enter** to indicate that the selection is correct.

6. Repeat this process in cells **E6 through E9**. Your screen should now look like **Figure 1.2**.

Fig. 1.2:

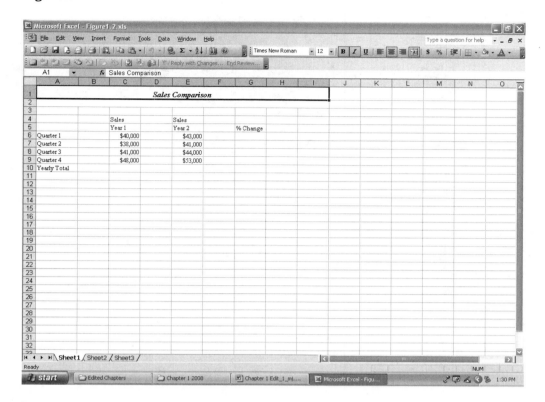

Entering Formulas

Now you want to add the figures for Year 1 Sales.

7. Click on cell **C10** (this is where you want the answer to be) and choose the **Auto-Sum (Σ)** symbol located in the Formatting Toolbar. You will notice that a flashing box forms around the data you entered in cells C6 through C9 and a formula appears in the active cell (C10). This formula, **=SUM(C6:C9)**, will add the data in the cells that are encircled by the flashing box. Press **Enter**. Your answer, 167,000, appears in cell **C10**.

> *HINT:* If the formula is incorrect, press the backspace key one time and your cursor will flash within the parentheses in the selected cell. Without moving the cursor, type the following: **C6:C9** (make sure you do not add any spaces). Then press **Enter** or click on the check mark (✓). A correct yearly total should then appear in cell **C10**.

8. Your screen should resemble **Figure 1.3**.

Fig. 1.3:

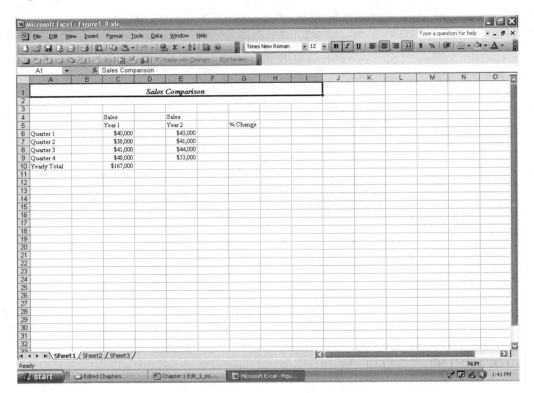

HINT: You should always estimate the sum in your head as a double-check method. The estimated number and the formula should yield approximately the same answer.

Copying Formulas

9. Click on cell **C10** and then click on **Copy** in the Toolbar or choose **Edit>Copy** from the pull-down menu. You will see a flashing box form around cell **C10**. Next, click on cell **E10** and click **Paste** located in the toolbar or choose **Edit>Paste** from the pull-down menu. A yearly total should appear in cell **E10**. Refer to **Figure 1.4**.

Fig. 1.4:

Copy and Paste Tools

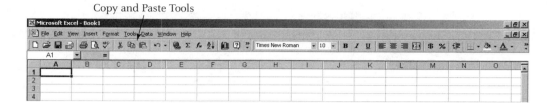

HINT: When you copy and paste a formula, Excel automatically adjusts the cell references in the pasted formula to the new cell. Check the formula in cell E10. Where your original formula reads =SUM(C6:C9) the newly pasted formula now reads =SUM(E6:E9).

Creating Formulas

10. Now determine the percentage change in sales over a two-year period. To do so, calculate

$$\frac{\text{TY Sales} - \text{LY Sales}}{\text{LY Sales}}$$

(Where TY = This Year and LY= Last Year or in this example TY = Year 2 and LY = Year 1)

11. Click on cell **G6** and enter the following formula; be sure that you do not type extra spaces: **=(E6-C6)/C6**.
    When you are finished typing the formula, press **Enter**. Your answer should read **0.075**. The cell is not formatted for percentages yet. The next few steps will describe how to format the cell for percentages.

12. Use Copy and Paste as you did in **Step 10** to find the % Change for the remaining three quarters and for the year. Your screen should now resemble **Figure 1.5**.

HINT: You can select a cell to copy and paste the formula to a **range** of cells. Click on cell **G6** (the cell you want to copy) and choose **Copy**. Then hold down the left mouse button to highlight each cell in which you would like the formula to be copied (**G7 through G10**). When the proper cells are highlighted the first cell (**G7**) will appear white but the following cells will be highlighted. You may then release the left mouse button and choose **Paste**.

Fig. 1.5:

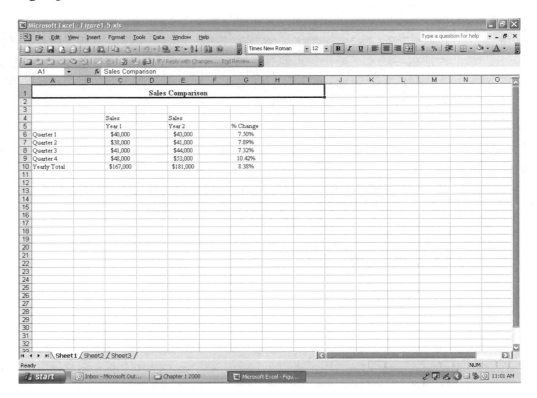

Completing the Formatting

13. Now that you have completed the % Change in sales for the two yearly periods, you will format the decimals into percentages. Click on cell **G6** and hold down the left mouse button while dragging down to **G10**.

14. When the cells are highlighted, choose **Format Cells**. Choose the **Number** tab from the dialog box.

15. Select **Percentage**. Make sure that the number of decimal places indicates **2**. Select **OK** to complete the formatting function.

> *HINT:* The number of decimal places can be changed as necessary by either clicking on the up arrow or simply typing in the desired number of decimal places in the **Format Cells** dialog box. Your instructor may have a preference about the number of decimal places to be used when formatting currency and percentages; otherwise, use what is indicated by the text.

16. Your calculations are complete for this assignment. Before you learn to save your work and print out a copy for grading, you need to format the spreadsheet so that is visually pleasing, easy to read, and professional.

17. Highlight cells **C6 through G10** by clicking on cell **C6** and holding down the left mouse button while dragging down to cell **C10 and over to cell G10.**

18. When this area is highlighted, choose **Format>Cells** just as you did in **Step 14**.

19. Choose the **Alignment** tab. You will see a small pull-down menu labeled **Horizontal**. Click the down arrow and choose **Center**. Then choose **OK**.

Bolding and Centering Headings

20. Holding down the left mouse button, drag to select the row titles Quarter 1 through Yearly Total (**A6 through A10**). Then choose Bold **B** in the Formatting Toolbar.

21. Now, center and bold the column headings by highlighting **C4 through G5** and selecting Center **≣** and Bold **B**.

Placing a Border under Column Headings

22. Highlight cells **C5 through G5**. Then select **Format Cells**.

23. Choose the **Border tab**. You will see to the right of the window a variety of **Line Styles**. Choose the double-lined rule in the bottom right column of **Line Styles** (or any other line that you prefer).

24. In the **Border** section of the window you can select from a variety of buttons that indicate where you want to place a border in the cell. Choose the button that places a border only on the **bottom** of the selected cells.

25. When you have completed these steps, click **OK**.

26. Although your formatting choices may differ slightly, your screen should resemble **Figure 1.6**.

Fig. 1.6:

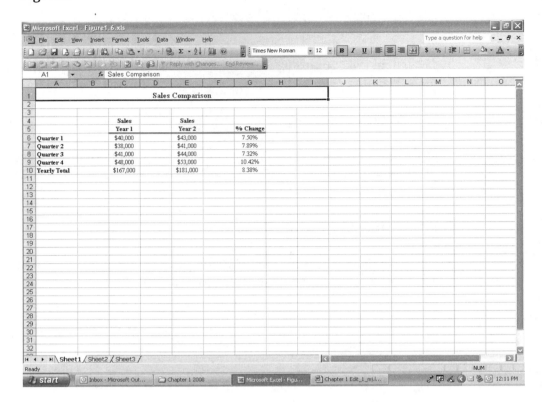

Setting a Print Area and Formatting the Page

27. Now you are almost ready to complete the assignment. First you need to choose the area of the spreadsheet that you would like to print. To set the print area, click on cell **A1** and highlight down to cell **I10**. Then select **File>Print Area>Set Print Area**.

28. Next, select **File>Page Setup**. Select the tab labeled **Sheet**. You will see that the gridlines and row/column headings have a check mark (✓) beside them. Click on these to eliminate the (✓) and turn off the gridlines and row/column headings. In most cases, the spreadsheet will look more professional without the row/column headings and gridlines.

29. You can select **Print Preview** to see how your spreadsheet will look when printed.

30. When you are through previewing the page you will need to choose **Close**, which will take you back to your working spreadsheet.

Saving Your Work and Printing

31. Before you print and turn in your assignment, always save your work.

32. To save your work, select **File>Save As**. Save your work on a travel drive and label it **Lesson1.1(your initials here with no spaces)**. For example, if your name is Amy Scott, your filename will read Lesson1.1AS.xls. By labeling the exercise in this way, you can retain the *original* spreadsheet file just in case you should need it at a later date.

33. To save the file on your travel drive, choose **File>Save As**. In the File name box, enter a new name for your file; in this case type **Lesson1.1(your initials here with no spaces)**. To save the copy to an external medium, click a different drive (as indicated by your instructor) in the **Save in** drop-down list or a different folder in the folder list, or both. Click **OK**.

34. Now print out your assignment by selecting **File>Print**, choose your printer and press **OK**.

> *HINT:* You may want to save each assignment in more than one place (e.g., your travel drive and on the hard drive in your own designated folder if you are allowed to do so).

Printing Formulas

35. Your instructor might request that you print out your spreadsheet assignment showing all the formulas you have written.

36. To do this, simply select **Tools>Options**. Click on the **View** tab and check the box next to **Formulas** under the **Window options** section.

37. You can also display formulas by pressing the **Ctrl** key and the tilde key (~) simultaneously.

Additional Spreadsheet Operations

The functions covered so far in this Tutorial are some of the most common and useful for representing retail mathematical operations in spreadsheet form. Here are a few more Excel functions that you might find helpful to employ.

Wrapping Text

When you type in text that is too large to fit in one cell the text will normally spill over into the next cell. If, however, that cell contains data, the text in your active cell cannot be seen.

1. You can **Wrap** the text in order to add another line to the desired cell. Simply place your cursor in the cell and click on **Format** and then **Cells**. When the window opens, select the **Alignment** tab and then place a check mark (✓) in the box indicating **Wrap Text**.

Formatting a Cell with

Sometimes when you insert a formula in a cell the result will be ######. This usually happens when the cell is not formatted yet (e.g., formatted as a percentage with two decimal places).

If the cell is formatted properly, you will simply need to widen the column using the **Format** menu and then selecting **Column** and then **Width**. You should widen only as much as necessary to reveal the results and remove the ###### symbol. You can also widen by placing your cursor on the dividing line to the right side of the column you wish to widen in the column headings (e.g., the line between A and B). When placed above the line, your cursor will become a two-way arrow pointing left and right with a thick center line. You simply hold down the left mouse button and drag the column to the width of your choice.

CHAPTER 2

Factors Affecting Profit

The principal function of every retail store is to procure merchandise to sell to consumers for a profit. Whether a retailer earns a profit or suffers a loss depends on three basic merchandising factors:

1. The dollar volume of merchandise sold, known as sales volume or net sales
2. The cost to the retailer of the merchandise sold
3. The cost of operating the business, commonly referred to as operating expenses

You will find the following concepts and definitions useful in calculating profit.

Billed cost Purchase price as it appears on the invoice.

Closing inventory at cost The cost value of the merchandise remaining in stock at the end of the period.

Cost of goods sold (a.k.a *Cost of merchandise sold)* Billed cost of the merchandise, plus freight or transportation costs, plus alteration/workroom costs, minus any cash discounts earned.

Customer returns and allowances (a.k.a. *Customer R&A)* Returns are goods returned to the store after initial purchase. Allowances are price adjustments made for customers when goods are found to be slightly damaged or soiled so that these customers can have the damage repaired (e.g., have a garment cleaned to remove a makeup stain or replace a button). These are the only percentages in a skeletal profit and loss statement that are based on Gross Sales.

Delivered Cost The purchase price as it appears on the invoice, plus any transportation costs incurred.

Direct expenses Department expenses that are directly related to that department's business. These expenses would cease to exist if the department ceased to exist. Usually includes such expenses as sales personnel salaries, selling supplies, travel for buying staff, and advertising expenditures for departments.

Gross margin Sometimes referred to as **gross profit**, this figure is obtained by subtracting the cost of goods sold from net sales. Gross margin can also be calculated by adding profit and expenses if the two figures are given.

Gross profit An alternative term used to describe gross margin.

Gross sales The total sales for any given period *before* deducting the retail value of goods returned to the store and/or making price allowances.

Indirect expenses Expenses that are incurred that are not directly related to a specific department. Examples might include store maintenance and security, senior executive salaries, and insurance. Such expenses are usually distributed among the individual departments on the basis of sales volume.

Landed Cost The purchase price as it appears on the invoice, plus any transportation costs incurred and any import/duty costs incurred.

Net sales The total sales for any given period *after* returns and/or price allowances are deducted. Always equal to 100% in a skeletal profit and loss statement.

Opening inventory The retail value of the merchandise at the beginning of the period.

Opening inventory at cost The cost value of the merchandise at the beginning of the period.

Operating expense The expenses incurred by the retailer during any given period. Usually divided into direct and indirect expenses on a profit and loss statement.

Profit and loss statement (a.k.a. *Income statement*) A summary financial statement prepared at the end of a specified period that indicates the relationship of the sales, cost of merchandise, and expenses to the profitability of an organization or business. These statements can also be prepared at the store or department level if desired.

Purchases Billed cost of new goods purchased during the period, minus any returns to, or allowances from, the vendor.

Skeletal profit and loss statement A shortened version of a profit and loss statement that allows quick calculation of profit and loss at any given time. The skeletal statement (a.k.a. skeletal P&L) utilizes net sales, cost of merchandise sold, and expenses to attain the gross margin, also known as gross profit, and profit figures.

Profit and Loss Statements

The **profit and loss (P&L) statement** is a summary of the income and expenses of a business. Frequently called an income statement, this document generally contains a wealth of information that is often expressed in both dollars and percentages. The dollar format allows us to determine the actual income, expenses, and profitability of the business, while the percentage format is useful for year-to year comparisons, business-to business comparisons, and industry comparisons.

For example, if a lingerie buyer and a shoe buyer each show a profit of $10,000 for their respective departments, can we say that they performed equally well? Not necessarily. The success of their results depends on the net sales of their particular department, last year's profits for the same period of time, and industry standards for their category. A profit of $10,000 based on net sales of $100,000 would represent a profit percentage of 10%, which may be considered quite successful, while a $10,000 profit based on $1,000,000 net sales would only represent a profit of 1% and may be considered quite dismal.

Skeletal Profit and Loss Statements

A shortened form of the income statement, referred to as a **skeletal profit and loss statement**, can be used for a quick examination of the relationship between income and expenses. A skeletal P&L is calculated as follows:

Gross Sales
– Customer Returns and Allowances
Net Sales
– Cost of Goods Sold
Gross Margin
– Operating Expenses
Profit (Loss)

The skeletal P&L format is most often expressed in both dollars and percentages. Since all of the factors are presented as a percentage of net sales, the net sales figure is always equal to 100%. When gross sales and customer returns (customer R&A) are given, you simply subtract customer returns from gross sales in order to determine net sales, and then complete the skeletal P&L:

Gross Sales	$120,000	
– Customer R & A	– 20,000	
Net Sales	$100,000	100%
– Cost of Goods Sold	– 52,000	52%
= Gross Margin	= $ 48,000	48%
– Operating Expenses	– 42,000	42%
= Net Profit	= $ 6,000	6%

Given the dollar amount of any of the factors affecting profit, you simply divide the given dollar amount by net sales to obtain the percentage:

> If Net Sales = $100,000 and Cost of Goods Sold = $52,000
> then %Cost of Goods Sold = $52,000/$100,000 = .52 = 52%.

Conversely, given the percentage of any of the profit factors, you can simply multiply the percentage by the net sales figure to obtain the dollar amount:

> If Operating Expenses = 42% and Net Sales = $100,000
> then $100,000 × 42% (or .42) = $42,000.

It is also possible to determine the dollar value of net sales if other profit factors and percentages are given. Here is an example:

> If Cost of Goods Sold is 38,000 or 55% and $Net Sales is not given,
> you can simply divide any of the $figures given by the % of net sales
> they represent. (Remember: Net Sales is always equal to 100%.)
>
> 38,000/55% = Net Sales   Remember that 55% = .55
> 38,000/.55 =
> 69,090.90 or $69,091 = Net Sales

Practicing What You Have Learned

Complete a skeletal profit and loss statement for each of the following (round to the nearest whole dollar amount and the percentages to one decimal place):

1. Cost of goods sold is $245,000, gross margin is 46%, and profit is 3%.

2. Net sales are $575,000, gross margin is $295,500, and operating expenses are 38%.

3. Gross sales are $1,200,000, customer returns and allowances are $67,000, cost of goods sold is 52%, and operating expenses are 35%.

4. Profit is $10,500, which is the equivalent of 4%, and gross margin is 45%.

5. Net sales are $75,000, gross margin is $45,000, and operating expenses are $37,000.

6. The men's furnishings department had net sales of $250,000 for the quarter. It experienced a profit of 3% during the period and gross margin was 51%.

7. Determine the net sales figure necessary to achieve a net profit of 5% when gross margin is planned at $175,000 (49%).

8. If net sales are $1,340,000, the cost of merchandise sold is $894,000, and expenses total $529,000 for the women's sportswear department, would the department earn a profit? What dollar amount would be gained/lost? What percentage?

9. If expenses totaling $39,500 are calculated at 44% and the cost of merchandise sold was $44,000, what net sales and profit would be achieved?

10. The linens department had net sales of $250,000, which resulted in a gross margin of 48%. The department experienced a loss of 3% during the period. Complete a skeletal profit and loss statement for the department.

11. Gross Margin $ 132,000
    Operating Expenses $ 134,500
    Loss   (− 1.0%)

12. Net sales $ 689,000
    Cost of Goods Sold $ 357,000
    Operating Expenses $ 202,000

13. Gross Sales $ 17,500
    Customer R&A $ 350
    Cost of Goods Sold $ 8,440
    Operating Expenses   33%

14. Net Profit   3.0%
    Gross Margin $43,000
    Operating Expenses $39,889

15. Net Sales $1,750,890
    Cost of Goods Sold   51.0%
    Loss   1.0%

Complete Profit and Loss Statement

The skeletal profit and loss statement provides a quick, concise look at the factors affecting profit. However, sometimes it is necessary to take a look at those factors in greater detail in order to monitor the transactions that have an impact on sales, cost of goods sold, and expenses.

GROSS SALES AND CUSTOMER RETURNS AND ALLOWANCES

Although in the skeletal P&L we are mainly concerned with net sales, it is also important for the business to monitor the relationship of gross sales to the volume of customer returns of merchandise sold. The gross sales figure represents the retail value of all merchandise initially sold through cash or credit to customers. However, there are times when customers return the merchandise after the sale for a refund, credit, or price adjustment due to damage or defect (e.g., a missing button or a small ink stain). The percentage of customer returns is calculated based on gross sales. This is the only percentage in the profit and loss statement based on gross sales. For example, consider the following:

> If gross sales for last year were $250,000 and customer returns and allowances totaled $18,000, then,
>
> LY Customer R&A% = $18,000 ÷ $250,000
> LY Customer R&A = 7.2%
>
> If gross sales for this year were $280,000 and customer returns and allowances totaled $26,000, then,
>
> TY Customer R&A% = $26,000 ÷ $280,000
> TY Customer R&A% = 9.3%

The dollar volume of customer returns may rise drastically during a given period. Why would such an increase occur? It could be a vendor issue such as a sizing problem, an improperly placed buttonhole, or an issue with excessive shrinkage or color fading when laundered. However, a rise could also be related to an increase in gross sales in which case the dollar volume of returns and allowances might rise, but the percentage remains relatively stable. There are also seasonal variations in returns such as in late December and early January when many people are returning gifts received during the holidays.

Retailers consider net sales the most significant figure when analyzing profit and calculate the percentages of all the key factors on the basis of net sales. Net sales is a more stable figure than gross sales because it represents the actual goods sold that remain sold. The gross sales figure does not take into account merchandise returned to the store. However, when gross sales are given, net sales are first calculated as a percentage of gross sales. Here is an example:

> If gross sales are given at $100,000 and customer returns are 3%, then

Gross Sales	$100,000	100%
– Customer R & A	$ 3,000	3%
Net Sales	$ 97,000	97%

> In order to calculate gross sales when net sales and customer returns and allowances percentages are known, the following formula will be necessary:
>
> Gross Sales$ = Net Sales$/100% – Customer R&A%

For the previous example, if net sales were given as $97,000 and customer returns were given as 3% then,

$$\text{Gross Sales} = \$97,000/(100\% - 3\%) = \$100,000$$

For the remainder of the P&L figures, percentages will be calculated based on net sales, which will represent 100%.

COST OF GOODS SOLD

The relationship of the cost of the merchandise (or goods) sold to net sales is also an important factor in determining whether a business can earn a profit. The cost of the merchandise to be sold is actually based on a combination of costs that include the actual billed cost of the merchandise, the cost of transportation (a.k.a. freight), any discounts received, and any costs incurred for alterations/workroom repairs to the merchandise.

Analyzing the individual components of the cost of goods sold can help keep costs low, which can result in greater profit for the business. For instance, a noticeable drop in discount dollars may merit investigation. Are cash discounts being taken? Are transportation/freight costs at the lowest levels possible? Can alteration/workroom costs be lowered?

In order to examine in detail the merchandise sold during a given time period, the opening and closing inventory of merchandise must be taken into account. The merchandise sold during a period is actually a result of considering all of the inventory on hand at the beginning of the period, adding any purchases received during the period, and subtracting all the merchandise left at the end of the period. For example consider the following:

Opening Inventory: $102,000
Closing Inventory: $ 93,500

If the billed cost of a shipment for the infants' department was $200,000 with cash discounts of $3,000 taken and transportation charges of $2,500 incurred, then,

Total Cost of Goods Sold = Opening Inventory
                          + Billed Cost (Purchases)
                          + Transportation (Freight)
                          – Closing Inventory
                          – Cash Discount
                          – Alterations/Workroom

Total Cost of Goods Sold = $102,000 + $200,000 + $2,500 – $93,500 – $3,000 (In this case there were no alterations/workroom expenses to account for.)

Total Cost of Goods Sold = $208,000

It is important to note that the cost of goods sold is a figure that is presented at the cost value rather than the retail value of the goods. The net sales figure is the retail value of all the goods sold to customers and not returned. This is an important distinction for inventory bookkeeping purposes, which will be discussed in detail later.

OPERATING EXPENSES

The expenses of operating a store are a significant component in determining if a retailer will earn a profit or have to withstand a loss. The various operational expenses are deducted from **gross margin** (a.k.a. **gross profit**) to determine the profit figure. Understanding and controlling these expenses can often be the difference between being in the black (profit) or in the red (loss).

Traditionally, **direct expenses** included such things as wages of sales personnel, departmental advertising, buyers' travel and expenses, etc. The figure includes those expenses that were incurred for the operation of a specific department that would not occur if the department did not exist. **Indirect expenses**, on the other hand, were those that benefited the entire store and would continue even if a particular department was eliminated. Executive salaries, maintenance, etc., were among the expenses included in this category. In the retail environment of today, expenses may be classified or categorized in any way that meets the objectives of the analysis or review. With the vast growth in specialty retailing where selling staff may no longer be assigned to a particular "department," it is increasingly difficult to cleanly separate direct and indirect expenses. For example:

A detailed profit and loss statement for the following information would resemble Table 2.1:

Gross Sales	$ 250,000
Customer Returns & Allowances	$ 21,000
Billed Cost of Goods	$ 101,000
Freight (Transportation)	$ 2,800
Alterations	$ 500
Cash Discounts	$ 6,900
Salaries (Buying & Selling)	$ 23,500
Executive Salaries	$ 20,000
Rent	$ 18,800
Utilities	$ 7,500
Maintenance	$ 5,200
Advertising (Department)	$ 10,000
Opening Inventory (cost)	$ 109,000
Closing Inventory	$ 75,000

TABLE 2.1

		DOLLAR	PERCENTAGE
Gross Sales		$ 250,000	
– Customer R&A		– $ 21,000	
= **Net Sales**		**$ 229,000**	100%
Opening Inventory (cost)		$ 109,000	
+ Billed Cost of Goods		$ 101,000	
+ Freight		$ 2,800	
Merchandise Handled		**$ 212,800**	
– Closing Inventory (cost)		– $ 75,000	
Gross Cost of Goods Sold	(–)	**$ 137,800**	
– Cash Discount		– $ 6,900	
Net Cost of Goods Sold		**$ 130,900**	
+ Alterations		+ 500	
Total Cost of Goods Sold	= **Gross Margin**	$ 131,400	57.4%
		$ 97,600	42.6%
Salaries (Buying/Selling)		$ 23,500	
Executive Salaries		$ 20,000	
Rent	(–)	$ 18,800	
Utilities		$ 7,500	
Maintenance		$ 5,200	
Advertising		$ 10,000	
Operating Expenses	= **Net Profit**	$ 85,000	37.1%
		$ 12,600	5.5%

Practicing What You Have Learned

Calculate a complete profit and loss statement for each of the following scenarios and provide percentages for net sales, total cost of goods sold, gross margin, total operating expenses, and net profit (round to the nearest whole dollar amount and round the percentages to one decimal place):

16. Net Sales $ 425,000
    Billed Cost of Goods (Purchases) $ 189,000
    Freight (Transportation) $ 20,500
    Cash Discounts $ 9,000
    Salaries (Selling & Buying) $ 48,000

Insurance	$ 10,000
Executive Salaries	$ 22,000
Insurance	$ 8,500
Rent	$ 26,000
Selling Supplies	$ 15,000
General Office	$ 8,500
Opening Inventory	$ 232,000
Closing Inventory	$ 197,000

17.

Gross Sales	$ 1,274,300
Customer R&A	$ 89,700
Opening Inventory	$ 393,100
Billed Cost of Goods (Purchases)	$ 698,000
Freight (Transportation)	$ 68,000
Closing Inventory	$ 402,000
Alterations	$ 12,300
Cash Discounts	$ 38,500
Salaries (Selling & Buying)	$ 82,000
Executive Salaries	$ 69,000
Rent	$ 98,000
Insurance	$ 19,000
Utilities	$ 14,900
Maintenance	$ 15,000
Advertising	$ 102,000
Office Supplies	$ 3,500
Wrapping & Selling Supplies	$ 22,000

18.

Gross Sales	$ 28,000
Customer R&A	$ 490
Opening Inventory (cost)	$ 5,100
Closing Inventory (cost)	$ 3,900
Billed Cost of Goods	$ 19,000
Freight (Transportation)	$ 950
Direct Expenses	$ 5,000
Indirect Expenses	$ 1,750
Alterations	$ 100

19. Determine the dollar and percentage gross margin given the following:

Gross Sales	$ 175,000
Customer Returns	$ 2,800
Billed Cost of Goods	$ 105,000
Freight	$ 5,000
Cash Discounts	5%

20. The juniors denim department experienced a 2.5% loss for the 6-month period. If the department had a gross margin of 44%, determine the percentage for operating expenses in the department.

Chapter 2 Review Exercise A

Report all figures in whole dollars and round percentages to the nearest tenth.

1. If gross margin is $49,500 and the gross margin percentage is 52%, calculate net sales dollars and percentage.

2. If a department suffers a loss of 2.50% with expenses totaling $35,000 and net sales of $98,000, calculate the following:

   a. Gross margin $
   b. Gross margin %
   c. Loss $

3. Complete a skeletal P&L given the following information:

Cost of Goods Sold	$ 189,250
Gross Margin	$ 143,500
Operating Expenses	32%

4. Set up a complete P&L statement using the following figures:

Opening Inventory (cost)	$ 25,000
Closing Inventory (cost)	$ 19,000
Gross Sales	$ 83,000
Customer R&A	$ 750
Purchases (cost)	$ 65,000
Freight (Transportation)	$ 1,250
Salaries (Selling & Buying)	$ 8,250
Rent & Utilities	$ 6,400
Cash Discounts Received	$ 1,200
Miscellaneous Expenses	$ 250

   Analyze the results obtained. What might the business consider if it desires to improve its profitability?

5. If customer R&A in the handbags department totaled $8,500 and net sales were calculated at $142,000, determine gross sales.

6. If gross sales totaled $245,000 and net sales were $239,000, determine the dollar and percentage value of customer R&A.

7. Set up a skeletal P&L given the following figures:

Net Sales	$69,000
Cost of Merchandise Sold	$35,000
Profit/Loss	$ 1,800

8. For the month of May, the men's sportswear department had gross sales of $389,000 and customer R&A totaling $13,200. If the selling costs (buying & selling) for the month were $38,500, calculate the percentage of selling costs.

9. Calculate gross sales given net sales of $250,000 and customer R&A of 2.8%.

10. The owner of Harry's Hardware store is not satisfied with the profit margins he is currently attaining. He wishes to increase his profits. Considering the factors affecting profits, discuss two strategies Harry might employ to realize his desired increase in profits.

Chapter 2 Review Exercise B

Report all figures in whole dollars and round percentages to the nearest tenth.

1. Find the dollar and percentage gross margin for the following data:

Gross Sales	$289,000
Customer R&A	$ 9,875
Billed Cost of Goods	$179,000
Freight	$ 4,300
Cash Discounts	$ 6,000
Opening Inventory (cost)	$ 59,000
Closing Inventory (cost)	$ 55,000

2. If the retailer attaining the figures in Problem 1 was able to negotiate a 5% discount from the vendor on the billed cost of goods, how would that affect the gross margin dollars and percentage?

3. Construct a skeletal P&L given the following:

Net Sales	$ 21,350
Cost of Merchandise Sold	55%
Expenses	$ 12,500

4. The men's accessories department had net sales of $87,700 and customer returns and allowances of 3.5%. Calculate gross sales in dollars.

5. Calculate a final P&L for the following information:

Gross Sales	$ 395,000
Customer R&A	$ 37,900
Total Cost of Goods Sold	$ 185,100
Direct Expenses	$ 105,000
Indirect Expenses	$ 65,100

6. Determine the net sales for an accessories department with a gross margin of $34,000 and profits of $4,000 totaling 4.5%.

7. Is it possible to increase profit percentages while experiencing a drop in net sales? Explain. Provide a scenario that can demonstrate your answer using skeletal P&Ls.

8. The tabletop department in a local retailer has monthly expenses totaling $10,500 and a cost of goods sold for the month of $32,500, which is 50% of net sales. If customer returns total $1,050, what were gross sales for the month?

9. Determine net sales for a business that experienced a loss of − (2.5%) or − ($2,500).

10. Why must percentages be included in a P&L statement?

Chapter 2 Review Exercise C

Report all figures in whole dollars and round percentages to the nearest tenth.

1. The designer sportswear department had net sales of $150,000 for the month of April. Billed cost of goods for the month was $87,000 and freight charges were $1,020. The department suffered $750 in workroom costs due to some minor damage to the shipment. If the department took advantage of a 6% cash discount, calculate the gross margin dollars and percentage.

2. Calculate a final P&L given the following information:

Net Sales	$ 599,000
Customer R&A	$ 58,000
Opening Inventory (cost)	$ 234,000
Closing Inventory (cost)	$ 203,000
Purchases (cost)	$ 275,000
Freight (transportation)	$ 10,500
Direct Expenses	$ 187,300
Indirect Expenses	$ 51,200

3. What was the profit percentage for an appliance department with a 52% gross margin totaling $144,000 and total operating expenses of 139,800?

4. Gross sales for the jewelry department were $1,225,000 and net sales were calculated at $1,087,990. Determine the customer returns and allowances percentage.

5.
Net Sales	$ 55,000
Gross Margin	42%
Expenses	$ 24,600

6. Last year, Sally's Luggage store experienced a loss of 1.5% on a gross margin of 43% and expenses of 44.5% totaling $37,000. Sally plans for a 3% increase in net sales and cost of goods sold this year. If she can lower her expenses by $3,000, can she earn a profit this year? How much?

7. If the profit is $4,000 and the profit percentage is 2.8%, calculate net sales.

8. Calculate the profit or loss dollars and percentage given the following information:

Net Sales	$532,000
Cost of Goods Sold	55%
Operating Expenses	42%

9. Nick and Kelly ran a lemonade stand for the entire summer in their neighborhood. At the end of the summer, they had $47.50 in sales. If the supplies cost $17.00 and they divide their profits evenly, how much will each child get?

10. Explain the difference between direct and indirect expenses. Which is easier for the department to control?

Basic Profit and Loss Calculations
Excel Tutorial 2

Opening the File

1. Open Excel. You can refer to the Excel Spreadsheet Concepts Tutorial in Chapter 1 at any time during this lesson if you cannot remember how to perform the assigned tasks.

    Choose **File>Open** and then locate the file entitled **Lesson2.1.xls**. You can open this file by double-clicking on the file name. Your screen should resemble **Figure 2.1**.

Fig. 2.1:

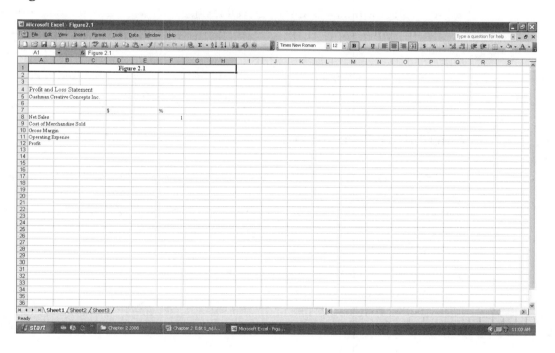

Completing the Spreadsheet

2. Enter the following data in Column D in the appropriate cells:

Net Sales	=	500,000
Cost of Merchandise Sold	=	270,000
Operating Expenses	=	240,000

HINT: The dollar amounts will be formatted in a later step. You simply
need to enter the figures as shown. If any of the variables had been given
as a percentage, you would simply enter the number as a decimal. (You
will note that the spreadsheet already indicates a **1** for net sales. This will
later be formatted to indicate 100%.)

3. Enter the formula = **D8-D9** in cell **D10**, which will calculate the gross margin for
   Carlton Creative Concepts, Inc.

   HINT: Remember that all formulas should begin with an equal sign (=)
   and subtraction (–) is represented by the hyphen (-) key.

4. Enter the formula = **D10-D11** (in cell **D12**), which will calculate the profit or (loss)
   for the company.

   HINT: You should always estimate the sum in your head and double-
   check that the formula you have created gives you the correct answer.

Calculating Percentages

The five major components of the P&L statement can be expressed as a percentage
of sales. Percentages allow the business to easily compare performance on a
year-to-year basis and a business-to-business basis. For example, a $5,000 profit on
$500,000 sales is not nearly as impressive as $5,000 profit on $50,000 sales (a 1%
profit versus a 10% profit).

   HINT: Remember that net sales will always be equal to 100% and all
   other components must be expressed as a percentage of net sales. Therefore, the formula for calculating cost of merchandise sold as a % to net
   sales should be = **D9/D8**. Calculate the remaining three components in
   the same manner dividing each component by net sales. Your screen
   should resemble **Figure 2.2**.

Fig. 2.2:

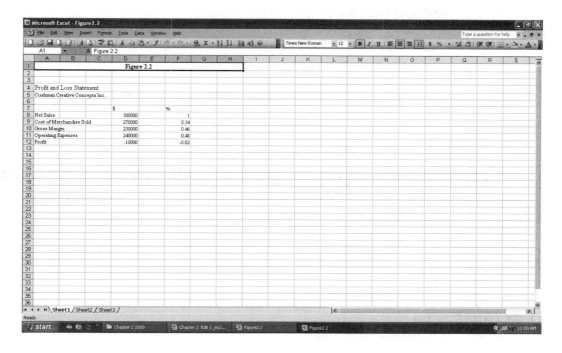

Formatting the Spreadsheet

In order to professionally present your spreadsheet calculations, complete the following formatting functions:

5. Center the title for the table. Click on cell **A4** and drag the mouse to **H4**. When the cells are highlighted, click on the merge and center button located in the formatting toolbar.

6. With cells **A4** through **H4** still highlighted, click bold **B** in order to bold the table heading.

7. Center the company name in the same manner as described previously, highlighting cells **A5** through **H5**.

8. Highlight cells **A8** through **A12** and bold the components text.

9. Beginning in cell **D7**, hold down the left mouse button and drag down to **D12** and over to **F12**. Now center the text within these columns by clicking center in the formatting toolbar.

10. Highlight from cell **D8** to **D12**. Then choose **Format>Cells** from the pull-down menu. A window will open with several tabbed pages. In this case the **Number** page is already visible. Select **Currency** from the category menu and make sure

that the decimal places are set at **0**. You should see another category entitled **Negative numbers**. Select the option that indicates the negative numbers in red and enclosed in parentheses.

11. Highlight from cell **F8** to **F12**. Then choose **Format>Cells** from the pull-down menu. Select **Percentage** from the category menu and make sure that the decimal places are set at **0**. Your screen should now resemble **Figure 2.3**.

Fig. 2.3:

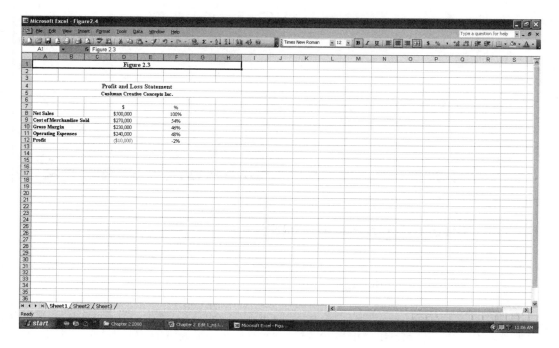

HINT: Although not evident in this case, you may find the text you enter will not fit properly in the cell. You can **Wrap** the text in order to add another line to the desired cell. Simply place your cursor in the cell and choose **Format>Cells**. When the window opens, select the **Alignment** tab and then place a check mark (✔) in the box indicating **Wrap Text**. Refer to **Figure 2.4**.

Fig. 2.4:

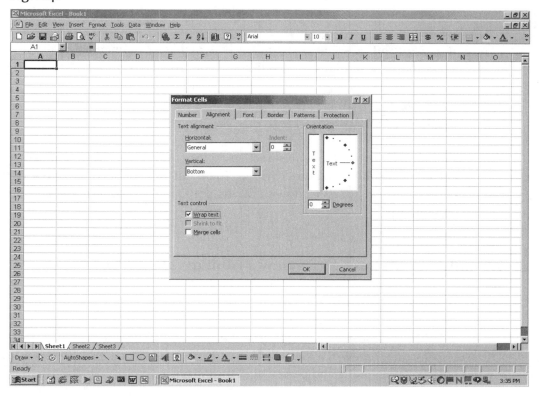

Setting a Print Area and Formatting the Page

Now you are almost ready to complete the assignment. First you need to set the area of the spreadsheet that you would like to print. Simply click on cell **A1** and highlight down to cell **H12**. Then choose **File>Print Area>Set Print Area**.

12. Next, select **File>Page Setup**. Select the tab labeled **Sheet**. You will see that the gridlines and row/column headings have a check mark (✓) beside them. Click on these to eliminate the (✓) and turn off the gridlines and row/column headings.

13. You can select **Print Preview** to see how your spreadsheet will look when printed. When you are through previewing the page you will need to choose **Close**, which will take you back to your working spreadsheet.

Saving Your Work and Printing

14. Before you print and turn in your assignment, you should always save your work. (In fact, you should save **often** during your work session to be sure that you have saved changes made to the worksheet.)

15. Save your work on the travel drive and label it **Lesson2.1(your initials here with no spaces)** just as you did in Chapter 1.

16. Now print out your assignment. It is highly recommended that you save your work to the hard drive in addition to your travel drive if permitted.

Printing Formulas

Your instructor may request that you print out your spreadsheet assignment showing all the formulas you have written. To do this, select **Tools> Options>View**. Check **Formulas** under the **Windows options** section. You can also display formulas by pressing **Ctrl ~**.

Profit and Loss Statement Review Problems Using Excel

Review Problem 2.1

Libby's Lampshades is assessing the holiday selling season. Given the following information, follow the steps below and create a skeletal P&L statement depicting both dollar amounts and percentages for the business.

- Gross Margin $ 236,000
- Cost of Merchandise Sold $ 124,000
- Expenses   40%

Open a blank Excel spreadsheet.

1. Save the blank spreadsheet and give it an appropriate filename. To be consistent, this file should be named **Review2.1(your initials here with no spaces)**. Now you are ready to begin working.

2. Be sure to round the dollar values to the nearest dollar and the percents to one decimal place. (You may want to refer to the formatting instructions in the basic Excel Tutorial in Chapter 1.)

3. Be sure to give your P&L statement an appropriate title and make sure to format it in a professional manner.

4. If you do not have access to a color printer that will allow you to indicate a loss in red, you should make sure to enclose any losses in parentheses to indicate that the dollar and percentage figures are losses and not gains.

5. When your assignment is complete, be sure to save your work (because you have already saved the file and named it **Review2.1(your initials)**, choose **File>Save**) and print out the final results.

Review Problem 2.2

After calculating this year's P&L, the owner of Libby's Lampshades realizes that she never completed a P&L for last year. Use the data listed next to create a skeletal P&L statement depicting both dollar amounts and percents.

- Net Sales $ 194,000
- Cost of Merchandise Sold $ 89,800
- Profit   6%

Open a blank Excel spreadsheet.

1. Save the blank spreadsheet and give it an appropriate filename. To be consistent, this file should be named **Review2.2(your initials here with no spaces)**. Now you are ready to begin working.

2. Be sure and round the dollar values to the nearest dollar and the percents to one decimal place. (You may want to refer to the formatting instructions in the basic Excel Tutorial in Chapter 1.)

3. Be sure to give your P&L statement an appropriate title and make sure to format it in a professional manner.

4. If you do not have access to a color printer that will allow you to indicate a loss in red, you should make sure to enclose any losses in parentheses to indicate that the dollar and percentage figures are losses and not gains.

5. When your assignment is complete, be sure to **save** your work (because you have already saved the file and named it **Review2.2(your initials)**, you can simply choose **File>Save**) and print out the final results.

Review Problem 2.3

Open a blank Excel spreadsheet.

1. Save the blank spreadsheet and give it an appropriate filename. To be consistent, this file should be named **Review2.3(your initials here with no spaces)**. Now you are ready to begin working.

2. Use the data from Review Problem 2.1 and Review Problem 2.2 to create a spreadsheet that compares last year's data for Libby's Lampshades to this year's data. Make sure to indicate the percentage change for the components of the profit and loss statements.

3. Be sure to round the dollar values to the nearest dollar and the percents to 1 decimal place. (You may want to refer to the formatting instructions in the basic Excel Tutorial.)

4. Be sure to give your P&L statement an appropriate title and make sure to format it in a professional manner.

5. If you do not have access to a color printer that will allow you to indicate a loss in red, you should make sure to enclose any losses in parentheses to indicate that the dollar and percentage figures are losses and not gains.

6. When your assignment is complete, be sure to **save** your work (because you have already saved the file and named it **Review2.3(your initials)**, you can simply choose **File>Save**) and print out the final results.

Review Problem 2.4

The men's accessories department at J.R. Moore's has the following figures available:

- Net sales of $266,000
- Customer R&A of 2.9%
- Gross Margin of 42%
- Operating Expenses of $97,000

Open a blank Excel spreadsheet.

1. Save a blank spreadsheet and give it an appropriate filename. To be consistent, this file should be named **Review2.4(your initials here with no spaces)**. Now you are ready to begin working.

2. Create a skeletal P&L statement that depicts both dollar and percentage values for all of the factors including gross sales.

3. Be sure to round the dollar values to the nearest dollar and the percents to 1 decimal place. (You may want to refer to the formatting instructions given in the basic Excel Tutorial in Chapter 1.)

4. Be sure to give your P&L statement an appropriate title and make sure to format it in a professional manner.

5. Save your work and print as directed by your instructor.

Review Problem 2.5

For this assignment, open the spreadsheet you saved in Review Problem 2.4 (Review2.4your initials).

The divisional merchandise manager is planning for a profit of 8% next year. He is convinced that the expenses can be controlled to attain this profit level while, at the same time, increasing sales 3% over last year. The manager intends to hold the cost of merchandise sold to this year's percentage by working to negotiate better transportation and vendor discounts.

1. Replicate the P&L for this year in order to have a point of comparison.

2. Create a second P&L statement that depicts the newly planned figures necessary to attain the 8% planned profit level.

3. Be sure to round the dollar values to the nearest dollar and the percents to 1 decimal place.

4. Be sure to give your P&L statement an appropriate title and make sure to format it in a professional manner.

5. What strategies might the buyer use to reduce the cost of goods? Is it possible to achieve these reductions without sacrificing sales? Write a brief paragraph to explain. You may place your statements at the bottom of the spreadsheet or in a separate Word document as indicated by your instructor.

6. Save your work and print as directed by your instructor.

Review Problem 2.6

Open a blank Excel spreadsheet.

The kitchen accessories buyer for The Silver Spoon experienced the following results during the summer season this year. She was disappointed by the lack of profitability and wanted to present an analysis of the results along with a skeletal P&L to his or her divisional merchandise manager.

Gross Sales	$ 110,000
Customer Returns & Allowances	$ 15,000
Gross Margin	37%
Loss	(− 3%)

1. Complete a skeletal P&L for the kitchen accessories that depicts both dollars and percentages for net sales, cost of merchandise sold, gross margin, operating expenses, and profit.

2. Provide two or three suggested opportunities that could help to ensure a more profitable result in the coming periods.

3. Be sure to round the dollar values to the nearest dollar and the percents to 1 decimal place.

4. Be sure to give your P&L statement an appropriate title and make sure to format it in a professional manner.

5. Save your work and print as directed by your instructor.

CHAPTER 3

Cost of Merchandise and Terms of Sale

In this chapter you will be introduced to the common terms of sale that are negotiated in a retail environment. In addition to the cost price negotiated by the buyer, successful negotiation of terms including discounts and transportation charges can have a significant impact on the bottom line. The factors discussed in this chapter include discounts, dating, anticipation, and transportation. Each of these can help to lower the cost of goods. The practice of **loading** will also be examined. Loading does not change the amount the store actually pays for the merchandise, but does allow the store's accounting office to maintain all inventory at the same cash discount rate.

You will find the following negotiating concepts and definitions useful:

Advanced dating or *Postdating* A situation where the vendor actually places a date on the invoice that is sometime in the future and then offers regular dating terms. For example, a vendor may ship merchandise on August 1 but place an invoice date on the merchandise of September 1. The vendor then offers 2/10, n/30 from the postdated invoice date, allowing the retailer an extended period of time to take the cash discount.

Anticipation An extra discount sometimes offered as an incentive for the retailer to pay as early as possible in an extended cash discount period. When offered and received, this discount is added to the cash discount and deducted from the billed cost. This is the only time discounts will be added together. For this text, we will use a 6% yearly rate based on a 360-day year (30 days per month).

Cash discount The most common type of discount. Cash discounts are offered as an incentive for the buyer to pay the amount due early. The time frame for taking the cash discount is often dependent on the dating terms agreed upon during the negotiation process.

Cash on delivery (COD) dating Payment must be rendered in full when the goods are delivered.

End of month (EOM) dating The cash discount period is offered 10 days from the end of the month in which the merchandise is invoiced. for example, 6/10 EOM where a 6% cash discount is offered 10 days from the end of the month. Traditionally, invoices dated after the 25th of the month allow 10 days from the end of the *following* month.

Extra dating The cash discount is calculated from the date of invoice but a specific number of extra days are added to the cash discount period. This type of dating can allow the retailer time to receive and even sell some or all of the merchandise before paying for the shipment and receiving the cash discount, for example, 2/10-30X where the 2% cash discount period is 10 days plus 30 extra (40 days) from the date of invoice. Otherwise the net (full amount) of the bill is due within 20 days after the last day to take the cash discount. (This is the usual net date, though it is often not stated.)

Loading An adjustment to the cost price of an item to allow for an additional cash discount. A retailer or store may prefer a standard cash discount that is greater than the cash discount being offered by the vendor. The price of the item is adjusted upward, or loaded, in order to accommodate the higher cash discount while resulting in the same payment to the vendor. (Loaded Cost = Net Cost ÷ Complement of the Desired Cash Discount.)

On percent or *Billed percent* The on percent or billed percent is the complement of a discount percentage given. For example, if a discount of 40% is given, then the complement would be 100% − 40% or 60%. Therefore, the on percent or billed percent is equal to 60%.

Quantity discount Percentage of the billed cost that is deducted when a pre-arranged quantity of merchandise is purchased. Often used as an incentive to get the buyer to commit to a larger quantity of goods from one vendor.

Receipt of goods (ROG) dating The cash discount period is offered for 10 days after the goods are received. In this case, the date of the invoice is not used in the calculation of the discount period.

Regular dating The cash discount period is calculated from the date of invoice (which is usually the same date that the merchandise is shipped). For example, 2/10, n/30 where a 2% cash discount can be taken if payment is made within 10 days of the date of invoice, otherwise the net amount (payment in full) is due within 30 days of the date of invoice.

Series discount A series of trade discounts deducted from the list price. See **Trade discount**.

Trade discount A percentage or series of percentages deducted from the list price. These discounts are not dependent on when the invoice is paid. If expressed as a series (for example, 40%, 15%, 10%), they must be taken individually and in order. You cannot add these discounts together (for example, a discount of 40%, 15%, 10% *is not* equivalent to a discount of 65%).

Terms of Sale: Discounts

A discount represents a percentage reduction in the billed cost of merchandise offered by the vendor to a buyer. The discounts offered can vary greatly by industry, vendor, type of merchandise, and negotiating power and skill of the buyer. The buyer must try to negotiate the best possible discounts to reduce the cost of merchandise sold.

As you learned in Chapter 2, lowering the cost of goods sold while holding revenues and expenses steady will result in greater profitability. There are several ways to lower the cost of goods sold. One way would be to lower the quality of materials or production of the goods offered (i.e., fabrications, tailoring details, etc.). Although this would reduce the cost of goods, it may also negatively impact sales revenues because consumers may see the goods as inferior and either demand a lower price or refuse to purchase the goods. Negotiating and taking advantage of discounts offered by the vendor is one way to lower cost of goods sold that will have no negative impact on sales revenues or expenses, thereby having a potentially positive impact on the bottom line.

There are generally three basic types of discounts that may be offered to retailers. These discounts are trade discounts, quantity discounts, and cash discounts. If the trade discount is offered, it is often expressed as a series of discount percentages off the list price (e.g., $100 less 40%, 20%, and 5%) and is usually deducted before other applicable discounts are calculated. The trade discount expressed as a series of discounts is sometimes referred to as a **series discount**.

Trade Discounts

The number or amount of **trade discounts** often varies by the category of the client (e.g., industrial buyer or retailer) as well as by the amount of support services (e.g., marketing) the client may offer. A promotion-driven, discount retailer may be eligible for larger discounts than a luxury retailer who very rarely advertises. List price minus trade discount quotes are not prevalent for apparel retailers but are more commonly offered in the wholesale and industrial trades.

The billed cost is calculated by deducting the trade discount offered from the list price of the purchased goods. Here is an example:

> A trade discount of 30% and 15% is offered on a 50-foot adjustable ladder that lists for $100.00. The discounts cannot be added together to obtain the billed cost. You must deduct each discount in the order listed as shown below.
>
> Billed Cost = $100.00 less 30% and 15%
> Billed Cost = $100 – $30.00 ($100 × 30%) = $70.00
> Billed Cost = $70 – $10.50 ($70 × 15%) = $59.50

It is possible to reduce the number of steps necessary to calculate the series trade discount by multiplying the complements of each of the discounts offered and then multiplying the result by the list price. The complement is equivalent to 100% – discount %. This is known as the **on percent method** or **billed percent method**.

The industry often uses the term *on percent* but it may be helpful to think of this method as *billed percent* because the result of your calculations represents the percentage of the list price that is the billed to the buyer:

> If the total list price of an order is $1,000.00 with trade discounts of 40% and 15%, then using the billed percent method:
>
> 60% (100% – 40%) × 85% (100% – 15%) = 51%
> 51% represents the percentage of the list price that must be paid to the vendor (a.k.a. billed cost)
> $1000.00 × 51% = $510

When using the billed percent method, the lowest possible percentage will be the most desirable because it will result in a lower billed cost.

Practicing What You Have Learned

Determine the billed cost for each of the following. Be sure to round currency to the nearest penny and percentages to the nearest tenth.

1. List price = $350
   Trade Discount Offered = 40% and 10%

2. List price = $1,200
   Trade Discount Offered = 30%, 20%, and 5%

3. List price = $475
   Trade Discount = 30%

4. A rug buyer placed an order for 3 dozen rugs. Twelve of the rugs had a list price of $575.00 each and the remaining rugs were listed at $650.00 each. The vendor offered the merchandise at list price less 30% and 15%. What was the billed cost of the order?

5. A manufacturer of wooden salad bowls and accessories offers its largest distributor a trade discount of 40%, 15%, and 5%. On an order of merchandise listed at $4,680 what would be the billed cost?

6. Calculate the billed percent for a trade discount of 30%, 15%, and 5%.

7. Calculate the billed cost of an outdoor patio set with a list price of $1,200 where a trade discount of 25% and 10% is offered.

8. Using Problem 7 above, calculate the billed cost of the same outdoor patio set using the billed percent method.

Quantity Discounts

Quantity discounts are sometimes offered to buyers when a specified quantity of goods is purchased. The discount is offered to encourage buyers to concentrate their purchases with one vendor if possible, rather than buying smaller amounts from a variety of vendors. Like the trade discount, this type of discount is not often used in the apparel trade but is more likely offered to buyers in hard goods or home furnishings.

The quantity discount is expressed as a percentage discount to be deducted from the billed cost when a predetermined quantity is purchased. It is important to note that unlike the trade discount, which is deducted from list price, this is a percentage deducted from billed cost. For this reason, if a trade discount is offered it must be taken first. Once the billed cost is calculated, then any quantity discount earned may be taken.

Application

A fabric manufacturer offers 1% discount on a particular fabric for orders of 500–1,000 square yards and a 1.5% discount for orders of more than 1,000 square yards. Millie's fabric store plans to order 900 square yards of the fabric at a billed cost of $2,700. Is the store eligible for a quantity discount? What would be the net billed cost?

Because 900 square yards is within the 500–1000 square-yard range, the store is eligible for a 1% discount.

Quantity Discount = $2,700.00 × 1% = $27.00
Billed Cost – Quantity Discount = Net Billed Cost
OR
$2,700.00 – $27.00 = $2,673.00 Net Billed Cost

Quantity discounts are legal due to the economies of scale but, when offered by a vendor, must be offered to all buyers whose purchase quantity qualifies.

Practicing What You Have Learned

Determine the answer for each of the following. Be sure to round currency to the nearest penny and percentages to the nearest tenth.

9. A supplier of wicker home furnishings offered a quantity discount of 10% on all purchases of 26 or more sofa tables. If The Home Store purchases 30 tables at a total billed cost of $4,500, what would the net billed cost be?

10. A carpet buyer placed an order for 1,500 square yards of carpet at a cost of $9.99 per square yard. If the vendor offered a trade discount of 25% and the quantity discount schedule below, what would be the net billed cost of the carpet?

Quantity (square yards)	Discount%
250–750	0.5%
751–1,500	0.75%
1,501–2,500	1%

11. The buyer at a local drugstore chain needed to replenish his stock of a popular brand of hair spray. Each unit costs $1.50 and he needs 480 units to restock his inventory. The vendor offers a 15% discount on all orders greater than 500 units. Should the buyer increase his order? Why? Calculate the billed cost for each scenario.

12. A riding lawn mower has a list price of $800 and trade discounts of 25% and 5%. If a local home improvement center orders a total of 3 mowers with a quantity discount of 10%, what would the net billed cost be on the total purchase?

13. If you were a buyer, which trade discount would you prefer?

    25%, 15%, & 5%
    OR
    40% and 10%

Cash Discounts

The **cash discount** is a percentage discount allowed on the billed cost if payment is made within an agreed upon period of time. The cash discount percentage is written on both the purchase order and the invoice. When trade and quantity discounts are offered, the cash discount is always the final discount taken. Billed cost is equal to the quoted cost or list price when a cash discount is the only discount offered.

The vendor offers the cash discount to the buyer to encourage payment as early as possible. The buyer, on the other hand, is best served by negotiating the longest cash discount period possible. This may allow the buyer time to receive and actually begin to sell the goods before payment is due, creating better cash flow. The negotiation of extensions to the cash discount period will be discussed later in this chapter.

The regular form of cash discount is stated in terms of the length of time the cash discount will be available and, if not taken, when the total billed cost is due. For example, the regular cash discount may be stated 3/10, **n**/30 where a 3% cash discount is allowed if the billed cost is paid within 10 days of the date on the invoice. If not paid in the 10-day discount period, the entire billed amount or **net** is due within 30 days of the date on the invoice. Net cost is the amount due after all applicable discounts are taken. If the retailer is unable to make payment by the end of the cash discount period, it must pay the net, or full, amount on the invoice. Alternatively, if the cash discount is desired, the discount is deducted from the billed cost and the net (billed cost minus cash discount) is paid within the discount period stated.

Application

If a shoe buyer places a $3,000 order and is granted a 5% cash discount for prompt payment, what would be the net cost remitted by the buyer?

$3,000.00 × 5% = Cash Discount
$3,000.00 × 0.05 = $150
Billed Cost − Cash Discount = Net Cost
$3,000.00 − $150.00 = $2,850.00

Practicing What You Have Learned

Determine the answer for each of the following. Be sure to round currency to the nearest penny and percentages to the nearest tenth.

14. If a leather goods buyer places an order for men's wallets with a billed cost of $1,475 and takes advantage of a 3% cash discount, what would be the net cost to the buyer?

15. A buyer places an order totaling $580. If the buyer is offered a trade discount of 25% and 5% as well as a 2% cash discount for prompt payment, how much would the buyer pay if all discounts were taken?

16. What is the net cost for a $2,375 order of silver jewelry if the cash discount of 6% is earned?

17. What is the net cost due on a gross of athletic socks priced at $36.50/dozen if a 3% cash discount is taken?

18. If a buyer negotiates regular terms (e.g., 6/10, n/30) for a cash discount and pays an invoice for $750 dated November 10 on November 26, can the cash discount be taken?

19. What would be the net cost due for an order totaling $1,899.00 if a 4% cash discount is taken?

20. A luggage buyer is offered a quantity discount of 1% on orders of 25–50 garment bags and a 2% discount for all orders greater than 50 garment bags. The cash discount negotiated is 2/10, n/30. If the buyer purchases 75 garment bags at $55.00 each and pays within the 10-day discount period, what would be the total amount remitted to the vendor?

Terms of Sale: Dating

Dating refers to the negotiated length of time the retailer has to pay the invoice with or without the cash discount. Dating terms often state the amount of the cash discount, the length of the cash discount period, and the length of time allowed to pay the amount in full without penalty.

For example, if a retailer is given regular terms of 2/10, n/30, then a 2% cash discount can be taken if payment is made within 10 days or else the total amount of the invoice is due within 30 days of the date of invoice. (Note that the 30-day net period does not begin at the end of the 10-day cash discount period but rather allows an additional 20 days after the discount period to pay the full amount of the bill.)

In the retail industry, successful negotiation often includes extending the cash discount period and payment dates as long as possible to allow the merchandise time to arrive and begin selling.

COD Dating

Cash on delivery (COD) dating refers to negotiated terms of cash on delivery. When a purchaser or retailer has no payment history or a poor payment history, the vendor may only be willing to enter into a transaction where the full amount of the invoice is paid upon delivery of the goods. For example, an invoice totaling $275 with COD terms is received by a retailer. The retailer must pay (remit) $275 upon receipt of the goods. In this case, no discount is granted and no grace period provided.

Regular Dating

Regular dating is among the most common types of dating. Regular terms allow the cash discount to be taken within a specified period (usually 10 days) of time from the date of invoice. The invoice is usually dated on the date that the merchandise is shipped.

Application

What amount should be remitted for an invoice totaling $600.00 dated July 1 with terms 8/10, n/30 if payment is made on July 5?

> Because payment is made on July 5, the cash discount can be deducted; therefore,
> Net Cost = Billed Cost − Cash Discount
> Net Cost = $600.00 − $48 ($600.00 × 8%)
> Net Cost = $652.00

Extra Dating

Extra dating (sometimes known as *X-dating* because it is notated by an "X" in the terms) is calculated from the date of invoice just like regular dating terms. However, unlike regular dating, extra dating grants a specified number of extra days in which to take advantage of the cash discount period.

Extra dating terms would be stated 3/10-30X where the cash discount period would last the original 10 days from the date of the invoice plus 30 extra days. This allows the retailer 40 days to take advantage of the cash discount. Just as in regular dating, if the cash discount is not taken, the net amount is due 20 days after the cash discount period expires. For example:

> A $1,000 invoice dated January 10 with terms 3/10-30X would remit:
> 1,000 − $30 ($1,000 × 3%) = $970 if paid by February 19 (21 days remaining in January plus 19 days to fulfill the remainder of the 40-day cash discount period)
> $1,000 would be due on March 11 (assume 28 days in February unless noted).

End of Month (EOM) Dating

End of month dating, like extra dating, extends the cash discount period. However, instead of adding days to the discount period, end of month dating indicates that the cash discount period is calculated from the end of the month in which the invoice is dated.

End of month dating is negotiated specifically to give the buyer an extended period of time within which to take the cash discount. For example, if an invoice is dated the first of the month with terms 6/10 EOM, a retailer would have the remaining days of the month plus 10 days to take the cash discount. If, however, the invoice is dated on the 26th of the month or later, the retailer will have until the end of the *following* month to take the discount in order to make the extension meaningful. For example:

> For an invoice with terms 6/10 EOM dated July 28, the retailer would have until the end of August plus 10 days (September 10) to take the cash discount of 6%.

> If the cash discount is not taken, the net amount would be due September 30 (20 days after the end of the cash discount period).

Receipt of Goods (ROG) Dating

Receipt of goods dating calculates the terms of the discount period from the date the goods are received. A buyer may request these terms when the goods have a significant distance to travel and may not arrive until the cash discount period offered by regular dating has expired. For example:

> An invoice dated July 1 with terms 3/10 ROG was received on July 10. This shipment would be eligible for a 3% cash discount until 10 days after the goods are received (e.g., July 20).

> If the cash discount is not taken, payment in full would be due 30 days after receipt of goods (10 days of the discount period plus 20 days or August 9).

Advanced or *As of* Dating

Advanced dating is often referred to as *as of* dating because the terms are usually stated as such: **3/10 as of July 1**. This means that a 3% discount can be taken for

10 days after July 1. The as of date negotiated is not necessarily the invoice date or the date the goods are received. For example:

> An invoice dated February 1 with terms 6/10 as of March 12 would require payment to be made by March 22 in order to receive the cash discount.

> If the cash discount is not taken, payment in full would be due April 11 (20 days after March 22).

In some cases, advanced dating terms will indicate that the actual invoice will be postdated (assigned some date in the future) and regular dating terms will then apply. For example:

> A shipment of merchandise may be made on February 1 but the invoice will be postdated to April 1. If terms are stated as 3/10, n/30, then the retailer will have until April 11 to take the 3% cash discount.

> If the discount is not taken, payment in full is due May 1 (20 days after April 11).

Practicing What You Have Learned

Calculate the last day to take the cash discount and the net payment due date for the following:

21. Invoice dated April 1 with terms 4/10, n/30 and shipment received April 4.

22. Invoice dated March 26 with terms 2/10 EOM and shipment received April 3.

23. Invoice dated July 1 with terms 4/10 ROG and shipment received on July 10.

24. Invoice dated October 3 with terms 6/10 as of November 15 and shipment received on October 18.

25. Invoice dated June 1 with terms 6/10-60X and shipment received on June 10.

26. Shipment received August 15 and invoice date October 1 with terms 3/10, n/30.

27. Invoice dated April 2 with terms 8/10 EOM and shipment received April 8.

28. Invoice dated December 2 with terms 4/10-30X and shipment received December 10.

29. Invoice dated March 17 with terms 2/10, n/30 and shipment received March 30.

30. Why might the buyer in the previous problem have wished to negotiate more favorable terms? What would you suggest?

Anticipation

Because the dating terms previously covered (e.g., as of dating) can significantly extend the cash discount period, some vendors allow an additional discount in addition to the cash discount to encourage early payment. This discount is referred to as **anticipation**. The total amount of the additional discount is based on the number of days remaining in the cash discount period when payment is made.

Anticipation rates will vary according to the prevailing interest rate but for calculations in this text, a 6% annual rate and 30 days per month (360 days per year) should be used. This is the equivalent of 0.5% for each month. As with the other discounts and terms of sale discussed in this chapter, the retailer will need to balance the desire to make early payments in order to receive the discounts offered with the need to create cash flow for the payment by selling the merchandise received.

The anticipation rate is a percentage that is calculated on the basis of the number of days remaining in the cash discount period. For example:

> If an invoice has terms of 2/10-30X, anticipation permitted, the retailer has 40 days to take the cash discount plus any anticipation earned. If the retailer pays the invoice on the 15th day, 25 days remain in the cash discount period.
>
> Anticipation = (25 ÷ 360) × 6%
> Anticipation = .0041666 = 0.42%
> Anticipation % + Cash Discount % = 0.42% + 2% = 2.42%

After the anticipation rate is calculated, it is added to the cash discount and multiplied by the billed cost to determine the amount to be remitted.

> *NOTE*: The anticipation rate and the cash discount are the only discounts that can be added together.

Practicing What You Have Learned

Determine the answer for each of the following. Be sure to round currency to the nearest penny and percentages to the nearest tenth.

31. The buyer of art supplies for a local retailer purchases goods totaling $1,040 with terms 8/10 EOM anticipation permitted. The invoice is dated April 5. How much should be remitted if payment is made on April 10?

32. An invoice for $2,400 dated February 11 has terms of 6/10-50X, anticipation permitted. If the invoice is paid on February 28, how much should be remitted?

33. Dorian's Book Emporium received an invoice for $825 dated August 25 with terms 4/10 EOM, anticipation permitted. If the invoice is paid on September 1, how much should be remitted?

34. An invoice for $650 is dated July 1 with terms 4/10 as of September 1, anticipation permitted. If the invoice is paid on July 10, how much should be remitted?

35. The linens buyer purchases $9,350 less 30% and 10% in organic, cotton bed linens. If the invoice is dated October 1 and the buyer negotiates terms of 5/10-40X, anticipation permitted, how much should be remitted on October 15?

Loading

There are times when a retailer desires to obtain a standardized cash discount on all goods purchased (e.g., 6%). If the cash discount offered by the vendor is less than the cash discount the retailer desires, the price of the invoice can be intentionally increased so that the desired cash discount can be offered. This practice, known as **loading**, allows the vendor to achieve the desired net cost and the retailer to achieve the desired cash discount.

Application

If a manufacturer quotes a cost for an invoice of down pillows totaling $1,500 with terms of 3/10, n/30, but the buyer desires a cash discount of 5%, then what would be the loaded cost?

First calculate the net cost of the invoice (i.e., the amount desired by the manufacturer).

Net Cost = $1,500 − ($1,500 × 3%)
Net Cost = $1,500 − $45 or $1,455

Next calculate the loaded cost necessary to provide the desired 5% discount.

Loaded cost = Net Cost ÷ Complement of the Cash Discount Desired
Loaded cost = $1,455 ÷ (100% − 5% loaded discount) or 95%
Loaded cost = $1,531.58

You can double-check your work:

Net Cost desired by manufacturer = $1,455
Net Cost (with loaded discount) = $1,531.58 less 5% = $1,455

Practicing What You Have Learned

36. An order totaling $790 is normally sold with terms 3/10, n/30. What will be the loaded price sold with terms 6/10, n/30?

37. A shipment of computer printers totaling $4,000 is normally sold with a cash discount of 4%. If a cash discount of 8% is desired, what would be the loaded cost?

38. Most cashmere scarf vendors are quoting a cash discount of 5% on all purchases. If the buyer from Heckman's Accessories Boutique desires an 8% discount on an order of 3 dozen scarves priced at $21 each, what would the loaded cost of the order be?

39. If an order totals $11,450 with terms 2/10, n/30, what would be the loaded cost if a 4% discount is desired?

40. A lawn mower that costs $225 is sold with a 3% cash discount. What would be the loaded cost if a 6% discount is desired?

Negotiating Transportation Terms

Just as with the discounts and the terms of sale previously discussed, negotiation of the terms of shipping (transportation) and handling can be critical factors in the profitability equation. Retailers are purchasing products from an ever-broadening variety of manufacturers in an ever-growing number of geographic locations. Many of these manufacturers are attractive due to the low costs at which they are able to provide the merchandise. However, if a buyer is not diligent in the process of negotiation including the negotiation of the terms of transportation, all of the savings to be gained from these lower manufacturing costs could be lost in the process of transporting the merchandise.

Free-on-board (FOB) is the common term used to express the terms of the transportation. FOB is commonly followed by a particular destination (e.g., factory or warehouse) indicating that the costs of transportation are free to the retailer up to that point. The terms also indicate the point at which the ownership of the merchandise changes from the manufacturer or vendor to the retailer. The owner of the merchandise at any point in time is responsible for the merchandise and bears the risks of loss or damage.

You will find the following definitions useful in negotiating the terms of transport:

Charges Reversed   Used in conjunction with one of the negotiated FOB terms (e.g., FOB Warehouse, Charges Reversed). Under these conditions, the vendor will maintain ownership of the goods and incur the risks to the negotiated destination but the buyer will pay the transportation charges from the factory.

FOB Destination   Term commonly used to indicate that the vendor is responsible for all transportation costs and owns the merchandise until it reaches a point designated by the retailer. This specified destination is commonly the store or a warehouse utilized by the retailer but could also be a port of entry into the country. This term can also be written *FOB Store*; *FOB Warehouse*, *FOB City*, or *FOB Port* are also destination points that the buyer may negotiate. The terminology indicates that the vendor pays for transportation up to the destination selected and then the buyer must pay to transport the merchandise from that point to the final point of sale (usually the store).

FOB Factory   Term commonly used to indicate that the buyer is responsible for all transportation costs and owns the merchandise from the moment it leaves the factory.

Freight Prepaid   Most commonly used in conjunction with one of the negotiated FOB terms (e.g., FOB Factory, Freight Prepaid). If, under the negotiated terms, the buyer is responsible for transportation costs, the vendor must be reimbursed when the costs for the merchandise are paid.

Practicing What You Have Learned

41. If the buyer receives a shipment of sweaters from a factory in China direct to her store with terms FOB Store,
    a.   Who pays the transportation charges?
    b.   Who takes ownership and risks for the sweaters during transportation?

42. If a shipment of merchandise from Guatemala arrives at a retailer's warehouse in California with terms FOB Factory, Freight Prepaid,
    a.   Who pays the transportation charges?
    b.   Who takes ownership and risks for the merchandise during transportation?

Chapter 3 Review Exercise A

Answer each of the following and be prepared to show all your work. Be sure to round all currency to the nearest penny and all percentages to the nearest tenth.

1. An invoice dated August 3 totaling $3,215 had terms 3/10-40X, anticipation permitted. If the net cost was paid on September 12, what was the total amount remitted to the vendor?

2. An invoice was received by Kay's Kloset in the amount of $980. If the negotiated terms were 3/10 as of June 1 and the invoice is dated May 2, what payment should be made if the invoice is paid on May 6?

    If the buyer desires an 8% cash discount, what would be the loaded cost?

3. What is the last day to take the cash discount on an invoice dated January 27 with terms 2/10 EOM?

4. A buyer for glassware orders merchandise from a vendor in China totaling $1,050.00. The buyer negotiates terms of 5/10-30X, FOB Store, anticipation permitted. If the invoice is dated July 9 and is paid on July 29, what amount should be remitted to the vendor?

5. If merchandise is shipped FOB Buyer's Warehouse, Freight Prepaid, who should pay for transportation of the goods? Who is the owner of the merchandise while in transit?

6. A sporting goods buyer made a purchase of golf equipment totaling $5,675. A 10% quantity discount was offered on the order with terms of 6/10 ROG. Transportation charges were $250 with terms FOB Store, Freight Prepaid. If the invoice was dated April 15 and the merchandise was received on May 1, how much should be remitted by the buyer on May 10?

7. What is the last day to take the cash discount on an invoice dated October 1 if the terms offered are 6/10-60X?

8. Determine the net cost on a shipment of men's leather goods with a list price of $2,740 if the vendor offers a trade discount of 40% and 15%.

9. A music store purchased a shipment of CDs for an upcoming promotional event. If the invoice of $2,500 was dated November 30 with terms of 8/10-40X, anticipation permitted, how much should be remitted to the vendor if paid on December 8?

10. A buyer was offered the following trade discounts. Which discount should he take?

30%, 15%, and 5%
OR
50% and 5%

Chapter 3 Review Exercise B

Answer each of the following and be prepared to show all your work. Be sure to round all currency to the nearest penny and all percentages to the nearest tenth.

1. Determine the last day to take the cash discount for each of the following:

Date of Invoice	Merchandise Received	Terms	Last Day to Take Discount
a. Sept. 29	Oct. 25	2/10 ROG	_____
b. May 26	June 10	8/10 EOM	_____
c. Nov. 5	Nov. 22	6/10-30X	_____
d. Dec. 3	Dec. 10	2/10, n/30	_____
e. Jan. 24	Feb. 11	4/10 as of Mar. 1	_____

2. If a handbag vendor offers terms of 3/10, n/30 on a $2,000 order and the buyer desires a 5% cash discount, what would be the loaded cost?

3. If the linens buyer received a trade discount of 30% and 10% on an invoice of bed linens totaling $7,330, what would be the total remitted if the cash discount of 3% is taken and the transportation charges of $335 are negotiated as FOB Factory, Freight Prepaid?

4. Vendor A offers an invoice of luggage totaling $1,975 with a trade discount of 30% and 10% and vendor B offers the same purchase with a trade discount of 25%, 10%, and 5%. Which vendor should the buyer select?

5. A dress buyer received an invoice dated February 26 that carries terms of 2/10-30X, anticipation permitted. If the invoice for $18,450 is paid on March 3, how much should be remitted?

6. Calculate the net cost for an invoice of 3 dozen pairs of women's tights priced at $4.00 per pair if a cash discount of 6% is earned.

7. An invoice was received by Mary Claire's Party Shop in the amount of $6,490 with a quantity discount of 25% and terms of 6/10 ROG. If the goods were received on May 20 and the invoice was paid on May 23, what net cost should be remitted?

8. If shipping terms of FOB Greensboro (Buyer's Warehouse), Charges Reversed are negotiated for an invoice,
   a. Who pays shipping?
   b. Who owns the merchandise while in transit?

9. An order totals $1,610 for merchandise normally sold with 1/10, n/30 terms. What would be the loaded cost if the merchandise was sold with 4/10, n/30 terms?

10. Consider merchandise totaling $465 with an invoice dated September 2 and terms of 2/10 ROG, FOB Store. The goods were received on September 10 and transportation charges totaled $21.50. If the invoice is paid on October 12, how much should be remitted?

Chapter 3 Review Exercise C

Answer each of the following and be prepared to show all your work. Be sure to round all currency to the nearest penny and all percentages to the nearest tenth.

1. A men's furnishings order was received on March 26 with an invoice dated March 21. The merchandise totaled $2,178 with terms 2/10 EOM. How much should be remitted if the invoice is paid on April 4?

2. A buyer placed an order for sporting equipment totaling $14,710. The vendor offered terms of 4/10, n/30, but the buyer required 6/10 terms. What would be the loaded cost for the order?

3. What is the on percent for a series discount of 40%, 15%, and 5%?

4. On November 5 a payment was made on a $4,080 order of swimwear with an invoice dated October 30 and terms listed as 2/10-40X, anticipation permitted. What was the amount remitted?

5. What is the last day to take the cash discount on an invoice dated June 12 with terms 6/10 as of September 1?

6. Vendor A is offering a shipment of merchandise valued at $10,500 with a quantity discount of 5% and cash discount of 3%. Vendor B offers the same merchandise for $10,000 and a cash discount of 2%. Which is the better resource?

7. Which discounts, if any, can be added together before taking the deduction?

8. An order for jeans totaling $3,400 arrived at the store on August 5. Terms of the invoice dated August 1 were 5/10 ROG, FOB Store, Freight Prepaid. If transportation charges for the merchandise were $285 and the bill was paid on August 16, how much should be remitted?

9. If terms of a merchandise shipment are FOB Factory, Charges Reversed,
    a. Who is responsible for the cost of transportation?
    b. Who owns the merchandise while in transit?

10. What is COD? Why might a vendor only offer such terms to a retail client?

Cost of Merchandise and Terms of Sale
Excel Tutorial 3

Opening a File

1. Open Excel. You can refer to the Basic Math Concepts Tutorial in Chapter 1 at any time during this lesson if you cannot remember how to perform the assigned tasks.

2. Choose **File>Open** and then locate the file entitled **Lesson3.1.xls**. You can open this file by double-clicking on the filename. Your screen should resemble **Figure 3.1**.

Fig. 3.1:

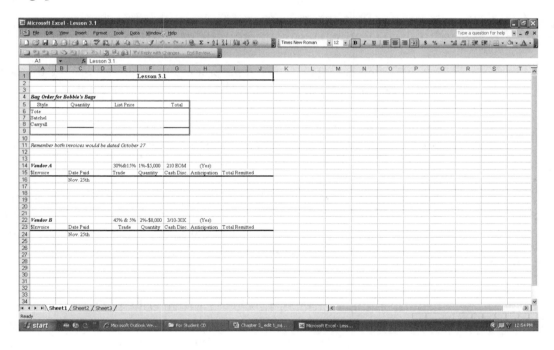

Completing the Spreadsheet

3. Bobbie's Bags needs to purchase the following shipment of bags:

Style	Quantity	List Price
Tote	200	$25.00
Satchel	100	$30.00
Carryall	250	$20.00

Each of the vendors shown below is able to provide a suitable product at the same list price. The terms each vendor is offering are listed. Determine the amount that Bobbie should remit to each vendor if payment is made on November 25.

- *VENDOR A*:
  - Terms 2/10 EOM
  - Invoice Dated: October 27
  - Anticipation permitted
  - Trade Discount 30% and 15%
  - 1% Quantity Discount on orders of $5,000 or more

- *VENDOR B*:
  - Terms 3/10-30X
  - Invoice Dated: October 27
  - Anticipation permitted
  - Trade Discount 45% and 5%
  - 2% Quantity Discount on orders of $8,000 or more

4. Enter the purchase data in the appropriate cells. Begin by placing the quantities in cells **C6 through C8**. Next, place the list prices in cells **E6 through E8**.

5. Format the data entries. Placing your cursor in cell **C6**, hold down the left mouse button and drag down to cell **C8** to highlight the quantity cells. After highlighting, select **Center** ≣ to center the data in the cells.

6. Format the list price entries. Placing your cursor in cell **E6**, hold down the left mouse button and drag down to cell **E8** to highlight the list price cells. After highlighting, center the data in the cells. Make sure the font is 10 pt. **Times New Roman**. Choose **Format>Cells** from the pull-down menu. Select **Currency** and make sure that the decimal places are set at **2**.

7. Calculate the total quantity to be purchased in cell **C9**. Place your cursor in that cell and click Σ on the standard toolbar. The formula reading [**=SUM(C6:C8)**] will appear in the cell and a flashing box will encircle the cells. Press **Enter**. While your cursor is still in this cell, center the total in the cell.

8. Enter the formula that will calculate the total purchase amount for each style. Begin with the Tote style. Place your cursor in cell **G6** and type (**=C6*E6**). Notice that the amount is already formatted in currency format. (If the amount is not properly formatted, use the directions in Step 6 to correct any problems.)

9. Copy the formula in cell **G6** to cells **G7** and **G8**. Your cursor should still be in cell **G6**. Select **Edit>Copy** from the pull-down menu or click 🖺 in the toolbar. A flashing box will encircle the cell you want to copy. Place your cursor in cell **G7** and, holding down the left mouse button, drag your cursor down to cell **G8** and release

the button. Now that the cells are highlighted, select **Edit>Paste** from the pull-down menu or click 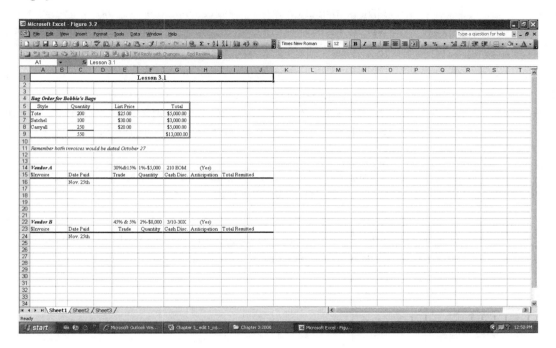 on the toolbar.

10. Calculate the total purchase amount by placing your cursor in cell **G9**. Click Σ on the standard toolbar. The formula reading [**=SUM(G6:G8)**] will appear in the cell and a flashing box will encircle the cells. Press **Enter**.

11. Format the totals figures by highlighting cells **G6 through G9** and selecting **Center** . Also make sure that the font type and size are consistent. Your screen should resemble **Figure 3.2**.

Fig. 3.2:

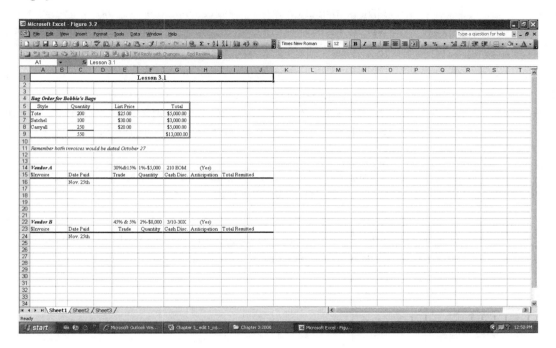

12. Enter the total purchase **$** calculated in cell **G9** in cells **A16 and A24** (for vendors A and B, respectively). Because copying the formula in that cell will cause the formula to change, it is best to simply type the amount in each of the cells.

13. Enter the formula that will calculate the purchase price less the trade discount for Vendor A in cell **E16** [**=(A16*0.7)*0.85**]. This formula uses the **on percent method**, taking the discounts in order by first multiplying by the complement of the 30% discount and then by the complement of the 15% discount.

14. Enter the formula in cell **F16** that will deduct the quantity discount of 1% from the newly discounted purchase amount (**=E16*0.99**). The total purchase price of the order entitles Bobbie to the 1% quantity discount because it surpasses the $5,000 minimum indicated.

15. Determine eligibility for cash discount. Next, you must determine whether Bobbie is eligible for the cash discount. The terms indicate that a cash discount of 2% can be taken if the invoice is paid within 10 days of the end of the month, and in this case, the invoice date is *after the 26th* so we start from the end of the month of November, giving us a cash discount date of December 10. The data indicate a payment date of November 25 so the cash discount can be taken. Because anticipation is permitted and we are eligible for 16 days of anticipation (6 days remaining in November and 10 days in December), we are going to add the cash and anticipation discount together and deduct them in cell **I16**. For now, type 0.02 in cell **G16** and 0.0027 in cell **H16**. You can then format these as percentages by selecting **Format>Cells>Percentage** as you learned in the Chapter 2 Tutorial.

> *HINT:* The anticipation rate can be calculated as $16/360 \times 6\% = 27\%$. Then we add that to the 2% cash discount for a total deduction of 2.27% (the complement of which is 97.73%).

16. Enter the formula in cell **I16** that will deduct the cash discount and anticipation percentage and yield the amount to be remitted. The formula should read **=F16*(1-(G16+H16))**. The formula could also be written **=F16*.9773**.

> *HINT:* Note that the spreadsheet package will accept two sets of parentheses in a single formula as indicated in this step.

17. Format cells E16, F16, and I16 as currency. Highlight each cell and select **Format>Cells>Currency**. Your screen should resemble **Figure 3.3**.

Fig. 3.3:

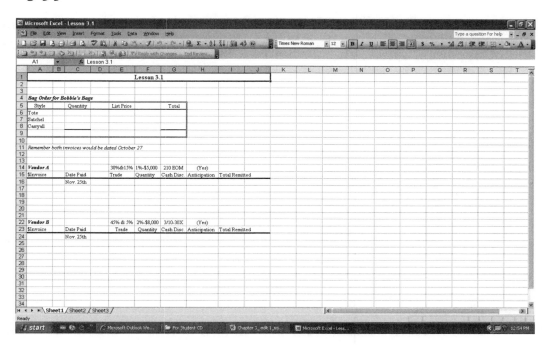

18. Follow steps 10 through 13 using the terms for trade given for Vendor B in order to determine the amount necessary for remittance to that vendor.

> *HINT:* You must determine whether Bobbie is eligible for the cash discount and anticipation with this vendor as well. The terms indicate that a cash discount of 3% can be taken if the invoice is paid within 10 days with 30 extra (a total of 40 days).
>
> The invoice date is October 27 so there are:
>
> 4 remaining days in October
> 30 days in November
> 6 days in December (December 6 is the last day to take the cash discount)
>
> Since the invoice was paid on November 25, you are entitled to the cash discount *plus* 11 days of anticipation. (Calculated as $11/360 \times 6\% = 0.18\%$)

19. As you have done previously, format all monetary amounts as currency with two decimal places and all percentages with two decimal places. Also be certain that the font is consistent throughout the spreadsheet as Times New Roman 10 pt. Your screen should resemble **Figure 3.4.**

Fig. 3.4:

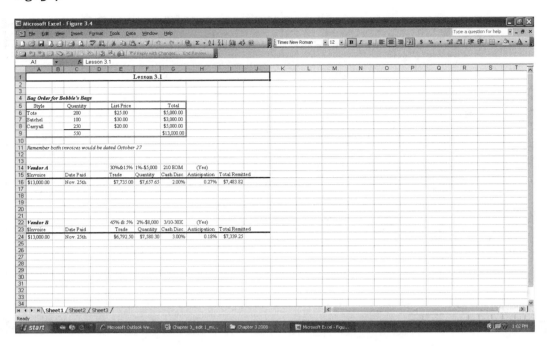

20. Now you are almost ready to complete the assignment. First you need to choose the area of the spreadsheet that you would like to print. To set the print area, click on cell **A1** and highlight down to cell **I24**. Then select **File>Print Area>Set Print Area**.

21. Next, select **File>Page Setup**. Select the tab labeled **Sheet**. You will see that the gridlines and row/column headings have a check mark (✓) beside them. Click on these to eliminate the (✓) and turn off the gridlines and row/column headings. In most cases, the spreadsheet will look more professional without the row/column headings and gridlines as you have done here.

22. You can select **Print Preview** to see how your spreadsheet will look when printed.

23. When you are through previewing the page you will need to choose **Close**, which will take you back to your working spreadsheet.

Saving Your Work and Printing

24. Before you print and turn in your assignment, you will always want to save your work.

25. To save your work, select **File>Save As**. You will want to save your work on a travel drive and label it **Lesson3.1(your initials here with no spaces)**. For example, if your name is Amy Scott, your filename will read Lesson3.1AS.xls. By

labeling the exercise in this way, you can retain the *original* spreadsheet file just in case you should need it at a later date.

26. To save the file on your travel drive, choose **File>Save As**. In the File name box, enter a new name for your file; in this case type **Lesson3.1(your initials here with no spaces)**. To save the copy to an external medium, click a different drive (as indicated by your instructor) in the **Save in** drop-down list or a different folder in the folder list, or both. Click OK.

27. Now, print out your assignment by selecting **File>Print**, choosing your printer, and pressing **OK**.

> *HINT:* You may want to save each assignment in more than one place (e.g., your travel drive and on the hard drive in your own designated folder if you are allowed to do so).

28. Your screen should resemble **Figure 3.5** when the steps are complete.

Fig. 3.5:

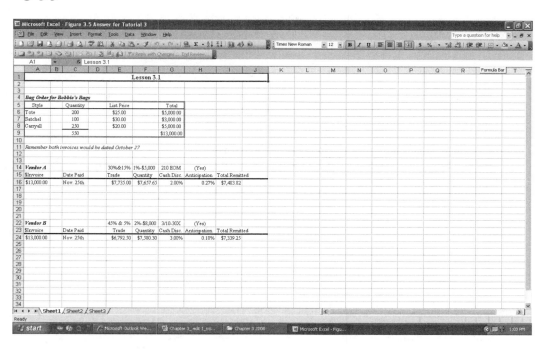

29. Your instructor may request that you print out your spreadsheet assignment showing all the formulas you have written. To do this, select **Tools>Options>View**. Check **Formulas**, under the **Window options** section. You can also display formulas by pressing **Ctrl ~**.

Cost of Merchandise and Terms of Sale Review Problems Using Excel

Review Problem 3.1

Open a blank spreadsheet.

1. Start by saving the blank spreadsheet to your travel drive and give it an appropriate filename. To be consistent, this file should be named **Review3.1(your initials here with no spaces)**. Now you are ready to begin working.

2. Create a table that will allow you to calculate the loaded cost for the following items:

    *   A handbag that normally costs $30.00 is sold with a 4% cash discount. If the buyer wants an 8% discount, what would be the loaded cost?
    *   A blazer that normally costs $54.00 is sold with a 2% cash discount. If the buyer wants a 6% discount, what would be the loaded cost?
    *   A small kitchen appliance that normally costs $35.00 is sold with a 5% cash discount. If the buyer wants an 8% discount, what would be the loaded cost?
    *   A costume jewelry buyer purchases a bracelet at a cost of $18.00. The terms normally offered are 2/10, n/30. What would be the loaded cost if the buyer desires 5/10, n/30 terms?

3. Be sure to give your chart an appropriate title, column headings, borders, and other appropriate formatting.

4. Present the data as well as your calculations in order to represent the results. For example you may want columns with the **Item**, **Cost**, **Cash Discount Offered**, and the **Cash Discount Desired**, as well as the **Loaded Cost**.

5. When you have completed your spreadsheet, set the print area and choose a format for the page that you feel presents the information in a professional manner. You can then save your work one last time and print. Because you have already saved the file and named it **Review 3.1(your initials)**, choose **File>Save** and print out the final results as directed by your instructor.

Review Problem 3.2

Open a blank Excel spreadsheet.

1. Save the blank spreadsheet to your own travel drive and give it an appropriate filename. To be consistent, this file should be named **Review3.2(your initials here with no spaces)**. Now you are ready to begin working.

2. Create a table depicting the total amount remitted for the following group of items if the trade discount and cash discount are taken:

- The accessories buyer placed an order for the following:
  - 20 Leather Totes – List Price $32.00 each
  - 40 Cell Phone Cases – List Price $9.00 each
  - 15 Leather Card Cases – List Price $12.00 each
  - 50 Watches – List Price $32.00 each
  - 25 Compact Umbrellas – List Price $6.50 each

- The buyer is quoted a trade discount of 30% and 10%.
- Terms are 6/10, n/30.

3. Be sure to give your chart an appropriate title, column headings, borders, and other appropriate formatting.

4. Present the data as well as your calculations in order to represent the results. For example, you may want columns with the **Item**, **Cost per Item**, **Total Cost**, **Trade Discount** (amount remitted), and **Cash Discount** (amount remitted) as well as the total amount remitted for all items. Make sure the information is professionally presented and easy to read.

5. When you have completed your spreadsheet, set the print area and choose a format for the page that you feel presents the information in a professional manner. You can then save your work one last time and print. Because you have already saved the file and named it **Review3.2(your initials)**, choose **File>Save** to save your work and print out the final results as directed by your instructor.

Review Problem 3.3

In the previous chapters, you practiced completing a pre-programmed spreadsheet and completing a spreadsheet of your own creation. In this practice problem you will be asked to complete a case study analysis for three vendors using the partially pre-programmed spreadsheet found in the file labeled **Review3.3.xls**. The case study below will ask you to use your knowledge of dating, discounts, terms of sale, and pricing to select the most appropriate supplier for a shipment of silk baby doll dresses necessary to complete the spring dress assortment for Amber's Attic.

Case Study: Amber Brown, the owner and fashion buyer of Amber's Attic, visited New York Fashion Week looking for a vendor who might have a suitable offering of the silk baby doll dresses she needs to complete the spring assortment for her boutique in Buffalo, New York. Amber's Attic is a trendy boutique on the east side of Buffalo that caters to middle-to-upper-income, fashion-forward women. Amber spent her first day meeting and negotiating with three vendors who she determined could offer the product she desired. Exhausted, she came back to the hotel with the following notes:

Total Need: 21 Dresses

Vendor A	Vendor B	Vendor C
$66 each	$62 each	$56 each
FOB Store	FOB Warehouse	FOB Shipping Point
	Trans. 1.5%	Trans. 4.0%
Location: Pittsburgh, PA	Location: California	Location: China
3/10, n/30	2/10 EOM	2/10, n/30
Ship: 2/7	Ship: 2/7	Ship: 2/7
		Supplies GAP

WE WILL TAKE CASH DISCOUNT!!!

Cream, Turquoise*, and Brown in sizes 2–14, 1 in each color, 3 each size?

*fashion colors/hot trends

As the assistant buyer, you spent the day at the hotel with your laptop inputting orders and vendor notes for the rest of the assortment Amber purchased. When Amber returns to the room, she hands you her notes and asks you to prepare an analysis of each vendor's offering along with your vendor recommendation for the boutique. She explains that she has made dinner arrangements with a key supplier for the boutique. Unfortunately, though she would love to have you along, she must have this analysis and recommendation by the time she returns so that she can make a final decision and fax the order before leaving for a 7:30 flight tomorrow morning. You order room service and get to work.

1. Open the Excel file labeled **Review3.3.xls**. A partial view of what the spreadsheet looks like is represented in Figure 3.6.

Fig. 3.6:

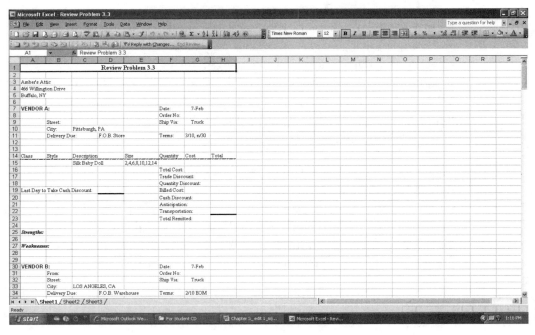

2. Using the notes Amber gave you, complete the vendor analysis form and then fill in the recommendation form provided at the bottom of the page. List at least one strength and one weakness for each vendor based on the information given (i.e., location, price, cash discount, transportation, etc.).

3. Refer to the terms provided at the beginning of this chapter to help you with the formulas. By now, you should be quite comfortable working with Excel spreadsheet formulas.

4. You can type in strengths and weaknesses much like you would in a word processing program. Just place your cursor in the cell in which you wish to start typing and do not press **Enter** until you have completed your comment.

5. Be sure to read the notes carefully and refer back to them often. **Remember:** The results are only as good as the information and formulas *you* enter!

6. Set the area of the spreadsheet that you would like to print.

7. Before you print and turn in your assignment, save your work.

In this case type **Review3.3(your initials here with no spaces)**. Then click **OK** and print out your assignment. Your instructor may also want you to print the assignment showing the formulas.

CHAPTER 4

Reductions

This chapter is devoted to the retail reductions that ultimately impact the profitability of a retail store or department. These retail reductions include markdowns, employee discounts, and shortages.

You will find the following concepts and definitions useful in the repricing of merchandise:

Employee discount A percentage reduction off the retail price of merchandise often extended as a fringe benefit to personnel.

Markdown A reduction in the original or previous price of an item or a group of items.

Markdown cancellation An increase in the retail price of an item or group of items that offsets all or a portion of a previously taken markdown.

Net markdown The difference between **total markdowns** and any **markdown cancellations** that occur.

Shortages Retail dollar difference between the book inventory (numerical or statistical count) and the physical inventory (actual physical count) of merchandise where the book inventory indicates that there is more merchandise on hand than is actually found when the physical inventory count is completed.

Retail reductions Any factor that reduces the value of the inventory a retailer carries. Can include markdowns, shortages in stock, (e.g., shipping shortage, damaged goods, theft), employee discounts, etc.

You will find the following formulas useful in your calculations:

- Reductions = Markdowns, Employee Discounts + Shortages
- $Markdown = Original Retail Price – New Retail Price
- Markdown% = $Markdown ÷ Net Sales
- Markdown Cancellation = Retail Price – Markdown Price (Usually multiplied by the number of items marked back up)
- Net Markdown = Total Markdown – Markdown Cancellation

Calculating Markdowns

Markdowns are the most common type of repricing. Markdowns are a reduction in the retail price of an item or group of items. They can be temporary (e.g., a 25% back-to-school special on tennis shoes), in which the price adjusts back to the original retail price after a specified period of time, or they can be permanent (e.g., an "every day low pricing" strategy results in a permanent markdown to a lower retail price).

Retailers use markdowns to attract customers to the store, to help to move merchandise that is not selling well, to match or beat competitor pricing, and to move merchandise already purchased in order to have money available for new purchases.

In order for a markdown to be most effective, the reduction must be taken before the merchandise movement has begun to slow significantly. Retailers often take an initial markdown of 15%–20% or more on new arrivals. Any reduction less than 20% is not likely to attract customer attention, especially in the fashion apparel business. Slow-selling merchandise, which often requires clearance pricing, can reduce the amount of dollars available for the purchase of new merchandise and may cause significant losses in profit for the retailer.

Markdown is most often discussed as a percentage of net sales for ease of comparison, for example, a comparison of one store to another or one department to another. Just as you learned with the other factors affecting profits, such as expenses, the markdown percentage is calculated by dividing the markdown dollars by the net sales figure.

Application

If 300 sweaters with an original retail of $39.99 are marked $24.99 for an Easter sale, and 125 sweaters were sold during the event while the rest sold at regular price, what would be the markdown in dollars and percentage?

$Markdown = Original Retail Price – New Retail Price
$Markdown = $39.99 – $24.99
$Markdown = $15.00 × 125 sweaters
$Markdown = $1,875

Then:

$$\text{Markdown\%} = \$\text{Markdown} \div \text{Net Sales}$$
$$\text{Net Sales} = (125 \text{ sweaters} \times \$24.99) + (175 \text{ sweaters} \times \$39.99)$$
$$\text{Net Sales} = \$3,123.75 + \$6,998.25 \text{ or } \$10,122$$
$$\text{Markdown\%} = \$1,875 \div \$10,122$$
$$\text{Markdown\%} = 18.52\%$$

Practicing What You Have Learned

For each problem, round dollar amounts to the nearest whole dollar and percentages to the nearest tenth.

1. During the month of December, a children's toy buyer took markdowns totaling $2,443. If net sales for the month were $11,560, what was the markdown percentage?

2. If a luggage buyer plans a markdown percentage of 12% on net sales of $9,870, what would be the total dollar amount of markdowns?

3. If markdowns for October totaled $14,900, which represented 16%, what would be the net sales achieved during the month?

4. The fragrance department planned net sales for the month of February of $105,000. If markdowns for the month were planned at 22%, determine the planned markdown dollars.

5. The buyer for Tabletop at Smithley's Department Store planned net sales of $225,000 for the 6-month period ending in December. If the planned markdown for the period totaled $20,500, what would be the planned markdown percentage?

6. The small leather goods buyer received a special deal on a trendy group of leather cell phone cases. If markdowns are planned at 15% and are expected to total $1,275, what are the expected net sales?

Calculating Markdown Cancellations

Retailers frequently hold special sales during which merchandise is marked down temporarily for the sale and then the remaining merchandise returned to the original price or some price point higher than the markdown price when the sale is over. This upward price adjustment is known as a **markdown cancellation**.

Technology has all but eliminated the need for markdown cancellations. Point-of-sale terminals can be programmed to take the markdown at the register when a sale item is purchased. Because the merchandise is not marked down until it is actually sold, there is no need to mark the remaining merchandise back up.

Ultimately, the net markdown figure is what interests the retailer. **Net markdowns** result from calculating the total value of markdowns and subtracting the total value of markdown cancellations.

Application

For a Labor Day sale, 40 fall sports jackets were marked down from $125.00 to $99.00. During the sale, 22 of the jackets sold and the 18 remaining jackets were returned to the original price. Calculate the total markdown, markdown cancellation, and net markdown figures.

Net Markdowns = Total Markdowns − Markdown Cancellations
Net Markdowns = [40 jackets × ($125.00 × $99.00)] − [18 jackets × ($125.00 − $99.00)]
Net Markdowns = (40 × $26.00) − (18 × $26.00)
Net Markdowns = $1,040.00 Total Markdowns − $468 Markdown Cancellations
Net Markdowns = $572.00

In some cases, the merchandise remaining after the sale will not be marked back up to the original price. Perhaps the end of the season is near or perhaps the merchandise remaining is not a full representation of sizes, colors, etc.; the retailer may feel that the remaining merchandise will move faster if the new price is somewhat lower than the original retail price.

For a special July 4 sale, 50 sundresses were reduced from $69.00 to $39.00. During the sale, 34 dresses were sold at the markdown price. After the sale, the remaining 16 dresses were marked back up to $45.00. Calculate the total markdowns, markdown cancellations, and net markdown achieved.

Net Markdown = Total Markdowns − Markdown Cancellations
Net Markdown = [50 dresses × ($69.00 − $39.00)] − [16 dresses × ($45.00 − $39.00)]
Net Markdown = (50 × $30.00) − (16 × $6.00)
Net Markdown = $1,500.00 − $96.00
Net Markdown = $1,404.00

Practicing What You Have Learned

For each problem, round dollar amounts to the nearest whole dollar and percentages to the nearest tenth.

7. During the month of April, the Pool & Patio Shop had total markdowns of $2,950.00 and markdown cancellations of $875.00. What were the net markdowns for the shop?

8. A swimsuit buyer reduced a group of designer swimwear from $75.00 to $50.00 for a special sale. If 40 swimsuits sold at the reduced price and the remaining 25 swimsuits were returned to the original price after the sale, calculate the total markdowns, markdown cancellations, and net markdown achieved.

9. A buyer purchased 200 ties for a special Father's Day sale. The buyer set an original retail price of $35.00 each, but planned to sell the ties at 25% off during the sale. During the sale, 130 ties were sold and the remaining 70 ties were marked back to the original price. Calculate the total markdowns, markdown cancellations, and net markdown achieved.

10. For a midnight sale in early May, a buyer priced 75 spring raincoats at $34.00 compared to their original retail price of $50.00. If 52 coats sold during the sale and the remaining coats were priced at $39.00 after the sale, what was the net markdown achieved?

11. A buyer reduced 30 men's dress coats from $250.00 to $199.00 for the anniversary sale. After the sale, the 8 remaining coats were marked back to the original price. Calculate the total markdowns, markdown cancellations, and net markdown achieved.

Shortages

Although the calculation of shortages will be covered in great detail with the retail method of inventory later in this text, the definition and possible causes of shortages are explained here as they relate to reductions in the value of inventory. The value of inventory in a retail store is constantly available in the form of a **book inventory**. The book inventory keeps a running statistical total of the retail value of additions and deductions to stock. Periodically, usually at the beginning of a new accounting period, the retailer will take an actual physical count of the inventory on hand. This count is known as a **physical inventory. Shortages** occur when the physical inventory count is smaller than the book inventory indicates that it should be.

There are many possible causes for this type of shortage. It is possible that there was an incorrect physical inventory count or incorrect book inventory calculation. Other clerical errors such as failure to record markdowns, transfers, or returns to vendor properly are also a possible cause. The use of technology has greatly decreased these types of clerical errors. Today, the causes of shortages in inventory are much more likely to be a result of physical merchandise losses, such as broken merchandise that is not properly noted or theft (by customers or employees).

Employee Discounts

In addition to hourly or salaried compensation, many retailers offer personnel a percentage reduction on the price of merchandise, or an **employee discount**. This type of reduction lowers the value of the merchandise in inventory in much the same way as markdowns and shortages. The employee discount is most often expressed as a percentage off the retail price (e.g., 15% off retail) and may be higher for managerial level employees than for sales personnel.

Application

A salesperson at Burton's Lighting receives a 20% employee discount on all non-sale merchandise. The employee wishes to purchase a table lamp that retails for $129. What would be the charge to the employee for the purchase?

Retail Price$ = Retail $ – Employee Discount$
Retail Price$ = $129.00 – ($129 × 20%)
Retail Price$ = $129.00 – $25.80
Retail Price$ = $103.20 including employee discount

Practicing What You Have Learned

For each problem, round dollar amounts to the nearest whole dollar and percentages to the nearest tenth.

12. Phil's Electronics offers a 20% employee to all employees. Rebecca bought the newest slim-line cell phone, which retailed for $109, using her employee discount. How much did Rebecca pay for the phone?

13. If Sheila gets a 15% discount as a salesperson and Amy gets a 25% discount as a department manager, how much would each pay for a winter coat that retails for $250?

14. Jill receives a 25% employee discount and wants to purchase several items. What is the total cost of the following goods if the discount is taken?

    | Leather Pumps | $89.50 |
    | Silk Blouse | $69.50 |
    | Pin Stripe Suit | $249.99 |

15. Eric wants to utilize his 15% employee discount to purchase a new flat-screen TV. If the particular set he is interested in retails for $879, what price will Eric pay with the discount?

Chapter 4 Review Exercise A

For each problem, round dollar amounts to the nearest whole dollar and percentages to the nearest tenth.

1. During the month of December, Emmett's Electronics had sales of $87,500 and markdowns of $12,390. What was the markdown percentage for the month?

2. For a midnight madness event in the bed linens department, 1,000-thread-count sheet sets that originally sold at retail for $120.00 were sold at $89.99 per set. Of the 231 sets in stock at the time of the sale, 147 sets sold at the discounted price. The remaining sets were marked back to the original price at the end of the sale. Calculate the total markdowns, markdown cancellations, and net markdowns for the event.

3. Markdowns for the month of June totaled 18.5%. If net sales during the month were $1,205,500, calculate the markdown dollars.

4. The lingerie department had a net markdown of $4,380. If the total markdowns totaled $7,395, what were the markdown cancellations?

5. A buyer for draperies received 200 traverse rods that retailed for $48.00 each. After several weeks only 25 of the rods sold at the original price. The buyer ran a special 3-day sale selling 89 of the rods at a price of $30.00. After the sale, the buyer marked the remaining rods at $40.00. Calculate the total markdowns, markdown cancellations, and net markdowns experienced.

6. A children's shoe department took the following markdowns for the month of August:

   25 pairs of canvas tennis shoes from $25.00 to $19.00
   30 pairs of patent leather shoes from $30.00 to $22.00
   20 pairs of soccer cleats from $28.00 to $18.00

   What were the total markdown dollars taken in the department for the month?

7. A crystal flower vase retailing for $119.00 was offered at a 30% discount during a special sale. What was the price of the vase after the markdown was taken?

8. The buyer for the sporting goods department had 75 sets of golf clubs in stock with an original retail price of $259.00. During a special sale, 48 sets of clubs sold at a markdown price of $199.00. After the sale the remaining sets sold for $229.00. Calculate the net markdown dollars and net markdown percentage.

9. A store gives employees a 20% discount on all merchandise purchased. If a salesperson buys a coat for $159.00 and a handbag for $59.00, what will be the total amount owed including the employee discount?

10. An accessories buyer sold a pair of pearl earrings for $109.00. The earrings had an original retail price of $179.00. What was the markdown percentage on the earrings?

Chapter 4 Review Exercise B

For each problem, round dollar amounts to the nearest whole dollar and percentages to the nearest tenth.

1. For the month of February, an accessories department planned markdowns of 9%. Actual markdowns totaled $1,875 for total sales of $17,950. Calculate the actual markdown percentage experienced. Was the actual markdown percentage more or less than the planned percentage?

2. A suit buyer took markdowns totaling $4,700 in the month of October. The net sales for the month were $63,000. Calculate the net markdown percentage for the month.

3. For a special anniversary sale, a shoe buyer took 50% off of all belts that originally retailed for $30.00. The buyer had 200 belts in stock and 168 sold during the sale. The remaining belts were marked back to the original price and sold. Calculate the net markdown dollars and net markdown percentage for the belts.

4. During May, a candy store experienced net markdowns of $430. If the total markdowns for the month were $1,079, calculate the markdown cancellation.

5. A buyer reduced 38 recliners from $349 to $279 for a Labor Day sale. During the sale, 21 recliners were sold. After the sale, the remaining recliners were priced at $299 and eventually sold. Calculate the total markdown, markdown cancellation, and net markdown figures.

6. A local department store offers store sales personnel a 12% discount and store management a 15% discount. How much would a suit retailing for $400 cost a sales associate? A store manager?

7. Markdowns in the designer dress department totaled $52,390. If net sales totaled $313,000, calculate the markdown percentage.

8. Markdowns for a local leather goods retailer totaled 12.5% for the first quarter of the year. If the markdown dollars totaled $6,800, what were net sales for the quarter?

9. If a dinette set that normally retails for $1,995 is placed on sale for $1,200, what is the markdown percentage for the set?

10. A buyer reduced 100 swimsuits from $59.00 to $38.00 for a one-day sale. Seventy-five of the suits sold that day. The remaining suits were marked back to the original price and sold. Calculate the net markdown dollars and the net markdown percentage.

Chapter 4 Review Exercise C

For each problem, round dollar amounts to the nearest whole dollar and percentages to the nearest tenth.

1. During the month of April, paint sales at Julie's Home Improvement Center totaled $6,200. If markdowns for the month were $1,100, what was the markdown percentage for the month?

2. A buyer reduced 150 screen-printed T-shirts from $29.00 to $19.99 for a special sale. Eighty-two T-shirts were sold at the reduced price and the remaining shirts were returned to the original price and eventually sold. Calculate the total markdowns, markdown cancellations, and net markdown dollars.

3. Pearson's Books had total markdowns of $1,325 and a net markdown of $634 for the month of October. Calculate the markdown cancellations for the month.

4. The accessories department at Finley's Department Store had net sales of $47,600 with markdowns taken totaling $8,850. Calculate the markdown percentage.

5. A local furniture store offered a special markdown to any customer purchasing a grouping of furniture. Paula had selected the following items:

Leather Sofa	$ 2,850
Leather Loveseat	$ 2,150
End Table	$ 330 each
Coffee Table	$ 550

Paula learns that she can purchase a sofa, loveseat, two end tables, and a coffee table for $4,657.50. Calculate the markdown percentage offered on the grouping.

6. Markdowns for a local home goods retailer totaled 11% for the first quarter of the year. If the markdown dollars totaled $9,300, what were net sales for the quarter?

7. A manufacturer offered a comforter and sheet set for $129.00. During a special sale, a markdown of 30% was offered. Calculate the reduced price for the bedding set.

8. A buyer bought 200 girls' Easter dresses that were offered at retail for $55.00. During a three-day Easter sale, 117 of the dresses sold at $39.00. After the sale, the remaining dresses were repriced to $45.00 and sold. Calculate the total markdowns, markdown cancellations, and net markdown for the dresses.

9. As part of his employee benefits package, Bill receives an employee discount of 15% on all merchandise purchased. During the month of May, Bill purchased a shirt at $65.00, 2 pairs of jeans at $50.00 each, and a belt costing $29.00. Calculate the total cost to Bill including the employee discount.

10. Plans for the designer dress department included planned sales of $310,000 and planned markdowns of 18%. Find the planned markdown$.

Calculating Reductions
Excel Tutorial 4

Opening a File

1. Open Excel. You can refer to the Basic Math Concepts Tutorial in Chapter 1 at any time during this lesson if you cannot remember how to perform the assigned tasks.

2. Place the CD that comes with your textbook into the CD drive. Locate the file named **Lesson4.1.xls** and from the **File** Menu, choose **Open>Lesson4.1.xls**. Your screen should resemble **Figure 4.1**.

Fig. 4.1:

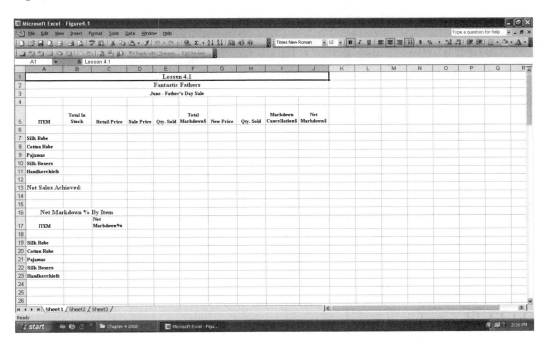

Entering Data

3. To enter data in a cell, click on the cell and enter the data, then press **Enter** or click on the green check mark (✔) in the formula bar. Now, enter the following data (as shown in whole numbers) in the appropriate cells:

	Total In Stock	Retail Price
Silk Robe	60	119
Cotton Robe	75	89

Pajamas	125	50
Silk Boxers	200	25
3 pk. Handkerchiefs	50	16

4. For a special Father's Day sale the items are sale priced and sold as follows. Enter the data for sale prices in **Column D** and the quantities sold in **Column E**:

	Sale Price	Qty. Sold
Silk Robe	89	32
Cotton Robe	60	40
Pajamas	34.99	83
Silk Boxers	12.99	125
Handkerchiefs	12	15

5. After the sale, the remainder of the items were marked back to the original prices and eventually sold. First highlight the regular retail prices by placing your cursor in **C7** and then drag the highlight down to **C11**. When the cells are highlighted, select **Edit>Copy** or . The flashing box will indicate the text to be copied.

6. Next place your cursor in cell **G7**. Select **Edit>Paste** or to indicate that the new, after-sale price was the same as the original retail price.

Formula Writing

7. Because the quantity remaining after the sale was eventually sold, you will need to calculate the remaining quantities in cell **H7**. Placing your cursor in H7, enter = (equal sign) and then click on cell **B7**. Now enter − (minus sign) to indicate subtraction and then click on cell **E7**. Press **Enter** to complete the calculation. Your screen should resemble **Figure 4.2**.

Fig. 4.2:

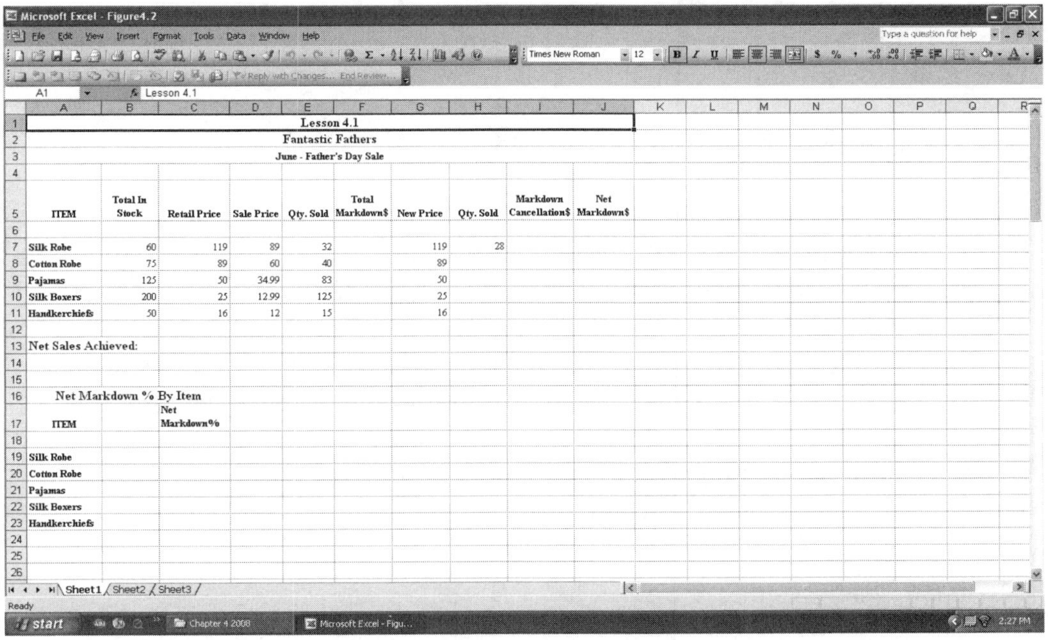

Copying Formulas

8. To calculate the remaining quantities sold for each of the other items, **Copy** the formula from cell H7 to cells H8 through H11. Place your cursor in cell **H7** and select **Edit>Copy** or ▣.

9. Move your cursor to cell **H8** and drag the cursor to **H11** to highlight the group of cells. Now select **Edit>Paste** or ▣ to copy the formula.

Formatting Numbers

10. The figures you have just entered need to be represented as quantities or dollar amounts where appropriate. Each cell in Excel defaults to a "general" format that works well for quantities. However, the retail price figures entered need to be represented as dollar figures, so you will need to format the data as currency.

11. Place your cursor in cell **C7**. Click on the cell and holding the left mouse button down, drag your cursor down to cell **C11** and then release the button. The highlighted area can now be formatted. Click on **Format>Cells**. Then, select **Number** from the box that appears and click on **Currency**. You will want to select the format with two decimal places to show dollars and cents. In the Sample box, you can see how your formatting will look. Press **Enter** to indicate that the selection is correct.

12. Repeat the process in the previous step to format the figures in cells **D7 through D11** as currency.

13. Repeat the process in step 11 to format the figures in cells **G7 through G11** as currency.

Completing the Formula Writing

14. Working in cell **F7**, calculate the Total Markdown dollars taken on silk robes. Type = to begin the formula writing process. Next, click **B7** to indicate the number of items marked down and then type * (the multiplication sign used in Excel). Then you will enter ((open parenthesis symbol) and click on cell **C7**. Type – and click on cell **D7** to determine the markdown dollars on each item. Type) (close parenthesis symbol) and press **Enter** to complete the calculation.

15. **Copy** and then **Paste** the formula from cell **F7** into cells **F8 through F11**. Your screen should now resemble **Figure 4.3**.

Fig. 4.3:

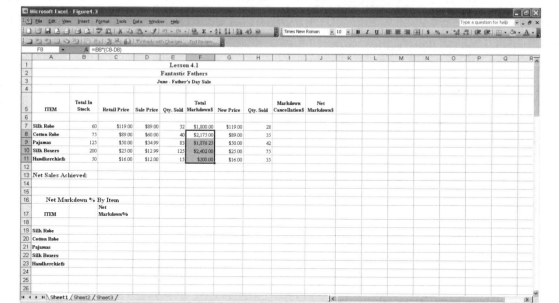

16. Because all of the items were not sold at the sale price, you must now calculate the markdown cancellations experienced on each item. Placing your cursor in cell **I7**, type = and then enter **H7*** to indicate the number of items remaining after the sale that must be multiplied by the upward price adjustment. Because the items went back to the original price, type **(C7-D7)** and press **Enter**.

HINT: Your formula in cell I7 should read = **H7*(C7-D7)** to calculate the total markdown cancellations.

17. **Copy** and **Paste** the formula entered in cell **I7** to cells **I8 through I11**.

18. Finally, you can calculate the net markdown dollars for each of the item categories. **Working in cell J7** type = to begin the formula. Now write the formula that will subtract the markdown cancellations from the total markdowns. Click on cell **F7** and –, then click on **I7**. Press **Enter** to complete the calculation.

19. **Copy** and **Paste** the formula entered in cell **J7** to cells **J8 through J11**. Your screen should now resemble **Figure 4.4**.

Fig. 4.4:

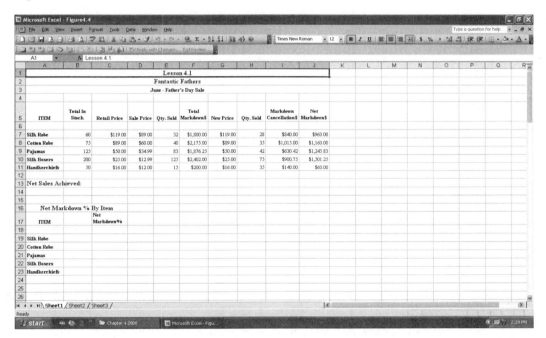

Completing the Spreadsheet

20. The management team of Fantastic Fathers wants to determine the net sales achieved on the merchandise as well as the Net Markdown percentage for each

item. This can easily be done by adding a column titled **Net Sales** to the right of the Net Markdown$ column.

21. After adding the column, place your cursor in cell **K7** and enter the formula to total the sales for the item during and after the sale. Enter = to begin the formula and then type **(E7*D7)+(H7*G7)**. Press **Enter** to complete the formula. Your screen should resemble **Figure 4.5**.

Fig. 4.5:

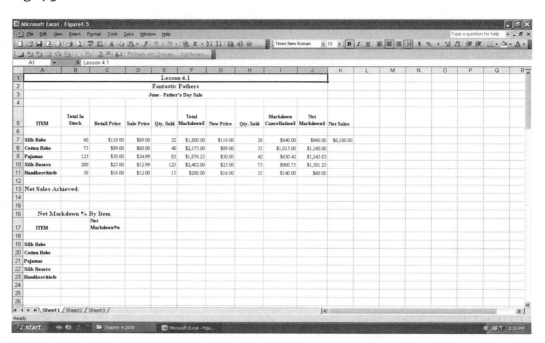

22. **Copy** and then **Paste** the formula entered in cell **K7** to cells **K8 through K11**.

23. Working in cell C13, total the net sales for the items by choosing **AutoSum(π)**. You will notice that a flashing box forms around the data you entered in cells C7 through C12 and a formula appears in the active cell (C13). This formula, **=SUM(C7:C12)**, will add the data in the cells that are encircled by the flashing box. Because this is NOT the correct formula, you simply need to place your cursor in the formula bar and change the cell selection to **K7:K11**. You will see a blue box form around the cells you have selected. If this is correct, press **Enter** to complete the formula.

24. Finally, the Net Markdown percentage can be calculated by placing your cursor in **C19** and entering the formula = **J7/K7**. You can then **Copy** and **Paste** the formula in cells **C20 through C23**.

25. Now format cells **C19 through C23** in percentage format. Show two decimal places for the percentages. Highlight the cells by clicking on **C19** and drag your cursor to **C23**. Next choose **Format>Cells**. The **Number** tab will be selected and you can select **Percentage** from the options. Make sure the decimal place to the right indicates 2 and then click **OK**. Your screen should now resemble **Figure 4.6**.

Fig. 4.6:

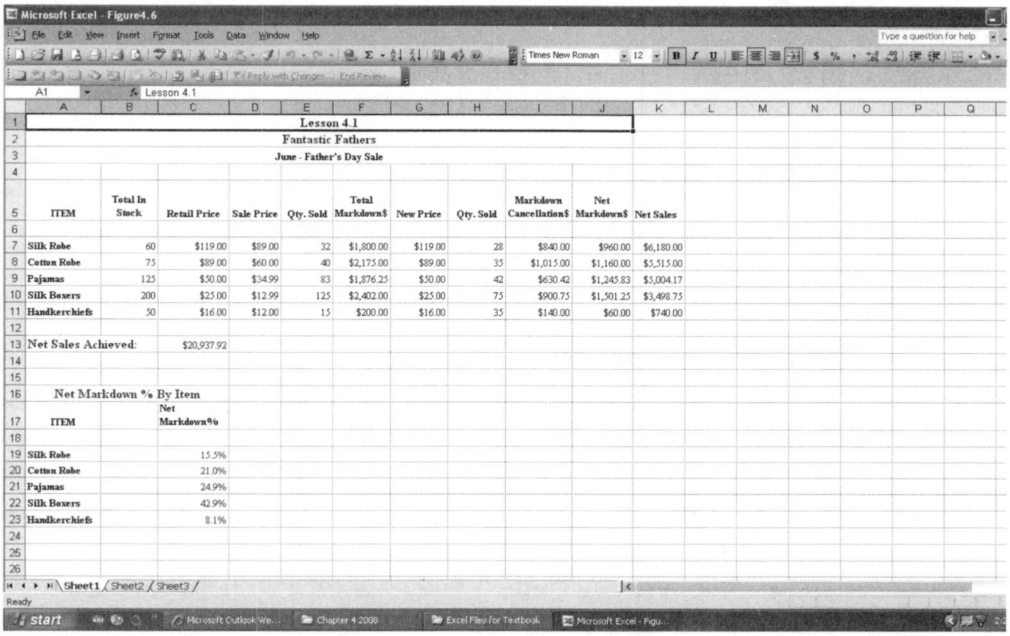

Setting a Print Area and Formatting the Page

26. Make sure to format the Net Sales heading in **K7** in bold by selecting the cell and clicking the **Bold** icon **B** from the toolbar. You will also want to center the heading by clicking **Center** ≡.

27. Now you are almost ready to complete the assignment. First you need to set the area of the spreadsheet that you would like to print. Click on cell **A1** and highlight down to cell **K23**. Select **File>Print Area>Select Print Area**.

28. Next, select **File>Page Setup**. A tabbed window will open and you will need to select the tab labeled **Sheet**. You will see that the gridlines and row/column headings have a check mark (✓) beside them. Click on these to eliminate the (✓) and turn off the gridlines and row/column headings.

29. You can select **Print Preview** to see how your spreadsheet will look when printed. When you are through previewing the page, choose **Close**, which will take you back to your working spreadsheet.

Saving Your Work and Printing

30. Before you print and turn in your assignment, save your work.

    HINT: You should save **often** during your work session to be sure that you have saved changes made to the worksheet.

31. Save your work on the travel drive and label it **Lesson4.1(your initials here with no spaces)**.

32. Now print out your assignment. It is highly recommended that you save your work to the hard drive in addition to your travel drive if permitted.

Printing Formulas

33. Your instructor may request that you print out your spreadsheet assignment showing all the formulas you have written. To do this, select **Tools> Options>View**. Check **Formulas**, under the **Window options** section. You can also display formulas by pressing **Ctrl ~**.

Calculating Reductions Review Problems Using Excel

Review Problem 4.1

The infant and toddler department at Broadbeck's Department Store held a special Easter sale with some special buys obtained from key vendors. The buyer purchased the items especially for the promotion. Create a chart that depicts the quantity, cost, and retail of the items as well as the indicated discount and sale price.

	Qty.	Cost	Regular Retail	Discount	Sale Price
• Hooded Pram	50	14.00	40.00	50%	
• Floral Cotton Easter Dress	90	9.00	24.00	30%	
• Sweater Vest Set	80	15.00	35.00		29.99
• Tulle Toddler Dress	50	18.00	40.00		29.99

Open a blank Excel spreadsheet.

1. Save the blank spreadsheet and give it an appropriate filename. To be consistent, this file should be named **Review4.1(your initials here with no spaces)**. Now you are ready to begin working.

2. Format the currency properly and the percentages to 1 decimal place.

3. Be sure to give your spreadsheet an appropriate title and make sure to format it in a professional manner.

4. When your assignment is complete, be sure to save your work (choose **File>Save** in the menu bar) and print out the final results.

Review Problem 4.2

The infant and toddler department at Broadbeck's Department Store completed its Easter sale as outlined in Review Problem 4.1. The figures below shows the results of that sale. Create a chart that depicts the total markdown dollars, markdown cancellation dollars, net markdown dollars, and net markdown percentage for each of the items.

- Hooded Pram: 45 sold at reduced price; remaining 5 were left at reduced price and eventually sold.
- Floral Cotton Easter Dress: 52 sold at reduced price; remaining dresses marked back to original price
- Sweater Vest Set: 47 sold at reduced price; remaining sets marked to original price
- Tulle Toddler Dress: 33 sold at reduced price; remaining dresses marked to $32.00

1. Save the blank spreadsheet and give it an appropriate filename. To be consistent, this file should be named **Review4.2(your initials here with no spaces)**. Now you are ready to begin working.

2. If you completed Review Problem 4.1, you can reopen that file and create a chart below the existing chart in order to utilize the information already entered. Be sure this is acceptable to your instructor before you begin.

3. Be sure to format the currency properly and the percentages to 1 decimal place.

4. Be sure to give your spreadsheet an appropriate title and make sure to format it in a professional manner.

5. When your assignment is complete, be sure to save your work (choose **File>Save** in the menu bar) and print out the final results.

Review Problem 4.3

Jenny has owned Lace & Lingerie, a small lingerie and sleepwear shop, for nearly three years. Net sales have recently dropped significantly and Jenny realizes that she often has a large portion of her merchandise on clearance at 50% off. Jenny is beginning to think that her current markdown strategy is not effective. Over the last few months, Jenny has experimented with two markdown strategies and now wishes to analyze the results. Create a chart that calculates the net markdown dollars and net markdown percentage for each of the events. Which strategy would appear to work best for Jenny?

- Jenny first tried purchasing 50 silk pajama sets that would retail for $85.00 per pair. When the new merchandise arrived, she ran a 20% off promotion and then returned the merchandise to the original price. During the sale, 29 sets were sold. After the sale, another 16 sets sold at the original price. The remaining 5 sets sold on 50% off clearance.
- For Jenny's next order, she again purchased 50 silk pajama sets that would retail for $85.00 per pair. This time, she did not run a promotion on the new merchandise but chose to run it at regular price for several weeks and then run a 30% off promotion midway through the selling cycle. Eighteen pairs of pajamas sold at regular price and all but two pairs sold at 30% off. The remaining 2 pairs were eventually sold at 50% off clearance.

1. Begin by saving the blank spreadsheet and giving it an appropriate filename. To be consistent, this file should be named **Review4.3(your initials here with no spaces)**. Now you are ready to begin working.

2. Be sure to format the currency properly and the percentages to 1 decimal place.

3. Be sure to give your spreadsheet an appropriate title and make sure to format it in a professional manner.

4. When your assignment is complete, be sure to save your work (choose **File>Save** in the menu bar) and print out the final results.

CHAPTER 5

Calculating Basic Markup

In this chapter you will be introduced to one of the basic pricing factors known as markup. **Markup** is the price that retailers must set for items offered for resale that covers the cost of the item and an added amount. This price must also be large enough to cover not only the expenses incurred in selling the item, but a desired profit as well. Markup percentages can be calculated as a percentage of the retail price of the item or the cost price. Generally, retailers express markup as a percentage of retail, although some retailers still use the cost-based method. Both methods will be presented in this chapter.

You will find the following negotiating concepts and definitions useful:

Cost or *cost price* The amount a retailer pays a vendor for merchandise purchased.

Cost complement The difference between 100% and the markup percent. (100% is often referred to as the retail percent.)

Markup The difference between the amount the retailer pays a vendor and the price of merchandise sold to the end consumer. Can be stated in dollars or percentage format.

Markup dollars The dollar difference between the cost price and the retail price of merchandise sold to the end consumer.

Retail or *retail price* The price of merchandise to the end consumer.

You will find the following formulas useful in your calculations:

- $Cost + $Markup = Retail
- $Retail − $Cost = $Markup
- $Retail − $Markup = $Cost
- $Cost ÷ $Retail = Cost%
- $Markup ÷ $Retail = Markup% on Retail
- $Markup ÷ $Cost = Markup% on Cost
- $Cost ÷ Cost Complement(100% − Markup%) = Retail
- $Retail × Cost Complement(100% − Markup%) = Cost
- Markup% on entire purchase = (Total $Retail − Total $Cost) ÷ Total $Retail

Calculating Markup

As you learned in the previous chapters, retailers must not only pay for the merchandise they wish to resale, but they have to cover the expenses of running the business (e.g., salaries, utilities, rent, etc.). A successful retailer will also need to earn a profit in addition to the cost of merchandise sold and expenses. The additional dollars needed to cover the planned expenses and earn a profit are known as **markup dollars**.

Calculating the Retail Price

The **retail price** of merchandise can be calculated by adding together the cost of the item and the dollars of markup necessary to earn a profit.

Application

If a retailer buys a peasant skirt for $20 and has a markup of $10, what is the retail price?

> Cost $ + Markup $ = Retail $
> $20.00 + $10.00 = $30.00 at Retail

Calculating the Markup Dollars

In some cases, a retailer will purchase an item at cost and have a planned retail price in mind. Given the cost of an item and the retail price, a retailer can easily calculate the markup dollars.

Application

If a retailer purchases a leather handbag for $25.00 and plans to retail the item for $58.00, what would the markup dollars be?

Retail $ – Cost $ = Markup $
$58.00 – $25.00 = $33.00 Markup

Calculating the Cost Price

Now that you understand the relationship of cost, markup, and retail, it is possible to calculate the cost dollars for an item when the retail price and markup are known.

Application

If a silver photo frame retails for $70.00 and is marked up $38.00, calculate the cost price.

Retail $ – Markup $ = Cost $
$70.00 – $38.00 = $32.00 at Cost

Practicing What You Have Learned

Calculate the retail price for each example, rounding each answer to the nearest penny.

1. If a retailer purchases a bamboo T-shirt for $13.00 and takes a $12.00 markup, what would be the retail price of the T-shirt?

2. If a retailer purchases a crystal vase for $45.00 and takes a $35.00 markup, what would be the retail price of the vase?

3. A sweater costing $39.00 was marked up $45.00. What price did the sweater retail for?

Calculate the markup dollars for each example:

4. A retailer purchases a designer brand handbag for $125.00. If the bag sells at retail for $260.00, calculate the markup dollars.

5. A buyer finds a great cost on a quality pair of men's black loafers. If she purchases the loafers for $32.00 per pair and sets a retail price of $95.00 per pair, what is the markup dollars on each pair?

6. The cost price of a checkerboard cut, amethyst ring with platinum band is $390.00. If the ring retails for $999.00, what would the markup dollars be?

Calculate the cost price for each example, rounding each answer to the nearest penny.

7. What is the cost price of a dress with a markup of $30.00 and a retail price of $49.99?

8. Calculate the cost price of a jewelry box that retails for $130.00 and has a markup of $75.00.

9. If a retailer sells men's dress socks at $7.50 a pair and achieves a markup of $4.50 per pair, what is the cost price per pair?

Calculating the Markup Percentage Based on Retail

Because retailers often work in terms of percentages, it is important to be able to calculate the markup percentage for a given item as well. Retailers most often speak of markup percentages based on the retail price of a good. To calculate markup percentage based on retail, divide the markup dollars by the retail dollars.

Application

Calculate the markup percentage for the peasant skirt in the Application on page x based on retail.

Markup $ ÷ Retail $ = Markup %
$10.00 ÷ $30.00 = 33.3% Markup at Retail

Calculating the Markup Percentage Based on Cost

Calculating markup percentages based on the cost price of goods is rare in the retail industry. However, markup expressed as a percentage of cost is the more intuitive way to express the concept. For instance, in the peasant skirt example, most students and consumers would say that the markup is 50% because the skirt cost $20.00 and was marked up $10.00 which is 1/2 or 50% of $20.00.

Application

Calculate the markup percentage for the peasant skirt based on cost.

Markup $ ÷ Cost $ = Markup %
$10.00 ÷ $20.00 = 50% Markup at Cost

NOTE: Because markup is rarely calculated based on cost in the retail field, you will always calculate markup based on retail for this text unless directed otherwise.

Practicing What You Have Learned

Calculate the markup percentage based on retail and cost for each example, rounding each percentage to the nearest tenth.

10. A leather belt retails for $29.99 with an original cost price of $10.00. Calculate the markup percentage:
     a. At Retail
     b. At Cost

11. A knit shirt selling at retail for $40.00 was purchased at a cost of $22.00. Calculate the markup percentage:
     a. At Retail
     b. At Cost

12. A wool blazer costs the retailer $110.00 and retails for $249.99. Calculate the markup percentage:
     a. At Retail
     b. At Cost

Calculating the Retail Price Given Cost Dollars and Markup Percentage

It is quite realistic for a retailer to know the cost price of an item and have a planned markup percentage in mind for that item. The retail price of an item can be calculated given this information as well:

Cost% + Markup% = Retail (100%)

In order to determine the retail price, first calculate the cost percentage, also known as the **cost complement**. We know that the retail price represents 100% of the retail of the good. Therefore, given the markup percentage, simply subtract the markup percentage from 100% to determine the cost percentage or cost complement.

Application

If we know that

> Markup $ + Cost $ = Retail $

then it follows that:

> Markup % + Cost % = Retail % or 100%

or

> Cost % (a.k.a. Cost Complement) = 100% − Markup %

If a buyer purchases a wool jacket for $65.00 and desires a markup of 60%, what must the jacket retail for?

First find the cost complement:

> Cost Complement = 100% − 60% or 40%

Then determine the retail price using what you learned in Chapter 2. In this case, you divide the cost price by the cost complement in order to determine the retail price because the retail price should *always* be *higher* than the cost price.

> Cost $ ÷ Cost Complement = Retail $
> $65.00 ÷ 0.40 = $162.50 at Retail

Practicing What You Have Learned

Calculate the retail price for each example, rounding the answers to the nearest penny.

13. If a buyer purchases a grandfather clock for $210 and desires a 52% markup, at what must he set the retail price?

14. What retail price must a buyer set to achieve a 50% markup on a set of wine glasses costing $24.00?

15. A men's furnishings buyer purchased a designer label, leather wallet for $15.50. If she desires a 60% markup, at what price must she retail the wallet?

Calculating the Cost Price Given Retail Dollars and Markup Percentage

To calculate the cost price of an item given the retail price and markup percentage, you will once again need to use the cost complement. For this calculation, however, it will be necessary to multiply the retail price by the cost complement because the cost price should be *lower* than the retail price.

Application

If we know that

Cost % (a.k.a. Cost Complement) = 100% − Markup %

then we can use the cost complement to determine cost price

Cost Price = Retail $ × Cost Complement

If a buyer retails a silk dress for $180.00, which establishes a markup of 52%, then what is the cost price of the dress?

Cost Price = $180.00 × 48%(100% − 52%)
Cost Price = $86.40

Practicing What You Have Learned

Calculate the cost price for each of the following, rounding each answer to the nearest penny.

16. Determine the cost price of a pajama set that retails for $35.00 and carries a markup of 55%.
17. A leather sofa retails for $1,599.00 with a 65% markup. Determine the cost of the sofa.
18. Calculate the cost price of a set of cookware that retails for $299.00 with a 60% markup.

Chapter 5 Review
Exercise A

1. Calculate the missing figure(s) for each of the following, rounding each dollar value to the nearest penny and each percentage to the nearest tenth.

	COST PRICE	RETAIL PRICE	MARKUP $	MARKUP % ON RETAIL
A.	$49.00	$95.00		
B.		$2,030.00	$1,350.00	
C.	$14.50		$9.90	
D.		$100.00		58%
E.	$138.00			45%
F.	$7.50	$18.00		
G.	$39.75	$89.50		
H.		$250.00		61%
I.	$32.45			52%
J.		$76.99	$35.00	

2. If a buyer purchases a plasma television for $895.00 and desires a 65% markup, what is the retail price?

3. If the retail price of a Valentine's gift basket is $45.00 and the total cost price of the basket is $21.00, what markup was achieved:
   a. in dollars
   b. in percentage (based on retail)

4. If the cost of a summer blazer is $48.50 and a 55% markup is desired, what should the item retail for?

5. If an electronics retailer sells a sound system for $430.00 with a markup of 65%, what is the cost price of the system?

6. Determine the retail price of a china vase that costs the buyer $69.99 and carries a 54% markup.

7. What is the cost complement of a pair of earrings that retails for $18.00 and carries a markup of 48%?

8. A buyer made a special purchase of 2 dozen wristwatches for $350.00. What must each watch retail for to achieve a 70% markup?

9. Calculate the markup dollars earned on a cashmere sweater with a retail price of $125.00 and a cost price of $52.00.

10. Find the retail price of a dress with a cost price of $64.50 and a markup of 57%.

Chapter 5 Review
Exercise B

Answer each of the following, rounding dollar values to the nearest penny and percentages to the nearest tenth.

1. What is the cost complement for a sweater vest that retails for $32.99 and has a 38% markup?

2. A set of golf clubs costs a sporting goods buyer $150.00. If a 52% markup is desirable, what must the set retail for?

3. If the retail price of an item is $38.75 and the markup on the item is 55%, then what is the cost price of the item?

4. Express the markup based on cost for an item that retails for $129.00 and costs $62.00.

5. Calculate the missing figure(s) for each of the following:

	COST PRICE	RETAIL PRICE	MARKUP $	MARKUP % ON RETAIL
A.		$32.00		58%
B.		$1,730.00	$950.00	
C.	$7.00	$16.50		
D.	$105.00			48%
E.		$77.00		45%
F.	$7.50		$12.50	
G.	$60.75	$129.00		
H.		$550.00		50%
I.	$12.95			53%
J.		$1,050.00	$695.00	

6. A buyer purchases 3 dozen hand towels for $44.00/dozen. If the buyer desires a 40% markup, what must the retail price of each hand towel be?

7. What is the cost of a leather briefcase that retails for $149.00 and has a markup of 60%?

8. A set of lawn furniture retails for $299.00 and costs $135.00. Express the markup:
   a. in dollars
   b. in percentage (based on retail)

9. A candy buyer stocks chocolate bars at a cost of $6.00 a dozen. If the buyer desires a markup of 45%, then what must each bar retail for?

10. If a decorative rug retails for $79.00 and costs $32.00, what is the markup% based on retail?

Chapter 5 Review
Exercise C

1. Calculate the missing figure(s) for each of the following, rounding dollar values to the nearest penny and percentages to the nearest tenth.

	COST PRICE	RETAIL PRICE	MARKUP $	MARKUP % ON RETAIL
A.		$1,055.00		52%
B.		$249.00	$135.00	
C.	$1.09		$1.00	
D.	$435.00			48%
E.		$199.00		45%
F.	$10.75	$21.00	$12.50	
G.		$189.99		
H.		$500.00		60%
I.	$2,350.00			50%
J.		$6.99	$3.50	

2. If a buyer purchases 6 dozen pairs of cashmere winter gloves for $149.00 per dozen and plans to sell the gloves at $30.00 per pair. What would be the markup figure:
   a. in dollars
   b. in percentage

3. What is the cost of a tweed jacket that retails for $249.00 and carries a markup of 55%?

4. If a buyer is able to purchase a leather tote bag for $39.00 and desires a 60% markup, what should be the retail price of the tote bag?

5. If a 24 × 36 oil painting costs $89.50 and retails for $199.00, what is the markup percentage achieved?

6. If a men's sportswear buyer sells a fleece hoodie at retail for $59.00 with a 60% markup, what is the cost price of the hoodie?

7. If a linen tablecloth costs $25.00 and retails for $49.00, representing a 96% markup, is that markup based on cost or retail?

8. Express the markup based on cost for a T-shirt that carries a retail price of $15.00 and a cost price of $8.50.

9. If a girl's silk Easter dress retails for $49.00 and carries a 48% markup, what is the cost price of the dress?

10. A buyer of silk flowers purchases an order of silk roses for a Valentine's sale at a price of $16.00 per dozen. What must each rose retail for to achieve a 50% markup?

Calculating Markup
Excel Tutorial 5

Opening a File

1. Open Excel. You can refer to the Basic Math Concepts Tutorial in Chapter 1 at any time during this lesson if you cannot remember how to perform the assigned tasks.

2. Choose **File>Open** and then locate the file entitled **Lesson5.1.xls**. You can open this file by double-clicking on the filename. The problems you will be solving in this tutorial are in the two tables in this file.

3. Using file **Lesson5.1.xls**, perform the following tasks. Your screen should resemble **Figure 5.1**.

Fig. 5.1:

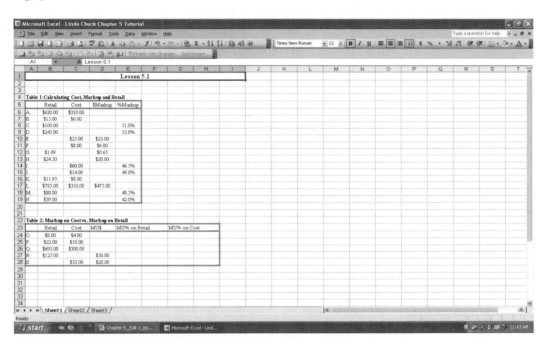

Completing the Spreadsheet

Enter the formula in cell **D6** to calculate the markup dollars for the retail and cost figures given in B6 and C6, respectively. This can be done by clicking on cell D6 and entering **= B6-C6**. When you have finished entering the formula press **Enter**.

HINT: Remember that $Retail − $Cost = $Markup

4. Enter the formula in cell **E6** that will allow you to calculate the markup percent based on retail in **Problem A**. This can be done by clicking on cell E6 and typing: **= D6/B6**. When you have finished typing the formula press **Enter**.

> *HINT:* The formula for calculating markup percent at retail can be written ($Retail − $Cost) ÷ $Retail. Because $Retail − $Cost = $ Markup, Markup% based on retail can also be calculated as $Markup ÷ $Retail.

5. Copy the formula for Markup dollars that you entered in **D6** into cell **D7**.

6. Repeat the process in step 5 so that you can copy the formula for Markup percent that you entered in cell E6 to cell E7.

7. Enter the formula that will calculate the Cost dollars necessary to complete **Problem C**, by entering **=PRODUCT(B8,1-E8)** in cell **C8**. Then you can complete the problem by entering the formula **= B8-C8** in cell **D8**.

> *HINT:* The formula for calculating Cost dollars when Retail dollars and Markup percent are known is:

$$\$Retail \times (100\% - \%MU) = \$Cost$$

Although your spreadsheet is formatted to show Markup in percentage format, Excel defaults to decimal form. Therefore, when you enter the formula to subtract Markup percentage from 100%, you must use a 1 instead of a 100. As you will remember from Chapter 1, 100% is equivalent to 1.00 in decimal format.

8. Use the previous steps to copy the formulas written in cells **C8** and **D8** to cells **C9** and **D9**, respectively, in order to complete **Problem D**.

9. Enter the formula in cell **B10** that will calculate the Retail dollars necessary to complete **Problem E**. This can be accomplished by typing **= SUM(C10,D10)**. Then you can complete Problem E by clicking on cell **E10** and entering the formula that will calculate Markup percentage (**= D10/B10**).

10. Use the previous steps to copy the formulas written in cells **B10** and **E10** to cells **B11** and **E11**, respectively, in order to complete **Problem F**. Your work should resemble **Figure 5.2**.

Fig. 5.2:

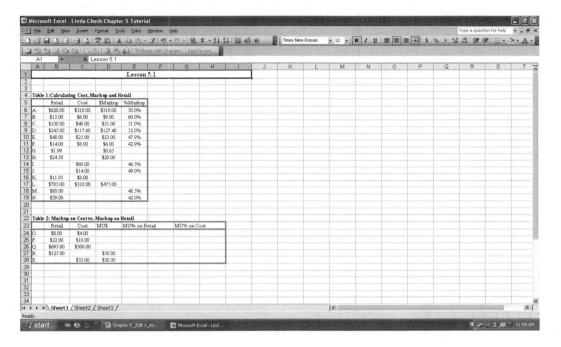

11. Copy the formula you entered in cell **E11** to cells **E12** and **E13**. This will calculate the Markup percentage given Markup dollars and Retail dollars.

12. Enter the formula that will calculate the Cost dollars for **Problems G and H**. This can be done by placing your cursor in cell **C12** and typing a formula that will subtract the markup dollars from the retail dollars. Your formula should be = **B12 − D12**. Copy this formula into cell **C13**.

13. Enter the formula in cell **B14** that will calculate Retail dollars given Cost dollars and Markup percentage. Because you are working with individual items in this example, you will want to include in your formula a function that calculates the cost of an individual unit, since cost is given per dozen. Your formula should read = **C14/(1-E14)**. You can then copy this formula into cell **B15** to begin **Problem J**.

   > *HINT:* When trying to calculate Retail dollars given Cost dollars and a desired Markup percentage, the formula is:
   >
   > Retail = $ Cost ÷ (100% − Markup%)

   Although your spreadsheet is formatted to show Markup in percentage format, Excel defaults to decimal form. Therefore, when you enter the formula to subtract Markup percentage from 100%, you must use a **1** instead of a **100**.

14. Enter the formula in cell **D14** to calculate Markup percentage by subtracting Cost dollars from Retail dollars. The formula reads **= B14-C14**. After you have typed the formula, press **Enter**. Copy the formulas into cells **D15 and D16** to calculate Markup dollars for **Problems J and K**.

15. Enter the formula in cell **E16** that will calculate Markup percentage given Markup dollars and Retail dollars. The formula will read Markup dollars ÷ Retail dollars or **= D16/B16**. Then copy the formula into cell **E17** to complete **Problem L**.

16. Enter the formula in cell **C18** that will calculate Cost dollars given Retail dollars and Markup percentage. Your formula will read **= PRODUCT(B18, 1-E18)**. Then copy this formula into cell **C19** to calculate Cost dollars for **Problem N**.

> *HINT:* Once you have pressed the **PASTE** function you will notice a clipboard icon 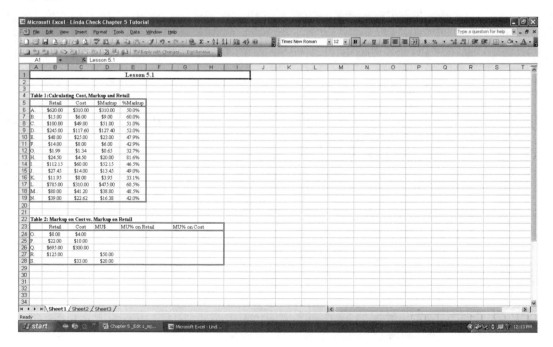 next to your highlighted cell. Press the arrow and select **Match Destination Formatting** from the pull-down menu. This will retain the cell formatting, leaving the table border intact.

17. Enter the formula in cell **D18** that will subtract Cost dollars from Retail dollars to give you Markup dollars. Your formula will read **= B18-C18**. Copy this formula to cell D19 to complete the exercise. Your screen should resemble **Figure 5.3**.

Fig. 5.3:

Completing the Table

Use the following steps to complete the table. (By now, the formulas should be familiar to you, but you can refer to the previous steps for help if necessary.)

18. Calculate MU$ for **Problems O, P, and Q**.

19. Calculate the $Cost for **Problem R**.

20. Calculate the $Retail for **Problem S**.

21. Calculate the Markup% based on Retail for **Problem O** in cell **E24**. The formula will read:

    Markup% = $Markup ÷ $Retail or **= D24/B24**

22. Copy this formula into cells **E25 through E28**.

    HINT: Remember that the retail calculation of markup is generally used because most other retail financial elements are also calculated as a percentage of retail sales.

23. Calculate the Markup% based on cost for Problem O in cell **G24**. The formula will read:

    Markup% = $Markup ÷ $Cost or **= D24/C24**

24. Copy this formula into cells **G25 through G28**.

25. Place your cursor in cell **E24**, hold down the left mouse button and drag over to **H24 and down to H28**. Release the left mouse button and the cells will be highlighted.

26. Format these cells to one decimal place. When you are done, press OK at the bottom of the window.

27. Before printing the lesson, place your cursor on the letter **A in Column A**. A down arrow appears and the entire column is now highlighted. Select **Insert>Columns** to add a new column. Your work should now reside in Columns B through I.

28. Take one last look at your work. Make sure that your font is consistent in every cell and table. In this case 10 pt. Times New Roman was used. Your work should resemble **Figure 5.4**.

Fig. 5.3:

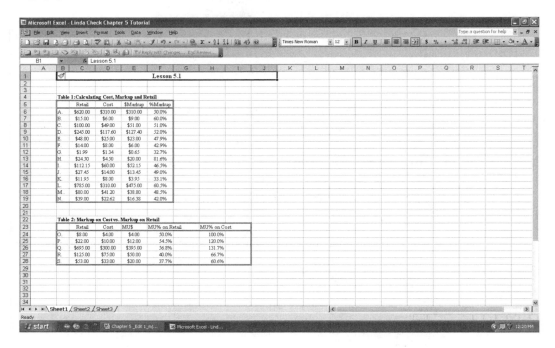

Setting the Print Area and Formatting the Page

29. Now you are almost ready to complete the assignment and print. First you need to set the area of the spreadsheet that you would like to print. Click on cell **A1** and highlight down to cell **I29**. Then select **File>Print Area>Select Print Area**.

30. Next, select **File > Page Setup**. A tabbed window opens. First select **Landscape** and then select the tab labeled **Sheet**. You will see that the gridlines and row/column headings have a check mark (✓) beside them. Click on these to eliminate the (✓) and turn off the gridlines and row/column headings. You can select **Print Preview** to see how your spreadsheet will look when printed. When you are through previewing the page, choose **Close** to take you back to your working spreadsheet.

Saving Your Work and Printing

31. Before you print and turn in your assignment, save your work.

32. Save your work on your travel drive and label it **Lesson5.1(your initials here with no spaces)**.

33. Your instructor may request that you also print out your spreadsheet assignment showing all the formulas you have written.

Calculating Markup Review Problems Using Excel

Review Problem 5.1

Open a blank Excel spreadsheet.

1. Save the blank spreadsheet to your own travel drive and give it an appropriate filename. To be consistent, this file should be named **Review 5.1(your initials here with no spaces)**. Now you are ready to begin working.

2. The buyer for Bonnie's Boutique made the purchase listed below. Create a chart that depicts the SKU, Quantity, $Cost per item, $Retail per item, $Markup per item, Markup%, Total Cost, and Total Retail for each SKU. Finally, calculate a Total $Cost, Total $Retail, and Total Markup% for the full order.

SKU	ITEM DESCRIPTION	QUANTITY	$COST	DESIRED MU%
1160781	Knit Skirt	40	$28.00/skirt	48%
2105476	Leopard Print Handbag	24	$144.00/dozen	60%
3350891	Cotton/Poly Blouse	50	$22.00/blouse	55%
3587049	Knit Shirt	60	$15.00/shirt	50%

> *HINT:* Remember that you are asked to represent the $Cost and $Retail *per item* so use a formula that utilizes the desired MU% and the $Cost per item to obtain the retail price you will charge for *each* item.

3. Be sure to give your chart an appropriate title, column headings, and other appropriate formatting.

4. When you have completed your spreadsheet, set the print area and choose a format for the page that you feel presents the information in a professional manner. You can then save your work one last time and print.

Review Problem 5.2

Open a blank Excel spreadsheet.

1. Save the blank spreadsheet to your own travel drive and give it an appropriate filename. To be consistent, this file should be named **Review5.2(your initials here with no spaces)**. Now you are ready to begin working.

2. For Valentine's Day, a jewelry buyer wishes to run a special $199.00 promotion on several different ruby and diamond items. The group consists of 114 pieces that cost:

   45 pieces @ $88.00 each
   25 pieces @ $71.00 each
   44 pieces @ $102.00 each

3. Create a table that depicts the Cost$, Retail$, and Markup% on each item.

4. Be sure to give your chart an appropriate title, column headings, and other appropriate formatting.

5. When you have completed your spreadsheet, set the print area and choose a format for the page that you feel presents the information in a professional manner. You can then save your work one last time and print.

Review Problem 5.3

Open a blank Excel spreadsheet.

1. Save the blank spreadsheet to your own diskette and give it an appropriate filename. To be consistent, this file should be named **Review 5.3(your initials here with no spaces)**. Now you are ready to begin working.

2. A buyer wants to spend $2,500 at retail on new purchases of nail polish for the cosmetics department. The department maintains a 60% markup. The buyer needs a minimum of 400 bottles of nail polish to create an adequate product display.

3. Create a table that depicts the minimum cost and retail per bottle that allows the buyer to maintain the required markup and not exceed the planned total expenditure.

4. The buyer also wishes to compare the possible assortment with an increase of the markup percent to 65%.

5. Add a row (or column depending on the way you have chosen to format your spreadsheet) to your spreadsheet that depicts the cost and retail per bottle that allows the buyer to achieve the maximum total expenditure ($5,000) with a 58% markup.

6. When your assignment is complete, be sure to save your work and print out the final results as directed by your instructor.

Review Problem 5.4

Open a blank Excel spreadsheet.

1. Save the blank spreadsheet to your own diskette and give it an appropriate file-name. To be consistent, this file should be named **Review 5.4(your initials here with no spaces)**. Now you are ready to begin working.

2. The buyer for men's swimwear purchases from several vendors. Create a table that depicts the cost, markup, retail, and total retail for each purchase given the following information:

VENDOR	QUANTITY	COST	MARKUP RETAIL	TOTAL RETAIL
A.	60	$23.00	50%	?
B.	75	?	55%	?
C.	30	$25.00	?	?
D.	60	$28.50	45%	?

3. Be sure to format the table in a way that is easy to read and professional in presentation with appropriate titles and headings.

4. When your assignment is complete, be sure to save your work and print out the final results as directed by your instructor.

Review Problem 5.5

Open a blank Excel spreadsheet.

1. Save the blank spreadsheet to your own diskette and give it an appropriate file-name. To be consistent, this file should be named **Review 5.5(your initials here with no spaces)**. Now you are ready to begin working.

2. A fabric buyer wishes to run a special $5.99 per yard promotion on several different bolts of discontinued fabric. The group consists of 800 yards of fabric that cost:

   75 yards @ $5.00 per yard
   150 yards @ $3.79 per yard
   300 yards @ $2.75 per yard
   275 yards @ $3.49 each

3. Create a table that depicts the Cost$, Retail$, and Markup% on each item.

4. Be sure to give your chart an appropriate title, column headings, and other appropriate formatting.

5. When you have completed your spreadsheet, set the print area and choose a format for the page that you feel presents the information in a professional manner. You can then save your work one last time and print as directed by your instructor.

Review Problem 5.6

Open a blank Excel spreadsheet.

1. Save the blank spreadsheet to your travel drive and give it an appropriate file-name. To be consistent, this file should be named **Review5.6(your initials here with no spaces)**. Now you are ready to begin working.

2. For the following items, create a chart that compares each item when markup is calculated on retail and when markup is calculated on cost:

COST$	RETAIL$	MARKUP$
$ 19.00	$ 39.00	$ 20.00
$ 45.00	$ 75.00	$ 30.00
$ 100.00	$ 250.00	$ 150.00
$ 1,000.00	$ 2,200.00	$ 1,200.00
$ 8.00	$ 15.00	$ 7.00

4. Be sure to give your chart an appropriate title, column headings, and other appropriate formatting.

5. When you have completed your spreadsheet, set the print area and choose a format for the page that you feel presents the information in a professional manner. You can then save your work one last time and print.

Markup and Pricing Strategy

In this chapter you will learn to identify several different types of markup that help a retailer develop a successful merchandising strategy. The following exercises will allow you to examine the pricing of merchandise from the first price placed on the merchandise (**Initial Retail**) to the price received when the item is eventually sold (**Final Selling Price**). Read the terms below carefully and look over the formulas given before beginning the lesson.

Average markup The average or mean markup taken on a group of merchandise where portions of the merchandise carry different or varying markups.

Cumulative markup The markup percentage achieved on a group of goods over a period of time. Usually all goods available plus any new purchases received for an extended period of time. Does not include markdowns.

Final selling price The price at which merchandise is sold. The price obtained could be equal to the initial retail price but often reflects a reduction from the initial retail price.

Initial markup The difference between the billed cost of merchandise as stated on the invoice and the initial retail price placed on the item. (Remember that the billed cost reflects any quantity and/or trade discounts but not any applicable cash discount.)

Initial retail or *Original retail* The original retail price at which merchandise is offered for sale.

Maintained markup The difference between net sales and the cost of merchandise sold. Does not include cash discounts, alterations, etc. While

Maintained Markup is related to Gross Margin, the latter is adjusted for cash discounts received and any alteration/workroom expenses encountered.

Reductions Any factor that reduces the value of the inventory a retailer carries. Can include markdowns, shortages in stock due (e.g., shipping shortage, damaged goods, theft), employee discounts, etc.

You will find the following formulas useful in your calculations:

- **Net Sales = Number Of Items Sold × Price Paid For Each Item**
- **Reductions = Markdowns, Employee Discounts + Shortages**
- Initial Markup% = $\dfrac{\text{Gross Margin\% (Expenses\% + Profit\%) + Reductions\% + Alterations\% – Cash Discounts\%}}{\text{Net Sales (100\%) + Reductions\%}}$
- **Cumulative Markup% = Cumulative \$ Markup ÷ Cumulative Retail Dollars**
- **Maintained Markup = Net Sales – Gross Cost Of Merchandise Sold where:**

  - **Gross Cost Of Merchandise Sold =**
    Opening Inventory
    +New Purchases
    +Inward Freight
    –Closing Inventory
- **Gross Margin = Net Sales – Total Cost Of Merchandise Sold where:**

  - **Total Cost Of Merchandise Sold =**
    Gross Cost Of Merchandise Sold
    –Cash Discount
    +Alteration/Workroom Costs
- **Gross Margin = Expenses + Profit**
- **Maintained Markup% = Initial Markup% – Reductions × (100% – Initial Markup%)**
- **Reductions % = $\dfrac{\text{Initial Markup\% – Maintained Markup\%}}{\text{Net Sales\% – Initial Markup\%}}$**

Calculating Initial Markup

The markup originally placed on merchandise when it arrives at the store is known as the **initial markup**. Initial markup can also be described as the difference between the *original* retail price of an item (or group of items) and the *billed cost* of the item (or group of items). This difference must be large enough to cover any expenses for the retailer, any reductions in inventory value that might be incurred (e.g., special sale prices, shortages including theft, and necessary alterations), plus a profit.

Because the initial markup must be large enough to cover expenses, reductions, necessary alterations and a planned profit, these factors are added together to form the numerator of the equation. The numerator also includes the cash discount, if taken, but because taking the cash discount actually adds to the value of the retail inventory, it is subtracted from the rest of the factors. The denominator represents the original retail value of the inventory, which can be calculated by adding any reductions necessary back to the net sales of the inventory:

$$\text{Initial Markup} = \frac{\text{Expenses} + \text{Profit} + \text{Reductions} + \text{Alterations} - \text{Cash Discounts}}{\text{Net Sales} + \text{Reductions}}$$

The initial markup figure can be expressed in dollars or percentages. For this text, the percentage format will be used unless otherwise noted.

Application

What would be the initial markup percent necessary to cover the following departmental figures?

Net Sales	$125,000
Expenses	$ 47,000
Profit	$ 12,000
Markdowns	$ 23,000
Employee Discounts	$ 900
Shortages	$ 500

$$\text{Initial Markup} = \frac{\text{Expenses} + \text{Profit} + \text{Reductions}}{\text{Net Sales} + \text{Reductions}}$$

(Reductions = Markdowns + Shortages + Employee Discounts = $24,400)

$$\text{Initial Markup} = \frac{\$47,000 + \$12,000 + \$24,400}{\$125,000 + \$24,400}$$

Initial Markup = 55.82%

Practicing What You Have Learned

Determine the initial markup percentage for each of the following. For each problem, round currency to the nearest whole dollar and percentages to the nearest tenth.

1. A department store plans for sales of $350,000 in the lingerie department with retail reductions of $130,000. If expenses for the department are $89,000 and profit is planned at $25,000, what must the initial markup be?

2. A specialty Christmas shop plans a gross margin (expenses + profit) of 45% and expects markdowns and shortages to total 30% and 2%, respectively. Net sales are planned at $202,000. If the shop desires an 8% profit figure, what must the initial markup percentage be?

3. Find the initial markup for a men's suit department with the following figures:

Net Sales	$435,000
Expenses	$137,500
Profit	$ 32,000
Markdowns	$111,500
Shortages	$ 8,700
Employee Discounts	$ 10,200
Alterations	$ 2,100
Cash Discounts	$ 13,000

4. A vintage clothing store has estimated expenses of 24%, markdowns of 17%, and stock shortages of 2%. If a 6% profit is desired, calculate the necessary initial markup.

5. Determine the initial markup percentage for the following figures:

Net Sales	$131,000
Gross Margin	$ 62,000
Markdowns	$ 18,000
Employee Discounts	$ 2,000
Cash Discounts	$ 6,000
Alteration costs	$ 750

Calculating Cumulative Markup

Initial markup, as previously demonstrated, is most commonly thought of as the markup over billed cost placed on an item. However, not every item in inventory will carry the same initial markup. Retailers commonly report a single initial markup figure for a given inventory for a six-month period. This markup figure results from combining the markup achieved for all the items in inventory during a given period plus the markup on any new purchases received into stock during the period. Commonly known as the **cumulative markup**, this figure represents the initial markup received on *all* goods in inventory during a given period.

The cumulative markup dollar amount represents the difference between the billed cost of all goods (including any transportation but excluding any applicable cash discounts) and the original retail of all goods in the inventory during a given period. This calculation will require knowing both the retail and cost dollars of the merchandise on hand as well as any merchandise purchased.

Application

As of July 1 the girls' dress department has an opening inventory of $75,000 at retail with a markup of 52%. On July 31, the new purchases to date have totaled $10,000 at retail with a markup of 49%. Find the cumulative markup achieved during the month of July.

$$\text{Cumulative Markup\%} = \frac{\text{Cumulative Markup \$}}{\text{Cumulative Retail \$}}$$

In order to complete the equation you must calculate the markup dollars on each group of merchandise. It is helpful to put all the information in chart form:

	COST	RETAIL	MU%
July 1 Inventory	(a)	$75,000	52%
New Merchandise	(b)	$10,000	49%
Total	(c)	(d)	(e)

Once the given information is in place, each of the empty cells must be filled in order to determine the cumulative markup.

a. Start by finding the cost value of the July 1 inventory:
   Cost Price = Retail Price × Cost Complement (100% – MU%)
   Cost Price = $75,000 × (100% – 52%)
   Cost Price = $36,000

b. Next find the cost value of the new merchandise purchased during the time period:
   Cost Price = Retail Price × Cost Complement (100% – MU%)
   Cost Price = $10,000 × (100% – 49%)
   Cost Price = $5,100

c. The total cost of merchandise handled during the period can then be calculated by simply adding together (a) and (b).
   Total Cost Price = $36,000 + $5,100 = $41,100

d. The total retail price is also an easy calculation of simply adding together the retail value of the merchandise on hand July 1 and the purchases made during the month.
   Total Retail Price = $75,000 + $10,000 = $85,000

e)　Finally, the cumulative markup can be calculated:

Cumulative Markup% = $\dfrac{\text{Total Retail Price} - \text{Total Cost Price}}{\text{Total Retail Price}}$

Cumulative Markup% = $\dfrac{\$85,000 - \$41,100}{\$85,000}$

Cumulative Markup% = 51.65%

You will note that the cumulative markup percentage *cannot* be obtained by subtracting the markup percentage of the new purchases from the markup percentage of the July 1 merchandise. Nor can it be calculated by adding the two markup percentage figures and dividing by 2. The cumulative markup percentage is actually much closer to the 52% markup on the July 1 merchandise. This is due to the fact that significantly more of the merchandise carries the 52% markup and a much smaller portion of the merchandise carries only a 49% markup. The outcome is actually a weighted average much like the cumulative grade point average calculated by most universities.

Practicing What You Have Learned

Determine the cumulative markup percentage for each of the following. For each problem, round currency to the nearest whole dollar and percentages to the nearest tenth.

6. The toy department had an opening inventory on October 1 of $337,500 at retail that carried a 45% markup. During the month, purchases of $34,000 at cost were received with a 54% markup. Calculate the cumulative markup percentage for the department.

7. The hosiery department has an opening inventory on February 1 of $189,000 at cost with a 58% markup. During the month, the buyer purchased and received additional inventory valued at $72,000 at cost that carried only a 50% markup. Calculate the cumulative markup percentage for the department during the month of February.

8. A buyer planned to retail a group of sweatshirts already in stock costing $39,000 for $79,000 during November for a Halloween promotion. If, during the month, the buyer also received some Christmas sweatshirts costing $75,000 and planned a markup of 55.3%, what would be the cumulative markup on the sweatshirts?

9. A buyer for handbags showed an opening inventory on April 1 of $145,000 at retail that carried a markup of 45%. During the month, she managed to acquire

another $50,000 in handbags on which she could carry a 60% markup. What is the cumulative markup achieved in handbags for the month of April?

10. The opening inventory at The Tie Place consisted of the following:

15 dozen ties priced at $25.00 each
4 dozen sterling tie clips priced at $40.00 each
50 gift boxes priced at $1.50 each

The current inventory carries a markup of 50%. During the month, a buyer purchases 4 dozen special purchase ties that cost her $8.00 each. If she plans to retail them for the same price as all of the other ties, what will be the cumulative markup on the merchandise for the month?

Calculating Maintained Markup

Although retailers often plan a markup percentage that they would like to receive, the actual percentage received can fall short of meeting those plans. Some of the merchandise purchased by the buyer may sell at full price but some merchandise actually will be sold at discounted price (e.g., merchandise sold during a sale or on clearance). **Maintained markup** represents the amount of markup the retailer was actually able to achieve:

Maintained Markup = Net Sales – Gross Cost of Merchandise Sold

Unlike initial markup, which is based on the retail price originally placed on the merchandise, maintained markup is based on the net sales or the total dollar amount the merchandise actually sold for. The maintained markup dollars are calculated by subtracting the gross cost of the merchandise from the net sales achieved. The gross cost of the merchandise represents what the merchandise costs the retailer, including transportation, but not taking into account cash discounts and alteration expenses:

Gross Cost of Merchandise Sold =
Opening Inventory + New Purchases + Transportation – Closing Inventory

The value of the inventory remaining at the end of the time period (*EOM*, or *end of month*) must be subtracted from the value of the inventory on hand at the beginning of the period (*BOM*, or *beginning of month*) plus the value of any new purchases received. The result will be the value of the merchandise sold.

You might notice that this calculation is very similar to the calculation to obtain gross margin, but remember that the gross margin figure is based on total cost of merchandise sold, which includes any cash discounts taken and alterations/workroom costs incurred. Here is an example:

Opening Inventory
+Net Purchases (Gross purchases – Returns to Vendor)
+Transportation
<u>–Closing Inventory</u>
Gross Cost of Merchandise Sold (used for Maintained Markup)
–Cash Discounts earned
<u>+Alterations/Workroom Costs</u>
Total Cost of Merchandise Sold (used for Gross Margin)

We can also write:

Maintained Markup =
Gross Margin – Cash Discounts + Alterations/Workroom Costs

Or alternatively:

Gross Margin =
Maintained Markup + Cash Discounts – Alterations/Workroom Costs

Maintained markup cannot be determined until after the merchandise is sold, but it is an important figure for the retailer because it gives an accurate account of the success achieved with the merchandise.

Application

Calculate the maintained markup percentage for the following figures:

Net Sales	$100,000
Opening Inventory	$ 67,000
Net Purchases	$ 25,000
Closing Inventory	$ 51,000
Transportation	$ 750

First calculate the gross cost of merchandise sold.

Gross Cost of Merchandise Sold =   Opening Inventory
                                     + Net Purchases
                                     +Transportation
                                     –Closing Inventory
Gross Cost of Merchandise Sold = $67,000 + $25,000 + $750 – $51,000
Gross Cost of Merchandise Sold = $41,750

Then:

Maintained Markup$ = Net Sales$ − Gross Cost of Merchandise Sold$
Maintained Markup$ = $100,000 − $41,750
Maintained Markup$ = $58,250

Then to calculate Maintain Markup%:

Maintained Markup% = Maintained Markup$/Net Sales$
Maintained Markup% = $58,250/$100,000
Maintained Markup% = 58.25%

It is also possible to calculate the maintained markup percentage when you are given the initial markup and the reductions for the period. Remember that reductions are equal to any markdowns, shortages, and employee discounts incurred during the selling period.

Application

If a jewelry buyer has an initial markup of 55% and markdowns/shortages during the period total 22%, what would be the maintained markup?

Maintained Markup% = Initial Markup% − Reductions × (100% − Initial Markup%)

Then:

Maintained Markup% = 55% − 22% × (100% − 55%)
Maintained Markup% = .55 − .22(.45)
Maintained Markup% = .55 − .099 or 0.451
Maintained Markup% = 45.1%

Practicing What You Have Learned

For each problem, round currency to the nearest whole dollar and percentages to the nearest tenth.

11. A stationary department has sales of $47,000, with markdowns of 8% and shortages or 1%. If the initial markup was 54%, what was the maintained markup for the period?

12. Pete's Hardware recorded the following figures for the quarter:

Net Sales	$235,500
Opening Inventory	$ 87,000
New Purchases	$ 97,000
Transportation	$ 2,500
Closing Inventory	$ 8,500
Cash Discounts	$ 4,800

    a.   What was the maintained markup percentage for the quarter?

    b.   What was the gross margin percentage for the quarter?

13. The men's suit department had an initial markup of 52%. Operating results showed markdowns of 13%, employee discounts of 3%, and shortages of 1%. What was the maintained markup for the department?

14. Calculate the maintained markup percentage for the following figures:

Net Sales	$ 82,000
Inventory June 1	$ 58,650
Inventory June 30	$ 68,450
Purchases	$ 65,000
Transportation	$ 1,200
Cash discounts	$ 3,400

15. Calculate the gross margin percentage for the previous problem.

Calculating Average Markup

Often retailers utilize a **price lining** strategy. Price lining is the practice of determining retail price points that would be attractive to the target customer. A retailer will typically utilize several price lines in two or three price zones. A **price zone** is a group of price lines that might appeal to a particular customer. Merchandise is commonly classified into low, medium, and high price zones also known as **promotional** (low), **volume** (medium), and **prestige** (high) price zones.

The price line chosen for each item depends on a variety of factors including the cost of the merchandise, competitors' pricing of the same or similar merchandise, store policies on positioning and markdowns/sales, and projected or current demand for the item. Typically, the buyer purchases an assortment of merchandise at varying prices but selects several specific price points at which to offer the merchandise to the consumer. For example, the buyer may purchase several T-shirts varying in cost from $5.00–$7.50. The buyer may then determine that each of the T-shirts will retail at the $12.00 price point.

The practice of price lining facilitates the selling process by making choices easier for the customer and decreasing the marking costs. However, it also creates variations in the markup achieved on each item. In the T-shirt example above, the markup varies from 37.5% on the T-shirts costing $7.50 to 58.3% on the T-shirts costing $5.00. This variation must be planned and monitored regularly in order to ensure that a successful merchandising strategy and level of profitability are attained.

One of the most effective ways to monitor these markup variations is through averaging markup. Averaging markup refers to the process of adjusting the balance of an entire stock or a group of merchandise purchased at different markups to achieve a predetermined desired markup for the entire assortment. The cumulative markup calculation presented earlier in the chapter refers to the weighted average markup placed on a group of merchandise. The average markup calculation also addresses the weighted average markup of the total group of merchandise but, unlike cumulative markup, it actually determines the markup needed on new purchases at any given point in time that will allow the buyer to achieve the desired cumulative markup.

Finding Markup Percentage for Remaining Purchases

If a buyer has planned a target cumulative markup percentage for a total inventory, it may be necessary to determine the markup percentage necessary on the remaining purchases that will, when combined with the markup achieved to date, achieve the desired cumulative markup percentage.

Application

A buyer has 300 dresses costing $35.00 each and carrying a retail value of $75.00 per dress. If the buyer needs a total retail stock of $45,000 and wishes to average a 55% markup for the dress category, what markup percentage must the buyer obtain on the remaining purchases?

As with cumulative markup, a chart to organize the merchandise in stock and the merchandise needed will be helpful.

	TOTAL PLAN	MERCHANDISE IN STOCK	MERCHANDISE NEEDED
Retail	$45,000	$75.00 × 300 (a)	(d)
Cost	(c)	$35.00 × 300 (b)	(e)
Markup	55%		(f)

a. First calculate the retail value of the dresses already in stock.
   Retail$ = $75.00 × 300
   Retail$ = $22,500

b. Then calculate the cost value of the dresses already in stock.
   Cost$ = $35.00 × 300
   Cost$ = $10,500

c. Next, find the planned cost of the inventory given the retail value and markup percentage.
   Cost$ = Retail$ × Cost Complement (100% − Markup%)
   Cost$ = $45,000 × (100% − 55%)
   Cost$ = $20,250

d. Now that the retail value planned and in stock are known, find the retail value of merchandise needed.
   Retail$ of Merchandise Needed = Total Retail$ − Total$ of Merchandise in Stock
   Retail$ of Merchandise Needed = $45,000 − $22,500
   Retail$ of Merchandise Needed = $22,500

e. Calculate the cost dollar value of merchandise needed to meet the total plan.
   Cost$ of Merchandise Needed = Total Cost$ − Cost$ of Merchandise in Stock
   Cost$ of Merchandise Needed = $20,250 − $10,500
   Cost$ of Merchandise Needed = $9,750

f. Finally, calculate the markup percentage necessary on the balance of merchandise needed.
   Markup% = (Retail$ − Cost$) ÷ Retail$
   Markup% = ($22,500 − $9,750) ÷ $22,500
   Markup% = 56.67%

	TOTAL PLAN	MERCHANDISE IN STOCK	MERCHANDISE NEEDED
Retail	$45,000	$22,500	$22,500
Cost	$22,500	$10,500	$9,750
Markup	55%		56.67%

Finding Cost Dollars for Remaining Purchases

It is also a realistic scenario that the buyer in the previous dress department scenario may, for example, desire a certain number of dresses for an Easter sale. If the buyer desires 500 total dresses with a markup of 55%, it is possible to look at the number of dresses currently in stock and determine the most the buyer can spend on the remaining dress purchase in order to meet the plan.

Application

The buyer currently has 300 dresses at $35.00 each. She desires 500 total dresses on hand for the Easter sale and plans to retail all of the dresses for $75.00 each. What is highest price the buyer can pay for each of the remaining dresses?

a. First calculate the number of dresses remaining.
   # of Dresses Remaining = 500 dresses needed − 300 dresses currently in stock
   # of Dresses Remaining = 200
   You will utilize this figure later in the example.

	TOTAL PLAN	MERCHANDISE IN STOCK	MERCHANDISE NEEDED
Retail	(b) $37,500 500 at $75.00		
Cost	(d) $16,875	(c) $10,500 300 at $35.00	(e) $6,375 (f) $31.88
Markup	55%		

b. Next determine the total retail dollars.
   Total Retail$ = Total Number of Items × Retail Price
   Total Retail$ = 500 × $75.00
   Total Retail$ = $37,500

c. Next determine the cost dollars of merchandise already in stock.
   Cost$ of Merchandise in Stock = Number of Dresses in Stock × Cost Price
   Cost$ of Merchandise in Stock = 300 × $35.00
   Cost$ of Merchandise In Stock = $10,500

d. Then calculate the planned total cost dollars.
   Total Cost$ = Total Retail$ × Cost Complement
   Total Cost$ = $37,500 × (100% − 55%)
   Total Cost$ = $16,875

e. Now calculate the dollar value of merchandise needed.
   Cost $ = Total Cost$ Plan − Total Cost$ of Merchandise in stock
   Cost$ = $16,875 − $10,500
   Cost$ = $6,375

f. Find the highest unit value that can be spent on the remaining 200(a) dresses.
   Cost$ for remaining dresses = $6,375 ÷ 200 dresses
   Cost$ for remaining dresses = $31.88 per dress

Finding Single Retail Price for Varying Cost

Many retailers utilize a price line strategy when offering goods to the customer. As we discussed earlier in this chapter, the practice of selecting several price points to retail a certain category (e.g. dresses) is less confusing to the customer and can actually help impact their decision-making process.

Most often the buyer will predetermine the price points that goods will be offered and then select merchandise that he or she determines will sell well at those price point. The merchandise selected for a given price point may not cost the buyer exactly the same amount resulting in different markup percentages on each item. Before finalizing his or her purchase decision, the buyer must make sure that the markup achieved on each item is sufficient to meet the overall plan for the category or department.

Application

In one last example, a buyer might be at market purchasing the dresses for the Easter sale. She finds that some of the dresses she wishes to purchase cost $28.00 each and some of the dresses cost $37.00. If she purchases 200 dresses at $37.00 and 300 dresses at $28.00, what single retail price must she use for all of the dresses in order to attain the 55% markup she desires?

	TOTAL PLAN	MERCHANDISE IN STOCK	MERCHANDISE NEEDED
Retail		(b) $35,111 (c) $35,111÷500 = $70.22	
Cost		200 × $37.00 = $7,400 300 × $28.00 = $8,400	
Markup	55%		

a. First find the total cost value of the merchandise purchased.
Total Cost$ = (200 × $37.00) + (300 × $28.00)
Total Cost$ = $7,400 + $8,400
Total Cost$ = $15,800

b. Find the retail dollar value necessary to attain the desired 55% markup on the merchandise already purchased.
Retail$ = Cost$ ÷ Cost Complement
Retail$ = $15,800 ÷ (100% − 55%)
Retail$ = $35,111

  c. Find the retail price necessary for each dress.
    Retail Price = \$35,111 ÷ 500 dresses
    Retail Price = \$70.22 per dress

Practicing What You Have Learned

For each problem, round currency to the nearest whole dollar and percentages to the nearest tenth.

16. If a hosiery buyer purchases 30 dozen pairs of tights for \$1,800 and 15 dozen from a vendor offering a special sale of \$750 for the order, what single retail price will allow the buyer to attain the 52% markup desired for the entire assortment?

17. An electronics buyer needs a retail value of \$55,000 in cell phones for the holiday season. If a markup of 60% is desired and the merchandise in stock already totals \$22,300 at retail and \$9,875 at cost, what markup percentage will the buyer need to attain on the remaining purchases in order to achieve the desired 60% markup for the assortment?

18. A glassware buyer plans to purchase 250 wine goblets that will retail for \$12.00 each. If the buyer has already purchased 70 goblets at a cost of \$4.50 each, what is the most he can pay per unit for the remaining goblets in order to attain the desired 58% markup?

19. A leather goods buyer purchased the following items for a special sale:

  35 Designer key chains   \$8.00 each
  25 Business card cases   \$10.00 each
  50 Small coin purses   \$12.50 each

  At what single retail price can each of the items be sold in order to attain the 50% markup desired?

20. In the month of February, a buyer plans to purchase ladies' swimsuits with a total retail value of \$34,000. If he has already purchased 60 suits that will retail for \$85.00 each with a cost of \$35.00 each, what will be the markup necessary on the remaining swimsuits to allow the buyer to reach the 60% markup goal he desires?

Chapter 6 Review Exercise A

1. Determine the cumulative markup percentage given the following:

	Cost	Retail
Inventory March 1	$130,000	$295,000
New Merchandise	$ 40,000	$ 92,000

2. A cosmetics department with an initial markup of 60% experienced a markdown of 15% and shortages of 2%. What was the maintained markup percentage achieved?

3. Determine the initial markup for a designer handbags department with the following figures:

Planned sales	= $560,000
Markdowns	= $ 85,000
Cash Discounts	= 5%
Shortages	= 0.5%
Expenses	= $162,000
Profit	6%

4. The children's shoe department has an initial markup of 52% and needs to achieve a maintained markup of 45%. What percentage for reductions is allowable?

5. A local manufacturer can provide 200 canvas beach bags for a summer sale at a cost of $15.50 each. If the buyer plans to have a total of 450 bags on hand for the sale and will retail each bag at $29.95, what is the most the buyer can pay for the remaining 250 bags in order to meet the markup plan of 55%?

6. A toy department has an initial markup of 58% with markdowns of 12% and shortages of 3%. If employee discounts amount to 5%, what is the maintained markup achieved?

7. A linens buyer achieved the gross margin of 48%, cash discounts of 4%, and workroom costs of 0.5% needed to repair a damaged shipment of pillowcases. If net sales totaled $143,750, what was the maintained markup?

8. A jewelry department had an inventory on April 1, of $232,500 at retail with a 65% markup. New merchandise purchased during the month was valued $49,000 at cost and $147,000 at retail. What is the cumulative markup percentage for the inventory?

9. A home goods store plans sales of $180,000 for the third quarter. If planned gross margin is $72,000 and reductions at retail are planned at $16,750, what should be the initial markup percentage?

10. A wallpaper buyer operates with a 55% markup in her department. She needs 1,000 rolls of wallpaper to fully stock her area. Vendor A can offer 600 rolls of traditional wallpaper in a variety of patterns at colors at $7.50 per roll. The buyer plans to contact Vendor B for some textured wallpapers to fill in the remaining stock. What is the most she can pay for each textured roll if the entire wallpaper stock will retail at $15.99 per roll?

Chapter 6 Review Exercise B

1. A lingerie buyer plans to buy camisole sets that will retail for $39.00. She has already purchased 100 sets at a cost price of $16.90 each. What must the cost price of the remaining purchases be in order to attain a 54% markup for the department with a retail stock value of $8,500?

2. What would be the maintained markup percentage for the following given net sales of $585,000?

Inventory on January 1	$325,000
New Purchases	$250,000
Transportation	$ 9,500
Cash Discounts	$ 12,000
Alterations/Workroom	$ 1,200
Inventory on January 31	$271,000

3. A buyer purchased 200 girls' Easter bonnets from 3 different vendors. If 40 of the bonnets cost $12.00, 100 bonnets cost $14.50, and the remaining 60 bonnets cost $15.25 each, what single retail price must be charged for each bonnet in order to attain the 62% desired markup?

4. Determine the initial markup percentage needed to achieve a 4% profit on the following figures:

Markdowns	12%
Expenses	33%
Cash Discounts	3%
Shortages	2%
Employee Discounts	2.5%

5. Find the cumulative markup for the month of October for a party supply store with an inventory on October 1 of $49,000 at retail ($21,000 at cost) and new merchandise received during the month totaling $36,000 at retail with a markup of 52%.

6. If a shoe department has an initial markup of 54% and total reductions of 12.5%, what would be the maintained markup percentage if there are no cash discounts earned or workroom costs incurred?

7. Calculate the gross margin percentage for the shoe department above.

8. A buyer plans to purchase a stock of leather jackets with a total retail value of $30,000 and a 55% markup. If 100 jackets have already been purchased at a cost of $95.00, what must be the maximum cost of each remaining jacket if all the jackets will retail for $199?

9. If the gross margin in bath accessories is 41.3% and reductions experienced in the department total 14.9%, what is the initial markup percentage?

10. A florist has sales of $88,000 with markdowns of 8% and shortages of 4%. If the initial markup was 62%, what was the maintained markup percentage?

Chapter 6 Review Exercise C

1. Calculate the maintained markup given the following figures:

Net Sales	$475,000
New Purchases	$239,800
Transportation	$ 4,000
Cash Discounts	$ 5,500
Workroom Costs	$ 750
Inventory on April 1	$330,000
Inventory on April 30	$357,000

2. If a department shows expenses of 31.3% and profits of 5% but experiences reductions totaling 15%, what is the initial markup percentage?

3. A table linens buyer needs $8,800 in merchandise at retail. If the buyer has placed an order for $4,000 at retail ($1,850 at cost) and desires a 52% markup for the department, what is the markup percentage necessary on the remainder of the goods needed?

4. If a buyer purchases 200 pairs of jeans at a cost of $28.00 and 340 pairs at $37.50, what single retail price can be utilized to achieve a 54% markup on the entire assortment?

5. A jewelry department has a retail inventory on December 1 of $173,000 and a cost value of $69,850. New merchandise purchased during the month carried a 58% markup and totaled $101,000 at cost. What is the cumulative markup achieved?

6. What would be the percentage of retail reductions experienced for a store with an initial markup of 52% and a maintained markup of 44.7%?

7. A candy store needs $17,500 worth of goods at retail and has a planned markup of 55% for the month of July. On July 3, the new merchandise received totaled $,800 at retail ($4,700 at cost). What markup percentage must be obtained on the remainder of the merchandise purchased in order to achieve the 55% markup figure?

8. If a local nursery buys the following merchandise to prepare for the summer, what would be the cumulative markup?

	Quantity	Cost	Retail
4' oak trees	30	$39.00	$99.00
2 gal. azaleas	100	$ 5.99	$18.99
Potting flowers	1,000	$ 0.79	$ 5.00 for 3

9. What would be the gross margin achieved from maintained markup of 47%, cash discounts of 6%, and workroom costs of 1.5%?

10. Determine the initial markup percentage for the following figures:

Expenses	37%
Profit	4%
Markdowns	10.5%
Employee Discounts	3.5%
Cash Discounts	5%

Markup Calculations and Pricing Strategies
Excel Tutorial

Opening the File

1. Open Excel.

2. Choose **File>Open** and then locate the file entitled **Lesson6.1.xls**. You can open this file by double-clicking on the filename.

3. Your screen should resemble **Figure 6.1**.

Fig. 6.1:

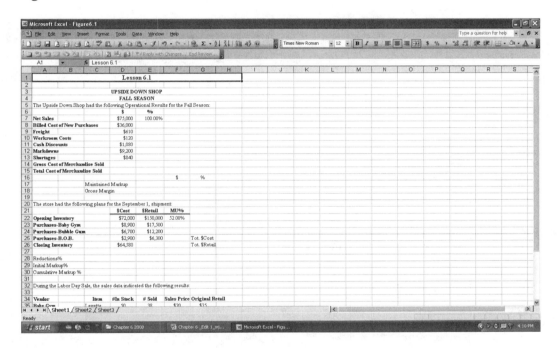

Completing the Spreadsheet

4. Enter the formula in cell **E10** that will allow you to calculate the percentage of net sales for the dollar figure given for Workroom Costs. Your formula should read: **=D10/D7**. When you have finished typing the formula press **Enter** or click on the green check mark (√) in the formula bar.

5. Enter the formula in cell **E11** that will allow you to calculate the percentage of Net Sales for the dollar figure given for Cash Discounts and copy this formula for the other operational results. Your formula will read: **= D11/$D$7**. (The dollar signs

in the formula let the spreadsheet know that those cells are absolute. The reference will not change when the formula is copied.)

> *HINT:* This time, you are going to copy the formula in cells **E8, E9, E12, and E13**. Because the percentage formula calls for each of these dollar amounts to be divided by Net Sales, you will need the numerator (e.g., Cash Discount dollars) to adjust while the denominator (**D7**, which is the dollar Net Sales figure) remains constant or absolute.

6. Copy the formula written in cell **E11** to cells **E8, E9, E12, and E13**. When this process is complete, the top of your screen should resemble **Figure 6.2**.

Fig. 6.2:

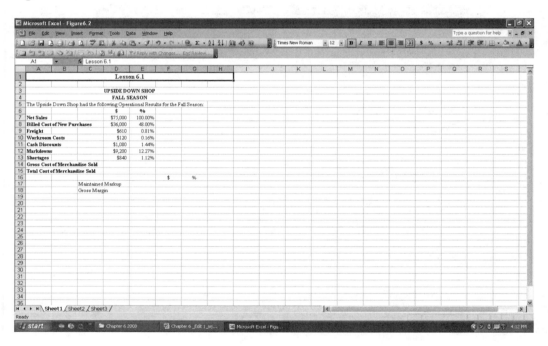

7. Enter the formula that will allow you to calculate dollar value of the **Gross Cost of Merchandise Sold** in cell **D14: = (D22+D8+D9)−D26**.

> *HINT:* Remember that the formula for Gross Cost of Merchandise Sold is Opening Inventory + New Purchases + Freight − Closing Inventory

You can find the Opening and Closing Inventory Levels listed in rows 22 and 26 respectively.

8. Enter the formula that will allow you to calculate dollar value of the **Total Cost of Merchandise Sold** in cell **D15: =D14–D11+D10.**

   HINT: Remember that the formula for Total Cost of Merchandise Sold is Gross Cost of Merchandise Sold – Cash Discounts earned + Workroom Costs

9. Enter the formula that will allow you to calculate **Maintained Markup dollars** in cell **F17.** Your formula should read: **= D7–D14.**

   HINT: Remember that the formula for Maintained Markup dollars is Net Sales – Gross Cost of Merchandise Sold

10. Enter the formula that will allow you to calculate **Maintained Markup percentage** in cell **G17.** Divide maintained markup dollars by net sales dollars or **=F17/D7.**

11. Enter the formula that will allow you to calculate **Gross Margin dollars** in cell **F18.** Your formula should read: **=D7–D15.**

    HINT: Remember that Gross Margin = Net Sales – Total Cost of Merchandise Sold.

12. Enter the formula that will allow you to calculate **Gross Margin percentage** in cell **G18.** Divide gross margin dollars by net sales dollars or **=F18/D7.**

13. Calculate the markup percentage obtained on the September 1 shipment. In cell **F23** enter the formula that will calculate the MU% achieved on the purchase of Baby Gym apparel. As you will remember from previous chapters, the formula should read: **=(E23–D23)/E23.**

14. Copy the formula entered in cell **F23** into cells **F24 and F25** to obtain MU% for the Bubble Gum and B.O.B. shipments.

15. In cell **H25,** enter **=D22+D23+D24+D25,** the formula for Total Cost dollars of beginning inventory and all new purchases.

16. In cell **H26,** enter **=E22+E23+E24+E25,** the formula for Total Retail dollars of beginning inventory and all new purchases.

    HINT: The totals found in steps 14 and 15 will help you to calculate Cumulative Markup percentage in a later step.

17. Find reductions percentage by entering **=E12+E13** in cell **D28**.

> *HINT:* Remember that Reductions = Markdowns + Shortages + Employee Discounts. In this example, the Upside Down Shop does not list any employee discounts so we will assume it did not grant any during this time period.

18. Enter the formula that will allow you to calculate Initial Markup percentage in cell **D29** by typing: **=(G18+E10–E11+D28)/(E7+D28)**.

> *HINT:* Initial Markup =
> $$\frac{\text{Gross Margin \% + Workroom Costs \% − Cash Discounts \% + Reductions \%}}{\text{Net Sales \% + Reductions \%}}$$

Since many of these components are already calculated on your spreadsheet, you can use the cell where the result of the calculation is placed rather than calculating that component again (e.g., Reductions percentage is calculated in cell D28 so you can use D28 in your formula rather than adding the Markup percentage and Shortages percentage separately into the calculation for Initial Markup percentage).

19. Enter the formula that will calculate the Cumulative Markup percentage for the period in cell **D30**. Your formula should read: **=(H26–H25)/H26**. Cumulative Markup percentage in this case is then calculated using the basic markup formula [(Retail – Cost) ÷ Retail]. However, because this figure represents an average markup over a period of time, you must utilize the Total Retail dollar figure of the opening inventory and all new purchases and the Total Cost dollar figure of the opening inventory and all new purchases. Your screen should resemble **Figure 6.3**.

Fig. 6.3:

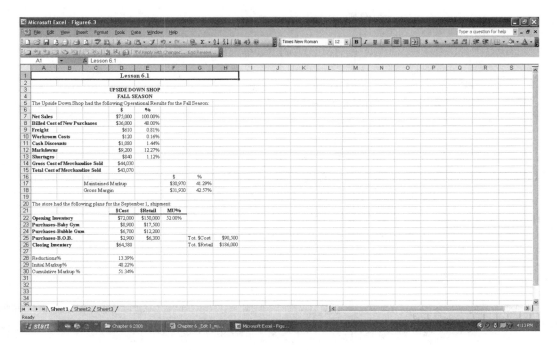

20. Enter the formula that will allow the Upside Down Shop to calculate the Total Markdown dollars for Baby Gym layettes during its Labor Day sale in cell **D40**. Your formula should read: **=PRODUCT(D35,(G35–F35))**. This formula calculates the total number of layettes in stock and multiplies them by the dollar amount that each layette was reduced for the sale resulting in Total Markdown dollars.

21. Enter the formula that will allow the shop to calculate the Markdown Cancellation dollars for Baby Gym layettes during its Labor Day sale in cell **D41**. Your formula should read: **=PRODUCT ((D35–E35),(G35–F35))**. This formula calculates the number of items left after the sale (Total Items – Number of Items Sold) and multiplies that number by the amount each item was marked back up (Original Retail Price – Sale Price).

> *HINT:* In this example, we assumed that the items were returned to their original retail price after the sale. What if, for example, the items originally retailed for $25 and during the sale were offered at $20? After the sale was over, the remaining items were only marked back up to $22. Your formula will read:
> (50 layettes – 38 sold) × ($22 – $20) = Markdown Cancellation $

22. Enter the formula in cell **D42** that will calculate the Net Markdown dollars for Baby Gym layettes during the Labor Day sale. Your formula will read **=D40–D41** because

Net Markdown = Total Markdown – Markdown Cancellations.

23. Find the Total Markdown $, Markdown Cancellation dollars, and Net Markdown dollars for Bubble Gum lamps and B.O.B. bibs during the sale. Make sure your calculations are in the appropriate cells.

24. Enter the formula in cell **D43** that will total the Net Markdown dollars for the three vendors during the Labor Day sale. Your formula should read **=D42+E42+F42**.

25. Your screen should resemble **Figure 6.4**.

Fig. 6.4:

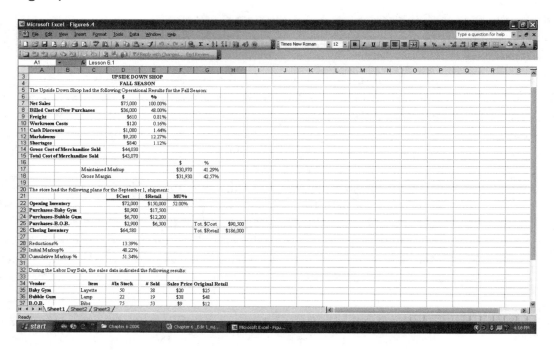

Setting a Print Area and Formatting the Page

26. Now you are almost ready to complete the assignment and print. First you need to set the area of the spreadsheet that you would like to print. Click on cell **A1** and highlight down to cell **H43**. Then select **File>Print Area>Select Print Area**.

27. Next, select **File > Page setup**. Select the tab labeled **Sheet**. You will see that the gridlines and row/column headings have a check mark (✓) beside them. Click on these to eliminate the (✓) and turn off the gridlines and row/column headings.

28. Check over your work one last time to ensure that the font size and style is consistent and that the printed work will look professional.

Saving Your Work and Printing

29. Before you print and turn in your assignment, Save your work and label it **Lesson6.1(your initials here with no spaces)**.

Printing Formulas

Your instructor may request that you also print out your spreadsheet assignment showing all the formulas you have written.

Markup Calculations and Pricing Strategies Review Problems Using Excel

Review Problem 6.1

Open a blank Excel spreadsheet.

1. Save the blank spreadsheet to your own travel drive and give it an appropriate filename. To be consistent, this file should be named **Review6.1(your initials here with no spaces)**. Now you are ready to begin working.

Create two tables that will allow you to calculate the following:

2. An accessories buyer has an opening stock figure of $69,000 at retail. The inventory carries a 59% markup. On August 31, new purchases for the month amounted to $47,000 at retail with a 52% markup. What is the cumulative markup percentage to date?

3. During the fall season, an electronics department determined that the amount of merchandise needed to meet the planned sales was $189,000 at retail with a 60% markup. At the beginning of the season, the merchandise on hand came to $108,000 at retail with a markup of 56%. What markup percentage does the buyer need to achieve on any new purchases?

HINT: Be sure to give each column and row a proper heading in order to present your work more professionally.

4. Be sure to save your work and print out the final results as directed by your instructor.

Review Problem 6.2

Open a blank Excel spreadsheet.

1. Save the blank spreadsheet to your own diskette and give it an appropriate filename. To be consistent, this file should be named **Review6.2(your initials here with no spaces)**. Now you are ready to begin working.

Create a table that will allow you to calculate the initial markup percentage, reductions percentage, and maintained markup percentage for each of the following problems:

2. A buyer plans an initial markup of 54% and reductions of 13.5%. What maintained markup can the buyer expect?

3. A shoe department has a planned initial markup of 53%. It expects markdowns of 10% and shortages of 2.8%. The department has an employee discount program that results in 3% employee discounts. What maintained markup can the department expect?

4. A junior department has the following figures for the holiday season: initial markup 51.5%, employee discounts 3%, markdowns 12%, and shortages of 1.0%. What maintained markup can the department expect?

5. A buyer plans an initial markup of 47.4% and reductions of 14%. What maintained markup can the buyer expect?

6. Select a different area on the same spreadsheet page and create a table for the following problem:

Calculate the gross cost of merchandise, total cost of merchandise, gross margin percentage, and maintained markup percentage for the following example:

- Net Sales $309,000
- Cost of Goods Sold $137,000
- New Purchases $285,000
- Inward Freight $ 6,800
- Cash Discounts $ 7,500
- Alterations/Workroom $ 1,800
- Closing Inventory $260,000

HINT: You may want to place a border around each of the two tables in order to present your work more clearly and professionally.

7. Be sure to save your work and print out the final results as directed by your instructor.

Review Problem 6.3

Open a blank Excel spreadsheet.

1. Save the blank spreadsheet to your own diskette and giving it an appropriate filename. To be consistent, this file should be named **Review6.3(your initials here with no spaces)**. Now you are ready to begin working.

2. The owner of Paul's Hardware Store is considering opening a new location in the retail space adjacent to the Elmwood Carpet Store. As a part of his research, the owner, Paul Parker, would like to analyze the information given below to determine whether the new location is viable with regard to gross margin and profit. You will need to provide one spreadsheet (which may contain separate tables) that provides the appropriate analysis to answer Mr. Parker's questions.

3. From his openings of previous locations of Paul's Hardware Store and years in the hardware business, Mr. Parker knows that the new location will need to be able to achieve a gross margin minimum of 42 % and Profit of 4%. Given the expected costs related to obtaining an opening inventory listed below and estimated net sales, will Paul's Hardware Store be able to achieve his goals? What gross margin dollars and profit dollars can be estimated

Planned Net Sales	$159,000
Cost of Goods Sold	$36,160
New Purchases–Opening Inventory for Grand Opening	$165,000
Inward Freight	$5,000
Closing Inventory	$122,000
Cash Discounts	$2,400

Mr. Parker has estimated the following reductions and would like to determine what initial markup would be necessary in the proposed location.

Markdowns	8%
Employee Discounts	3%
Shortages	1%

4. Because maintained markup is the markup actually achieved on the sale of merchandise, Mr. Parker would also like to see the maintained markup possible given the estimated figures above. Provide a small chart that depicts the figures you will need to use to calculate maintained markup as well as providing the calculation of maintained markup in percentage and dollars.

5. Be sure to give your charts appropriate titles, column headings, and other appropriate formatting.

6. Make sure your work is formatted professionally and addresses Mr. Parker's concerns in an easy-to-read format.

7. Be sure to save your work and print out the final results as directed by your instructor.

Review Problem 6.4

Open a blank Excel spreadsheet.

1. Save the blank spreadsheet to your own diskette and give it an appropriate filename. To be consistent, this file should be named **Review6.4(your initials here with no spaces)**. Now you are ready to begin working.

2. A buyer for the lingerie department at Selby's Department Store has recorded the following figures:

Gross Margin	43.0%
Markdowns	10.0%
Employee Discounts	2.0%
Cash Discounts	3.0%

3. Create a table that lists the figures given and determines the initial markup percentage.

4. After calculating the initial markup, the buyer sets out to determine the cumulative markup on the merchandise handled in her department to date. She would

like to present this information to the Divisional Merchandise Manager (DMM) at tomorrow's executive meeting.

Opening Stock	$135,000	MU% = 58
New Purchases	$201,000	MU% = 52

5. Create a table that lists the figures given and determines the cumulative markup achieved on merchandise handled.

6. Be sure to give your charts appropriate titles, column headings, and other appropriate formatting. Make sure your work is formatted professionally and is easy to read.

7. Be sure to save your work and print out the final results as directed by your instructor.

Review Problem 6.5

Open a blank Excel spreadsheet.

1. Save the blank spreadsheet to your own diskette and give it an appropriate filename. To be consistent, this file should be named **Review6.5(your initials here with no spaces)**. Now you are ready to begin working.

2. In preparation for a buying trip, a children's buyer determines that a 52% markup is required on purchases to meet expectations for the period. Her total purchases will amount to $750,000 at retail and while on the trip she made purchases from three vendors as follows:

	Cost	Retail
• Resource A	$50,000	$110,000
• Resource B	$15,000	$28,000
• Resource C	$75,000	$150,000

3. Create a table that depicts the purchases already acquired and indicates the markup percentage needed on the balance of the purchases to achieve the desired cumulative markup.

4. Be sure to give your chart an appropriate title, column headings, and other appropriate formatting.

5. Make sure your work is formatted professionally and is easy to read.

6. Be sure to save your work and print out the final results as directed by your instructor.

Review Problem 6.6

Open a blank Excel spreadsheet.

1. Save the blank spreadsheet to your own diskette and give it an appropriate file-name. To be consistent, this file should be named **Review6.6(your initials here with no spaces)**. Now you are ready to begin working.

2. An infants' buyer operates on a 53% markup and needs 300 layettes that will retail at $18.00 each and 400 blankets that will retail at $12.00 each. If the buyer pays $9.75 for the layettes, create a chart that represents the given information and how much can be spent for each blanket to attain the desired markup on the total purchase.

3. Be sure to give your chart an appropriate title, column headings, etc.

4. Make sure your work is formatted professionally and addresses the buyer's concerns in an easy to read format.

5. Be sure to save your work and print out the final results as directed by your instructor.

CHAPTER 7

Valuation of Retail Inventory

In a perfect world, every retailer would have both the quantity and variety of merchandise on hand that would satisfy every customer demand with no merchandise going unsold. However, reality is much different, and requires that most retailers find ways to balance the desire to have enough merchandise on hand to satisfy customers while keeping the investment in stock as low as possible. This strategy will allow the retailer to minimize the over-purchase of slow-selling items and reserve budget dollars to take advantage of unpredicted trends or **hot items**.

A **book inventory** indicates the retail value of stock that has been determined from records. The **physical inventory**, in contrast, is an actual count of stock on hand at any given time (usually the end of the period) valued at retail. In this chapter, you will learn to utilize the retail method of inventory to determine the book inventory and shortage/overage.

The **retail method** system begins with a complete physical count of all the goods on hand and a calculation of the retail value of those goods. The retail value obtained is used as the opening book inventory. Inventory is then reported on the books by taking into account all of those transactions that add to the retail value of the inventory (ins) and those that subtract from the retail value of the inventory (outs).

Once the period is complete, another physical count of the inventory occurs. The difference between the statistical value calculated in the book inventory and the actual physical inventory is stated in terms of shortage or overage. If the physical inventory is less than the book inventory indicates it should be, then a **shortage** has occurred. If the physical inventory is greater than the book inventory indicates it should be, then an **overage** has occurred.

You will find the following concepts and definitions useful in the valuation of retail inventory.

Book inventory or **perpetual inventory** A running total and record of the retail value of merchandise in the department or store including all movement of merchandise in and out of the department or store.

Overage Retail dollar difference between the book inventory (numerical or statistical count) and the physical inventory (actual physical count) of merchandise where the physical inventory indicates that there is more merchandise on hand than the books indicate.

Physical inventory The retail value of all goods physically counted in the store or department at a given point in time.

Shortage Retail dollar difference between the book inventory (numerical or statistical count) and the physical inventory (actual physical count) of merchandise, where the book inventory indicates that there is more merchandise on hand than is actually found when the physical inventory count is completed.

Retail method of inventory An accounting method used by retailers that assesses the retail value of merchandise in stock and allows for determination of the cost value.

You will find the following formulas useful in your calculations:

- **Book Inventory at Retail = Opening Physical Inventory + Additions (ins) – Deductions (outs)**
- **Book Inventory at Cost = Book Inventory at Retail × (100% – Markup%)**
- **Shortage (Overage) = Closing Book Inventory at Retail – Closing Physical Inventory at Retail**
- **Shortage(Overage)% = Shortage(Overage)$ ÷ Net Sales**

Calculating Book Inventory

The first step in calculating the book inventory figure at retail is to determine the opening amount of inventory on hand. A physical inventory count, usually completed at the beginning and end of each accounting period, will act as the opening book inventory. It is important to note that the beginning book inventory for a new accounting period can also be the closing physical inventory for the previous accounting period. For example, the physical inventory counted on July 31 would then become the beginning book inventory for the period beginning August 1.

Book inventory at retail is comprised of the opening physical inventory of merchandise, plus any additions to the retail value, minus any reductions in the retail value.

INCREASE RETAIL VALUE (ADDITIONS)	DECREASE RETAIL VALUE (DEDUCTIONS)
net purchases**	gross sales*
additional markup	net sales*
transfers in	transfers out
customer returns*	employee discounts
markdown cancellations	markdowns
gross purchases**	returns to vendor**

*Note: When given gross sales, customer returns, and net sales, only net sales should be used in calculating the book inventory at retail.

**Note: When given gross purchases, returns to vendor, and net purchases, only net purchases should be used in calculating the book inventory at retail.

Application

If the physical count of inventory on July 31 in the jewelry department yielded a retail inventory value of $37,000, what was the book inventory at retail on January 31 given the following figures for the period:

Gross Purchases	$68,000
Net Sales	$52,000
Markdowns	$8,300
Returns to Vendor (RTVs)	$1,100
Employee Discounts	$250
Markdown Cancellations	$750
Freight	$400

Additions to Retail Value = Gross Purchases + Markdown Cancellations
Additions = $68,000 + $750
Additions = $68,750

Deductions to Retail Value = Net Sales + Markdowns + Employee Discounts + RTVs

Deductions = $52,000 + $8,300 + $250 + $1,100
Deductions = $61,650

Book Inventory at Retail = Opening Physical Inventory + Additions – Deductions
Book Inventory at Retail = $37,000 + $68,750 – $61,650
Book Inventory at Retail = $44,100

Practicing What You Have Learned

Calculate the closing book inventory for each of the following. Round each answer to the nearest whole dollar.

1. Opening Physical Inventory $93,000
   Gross Purchases $182,000
   Returns to Vendor $7,000
   Markdowns $17,000
   Net Sales $202,000

2. Opening physical inventory at retail for the men's suit department is $342,000. Purchases at retail for the period of February through July totaled $294,000 and net sales were $402,000. The department also experienced markdowns of $68,000, transfers into the department of $3,900, transfers out of the department of $1,050, employee discounts of $8,300, and markdown cancellations totaling $7,900.

3. Opening physical inventory $37,500
   Net Sales $41,000
   Net Purchases $43,800
   Markdowns $4,500
   Markdown Cancellations $750
   Employee Discounts $250

4. Opening physical inventory at retail for the leather goods department totaled $73,000 on August 1. Purchases at retail for the following six-month period totaled $85,000 and net sales were $94,000. The department experienced markdowns of $6,500 and employee discounts on merchandise of $800. What was the closing book inventory on January 31?

5. Opening physical inventory $245,000
   Gross Purchases $201,000
   Gross Sales $310,000
   Customer Returns $41,000
   Returns to Vendor $10,000
   Markdowns $47,000
   Markdown Cancellations $11,000
   Transfers Out $400
   Additional Markup $200

Calculating Shortages and Overages

Each time a physical inventory count is completed, the book inventory is adjusted to agree with the physical count. As we discussed in Chapter 4, there are many reasons that the actual count of merchandise and the retail dollar value associated with that stock may differ from the value stated in the books.

Among the most common causes of differences between the book inventory and physical count are errors in recording markdowns, returns to vendor, transfers in and out, merchandise breakage, and employee/customer theft. It is also possible that human error could cause the physical count of the merchandise to be incorrect.

Application

Using the method for calculating book inventory, calculate the shortage or overage experienced by the department with the following figures:

Opening Physical Inventory	$45,000
Net Purchases at Retail	$65,000
Markdowns	$5,000
Employee Discounts	$1,000
Markdown Cancellations	$1,000
Net Sales	$61,000
Physical Inventory at End of Accounting Period	$43,000

First calculate the book inventory:

Additions to Retail Value = Purchases + Markdown Cancellations
Additions = $65,000 + $1,000
Additions = $66,000

Deductions to Retail Value = Net Sales + Markdowns + Employee Discounts
Deductions = $61,000 + $5,000 + $1,000
Deductions = $67,000

Then:

Book Inventory at Retail = Opening Physical Inventory + Additions − Deductions
Book Inventory at Retail = $45,000 + $66,000 − $67,000
Book Inventory at Retail = $44,000

Then:

Shortage(Overage) = Closing Book Inventory at Retail − Physical Inventory at Retail

Shortage(Overage) = $44,000 − $43,000

Shortage = $1,000

This is classified as a shortage because the physical inventory is less (or short) of what the book inventory states. If the result had been a negative number, indicating that the physical inventory was actually larger than what the books stated, an overage would have occurred.

Practicing What You Have Learned

Find the shortage or overage for each of the following. Round each answer to the nearest whole dollar.

6. Opening Physical Inventory $127,500
   Net Sales $141,000
   Net Purchases $95,500
   Markdowns $12,300
   Markdown Cancellations $1,400
   Employee Discounts $500
   Physical Inventory at End of Accounting Period $72,000

7. During the last accounting period, a closing physical inventory of $289,000 was counted. The book inventory was $291,000 for the same period. What was the shortage/overage?

8. Opening Physical Inventory at Retail $135,000
   Gross Sales $142,000
   Returns to Vendor $10,000
   Transfers Out $1,500
   Transfers In $1,750
   Gross Purchases $140,000
   Markdowns $16,000
   Markdown Cancellations $4,500
   Closing Physical Inventory at Retail $113,000

9. An accessories department showed an opening physical inventory of $58,000 at the beginning of a 6-month accounting period. During the period, net sales totaled $34,000, markdowns were $2,800, and net purchases were $43,000. At the

end of the 6-month period, a physical inventory count totaled $63,000. Calculate the shortage/overage.

10. | | |
|---|---|
| Opening Physical Inventory at Retail | $195,000 |
| Gross Sales | $325,000 |
| Customer Returns | $41,000 |
| Gross Purchases | $254,000 |
| Returns to Vendor | $15,000 |
| Markdowns | $63,000 |
| Markdown Cancellations | $8,000 |
| Employee Discounts | $4,000 |
| Additional Markups | $5,000 |
| Closing Physical Inventory at Retail | $99,500 |

Calculating Shortage and Overage Percentage

Because shortages vary widely from department to department and store to store, retailers calculate shortage as a percentage of net sales for easy comparison. Few, if any, retailers are immune to physical losses of merchandise. The National Retail Security Survey conducted by the National Retail Federation in conjunction with the University of Florida reported in June of 2007 that the national average for shortage (also known as *shrinkage*) in 2006 was 1.61%. The majority of this shrinkage resulted from employee theft and shoplifting, which accounted for 47% and 32%, respectively, of total shrinkage.[1]

Application

During the 6-month period from August 1 to January 31, the sporting goods department had net sales totaling $147,000. On January 31 a physical inventory totaling $102,000 was taken. If the book inventory for the same period totaled $104,200, what was the shortage percentage for the period?

First calculate the shortage or overage dollar figure:

Shortage(Overage) = Closing Book Inventory at Retail – Closing Physical Inventory at Retail
Shortage(Overage) = $104,200 – $102,000
Shortage = $2,200

---

[1]Grannis, K. (2007, June 11). Retail Losses Hit $41.6 Billion Last Year, According to National Retail Security Survey. NRF.com.

Then:

> Shortage% = Shortage$ ÷ Net Sales
> Shortage% = $2,200 ÷ $147,000
> Shortage% = 1.50%

Because shortages are a normal occurrence, retailers often plan for a certain percentage of shortage. This is an easy calculation to make given a planned net sales.

Application

The merchandising plan for the period ending July 31 shows a net sales figure of $245,000 and a planned shortage of 1.3%. Calculate the planned shortage dollars.

Because we know that:

> Shortage% = Shortage$ ÷ Net Sales$

We also know that:

> Shortage$ = Net Sales$ × Shortage%

Then:

> Shortage$ = $245,000 × 1.3%
> Shortage$ = $3,185

Practicing What You Have Learned

For each problem, round currency to the nearest whole dollar and percentage to the tenth.

11. During the 3-month period from February 1 to April 31, a lingerie department had a net sales of $39,000. On April 31 the physical count of the inventory totaled $51,000 and the book inventory totaled $52,200. Calculate the shortage or overage for the period.

12. For the lingerie department listed above, calculate the shortage or overage percentage during the same time period.

13. A children's shoe department was planning to achieve net sales of $114,000 with an estimated 2% shortage. Calculate the dollar amount of the planned shortage.

14. Calculate the shortage/overage dollars and percentage for a department with the following figures.

Opening Physical Inventory at Retail	$32,000
Net Purchases at Retail	$43,000
Markdowns	$4,500
Markdown Cancellations	$500
Net Sales	$39,000
Employee Discounts	$400
Closing Physical Inventory at Retail	$33,000

15. If the planned shortage for an electronics retailer is 2.5% during a 6-month period where net sales are $87,580, calculate the shortage dollars.

Calculating the Book Inventory at Cost

Up to this point, we have been discussing the value of merchandise in a store or department in terms of the retail value of the merchandise. Because most retailers utilize this retail method of inventory valuation, they also must obtain the cost value of the merchandise sold in order to calculate the profitability of the merchandise.

This process requires drawing on many of the concepts learned in previous chapters, including calculating total merchandise handled and cumulative markup percentage (Chapter 6) and converting retail figures to cost (Chapter 5).

Because not all inventory carries the same markup percentage, converting a book inventory to cost requires several steps.

1. Convert the opening book inventory figure (usually the opening physical inventory figure) from retail to cost.
2. Calculate the cost value of the total merchandise handled and the cumulative markup achieved.
3. Convert the closing book inventory figure (usually a closing physical inventory figure) from retail to cost.

Application

If we use the same problem for which we calculated the book inventory earlier in this chapter, given a markup percentage of 50% and the cost of new purchases of $32,000, we can calculate the book inventory at cost:

If the physical count of inventory on July 31 in the jewelry department yielded an inventory value of $37,000, what was the book inventory at retail on January 31 given the following figures for the period:

Gross Purchases	$68,000
Net Sales	$52,000
Markdowns	$8,300
Returns to Vendor (RTVs)	$1,100
Employee Discounts	$250
Markdown Cancellations	$750
Freight	$400

First, convert the opening book inventory from retail to cost:

Opening Book Inventory at Cost = Retail$ × Cost Complement (100% − MU%)
Opening Book Inventory at Cost = $37,000 × (100% − 50%)
Opening Book Inventory at Cost = $37,000 × 0.50
Opening Book Inventory at Cost = $18,500

Next, calculate the cost of the total amount of merchandise handled and find the cumulative markup achieved.

IMPORTANT NOTE: You will note that the freight figure is used in the cost calculation but not in the retail calculation. Freight is a factor that adds to the cost of the merchandise.

Cost of Merchandise Handled = Opening Inventory at cost + New Purchases at cost + Freight
Cost of Merchandise Handled = $18,500 + $32,000 + $400
Cost of Merchandise Handled = $50,900

Then:

Markup$ = Total Merchandise Handled at Retail − Total Merchandise Handled at Cost
Markup$ = [$37,000(Gross Purchases) + $66,900 (RTV)] − $50,900

Markup$ = $53,000
Markup% = Markup$ ÷ Total Merchandise Handled at Retail$
Markup% = $53,000 ÷ $103,900
Markup% = 51%

Finally, convert the closing book inventory from retail to cost. (Remember that the closing book inventory figure we calculated previously was $44,100 at retail.)

Closing Book Inventory at Cost = Retail$ × Cost Complement (100% − MU%)
Closing Book Inventory at Cost = $44,100 × (100% − 51%)
Closing Book Inventory at Cost = $44,100 × 0.49
Closing Book Inventory at Cost = $21,609

Practicing What You Have Learned

Round each answer to the nearest whole dollar.

16. A juniors' sportswear department buyer has the following data for the 6-month period beginning August 1:

	Cost	Retail
Opening Inventory	$85,000	$155,000
Purchases	$102,000	$205,000
Net Sales		$234,000
Markdowns		$18,000

Calculate the closing book inventory at cost.

> *HINT:* You may want to refer to the instructions for Calculating Cumulative Markup in Chapter 6.

17. Calculate the total merchandise handled and the closing book inventory at cost for the following data:

Opening Physical Inventory	$123,000
Gross Purchases	$211,000
Returns to Vendors	$2,500
Freight	$1,500
Markdowns	$8,400

Markdown Cancellations	$750
Employee Discounts	$1,050
Net Sales	$179,000
Markup Opening Inventory	52%
Net Purchases at Cost	$101,000

Total Merchandise Handled at Retail =

Closing Book Inventory at Cost =

17. The men's suit department had a closing book inventory at retail of $280,000 with a 52% markup on the total merchandise handled. Given this information, calculate the closing inventory at cost.

Reviewing Markup Concepts, Total Merchandise Handled, and Gross Margin

Many of the concepts covered in previous chapters actually provide the foundation for the retail method of valuing the merchandise inventory. Remember that in Chapter 6 you learned to calculate the total retail and cost value of merchandise handled in order to find the cumulative markup percentage. Here is a quick review of these concepts covered in the previous chapters.

Calculating the Closing Book Inventory at Cost: Remember that you can calculate the cost value of the closing book inventory by multiplying the closing book inventory at retail figure by the cost complement.

Closing Book Inventory at Cost =
Closing Book Inventory at Retail × (100% − MU% of Total Merch. Handled)

Where MU% = $\dfrac{\text{Total Merchandise Handled at Retail} - \text{Total Merchandise Handled at Cost}}{\text{Total Merchandise Handled at Retail}}$

Calculating the Closing Book Inventory at Retail: Remember that you learned to calculate the closing book inventory by subtracting all the deductions (e.g., net sales, net markdowns, employee discounts) at retail from the retail value of the total merchandise handled.

Closing Book Inventory at Retail = Total Merchandise Handled at Retail − Total Deductions at Retail
or

Closing Book Inventory at Retail = Opening Inventory at Retail + Additions + Deductions

Calculating the Cumulative Markup Dollars and Percentage for Total Merchandise Handled: Now that you have the dollar value of total merchandise handled at retail and cost, remember that you can find the cumulative markup dollars and percentage.

Cumulative Markup$ = Total Merch. Handled at Retail – Total Merch. Handled at Cost

Cumulative Markup % = Cumulative Markup$ ÷ Total Merch. Handled at Retail

Calculating the Gross Cost of Merchandise Sold: Remember that in Chapter 6 you learned that you could calculate the gross cost of merchandise sold by subtracting the closing inventory at cost from the value of the total merchandise handled at cost.

Gross Cost of Merchandise Sold =

Merchandise Handled at Cost (Opening Inventory + New Purchases + Freight) – Closing Inventory

Calculating the Gross Margin Dollars and Percentage: Now that you have the total cost of merchandise sold, you can calculate gross margin dollars by subtracting this figure from net sales. Gross margin percentage can then be calculated by dividing gross margin dollars by net sales.

Gross Margin $ = Net Sales – Total Cost of Merchandise Sold

Gross Margin % = Gross Margin $ ÷ Net Sales

Calculating the Maintained Markup Dollars and Percentage: In Chapter 6 you learned that maintained markup can be calculated by subtracting the gross cost of merchandise sold from net sales. The maintained markup percentage can then be calculated by dividing the maintained markup dollar figure by net sales.

Maintained Markup$ = Net Sales – Gross Cost of Merchandise Sold

Maintained Markup% = Maintained Markup$ ÷ Net Sales

Calculating the Total Cost of Merchandise Sold: Also in Chapter 6 you learned that the total cost of merchandise sold represented the subtraction of cash discounts and the addition of any alteration or workroom costs from the gross cost of merchandise sold.

Total Cost of Merchandise Sold =

Gross Cost of Merchandise Sold – Cash Discounts + Alterations/Workroom Costs

Calculating the Total Merchandise Handled at Cost: Remember that calculating the merchandise handled at cost requires the following formula utilizing the cost dollar figures for each factor:

Merchandise Handled at Cost =

Beginning Inventory + Net Merchandise Purchases + Freight

Calculating the Total Merchandise Handled at Retail: Remember that calculating merchandise handled at retail requires the following formula utilizing the retail dollar figures for each factor:

Merchandise Handled at Retail =
Beginning Inventory + Net Merchandise Purchased (not including freight) + Additional Markup

Practicing What You Have Learned

18. Determine the (a) closing inventory at cost and retail, the (b) gross margin percentage, and (c) shortage/overage percentage for the following data (round to nearest whole dollar amount as you work):

	Cost	Retail
Opening Physical Inventory	$27,500	$58,200
Net Purchases	$81,100	$189,500
Freight	$2,000	
Markdowns		$9,250
Markdown Cancellations		$800
Net Sales		$113,400
Cash Discounts	$3,055	
Alteration/Workroom	$250	
Closing Physical Inventory		$124,200

19. Find the (a) cumulative markup percentage, (b) maintained markup percentage, and (c) gross margin percentage for the department reporting the figures below (round to nearest whole dollar amount as your work):

	Cost	Retail
Opening Physical Inventory	$159,000	$310,000
Gross Purchases	$203,000	$495,000
RTVs	$13,000	$32,000
Freight	$2,700	
Net Sales		$383,000
Markdown		$24,900
Markdown Cancellations		$2,400
Employee Discounts		$4,100
Cash Discounts	$6,500	
Closing Physical Inventory		$363,800

Chapter 7 Review Exercise A

1. The net sales in the hosiery department for the month of August totaled $16,300. If a book inventory indicated a closing inventory level of $41,200 at retail and the physical count at the end of August totaled $39.850 at retail, calculate the shortage or overage percentage for the month.

2. Opening inventory at retail for the juniors' sportswear department is $310,000. Purchases at retail for the 6-month period beginning February 1 were $425,000 and net sales for the same period totaled $487,000. Find the closing book inventory at retail if markdowns were $89,000, transfers in were $7,200, transfers out were $1,050, and employee discounts were $16,000.

3. If the cumulative markup percentage on total merchandise handled was 50.5%, what would the closing book inventory be at cost for the juniors' department in Problem 2?

4. Find the closing inventory at (a) retail and (b) cost for Ted's Electronics Boutique given the following figures:

	Cost	Retail
Net Sales		$117,000
Opening Physical Inventory	$45,000	$103,000
Markdowns		$12,000
Net Purchases	$85,000	$169,000
Employee Discounts		$1,200

5. For Ted's Electronics Boutique (depicted in Problem 4), if cash discounts earned were $5,000 and workroom costs were $350, calculate the gross margin percentage.

6. Find the shortage or overage percentage for the department reporting the following figures:

Gross Sales	$437,000
Customer Returns	$26,000
Opening Physical Inventory (retail)	$491,000
Markdowns	$58,000
Employee Discounts	$ 8,000
Gross Purchases	$317,000
RTVs	$11,000
Closing Physical Inventory (retail)	$321,500
Net Sales	$289,000

7. A shoe department buyer received the following figures:

	Cost	Retail
Opening Physical Inventory	$125,000	$289,000
Gross Purchases	$211,000	$395,000
RTVs	$10,000	$23,000
Freight	$2,900	
Net Sales		$255,000
Markdown		$15,000
Markdown Cancellations		$1,000
Employee Discounts		$1,000
Cash Discounts	$3,000	
Closing Physical Inventory		$359,000

Calculate the (a) cumulative markup percentage on total merchandise handled, (b) gross margin percentage, and (c) maintained markup percentage.

8. Calculate the shortage or overage dollars and percentage using the information provided in Problem 7.

Chapter 7 Review Exercise B

1. Net sales in the men's furnishings department were $74,000. The book inventory at the end of the period was $139,500 at retail and the physical count at retail totaled $141,000. Did the department experience a shortage or overage? What was the percentage of shortage or overage?

2. A buyer in housewares showed a planned sales figure of $110,000 with an estimated shortage of 1.5%. Calculate the planned shortage dollars.

3. On January 31 a small appliances department recorded the following figures for the six-month period:

Opening Physical Inventory (retail)	$245,000
Gross Sales	$310,000
Customer Returns	$18,500
Net Merchandise Purchases (retail)	$290,000
Transfers In	$3,200
Transfers Out	$800
Additional Markup	$500
Markdowns	$44,000
Markdown Cancellations	$4,600
Employee Discounts	$3,900

Calculate the closing book inventory at retail for the department.

4. If the physical count of inventory at retail for the department depicted in Problem 3 totaled $201,000, was there a shortage or overage in the department? What was the percentage of shortage or overage experience?

5. Calculate the (a) total merchandise handled at retail, (b) at cost, and (c) the closing book inventory at cost for the department experiencing the following figures:

	Cost	Retail
Opening Physical Inventory	$26,750	$69,350
Net Purchases	$65,000	$108,400
Freight	$890	
Markdowns		$9,900
Markdown Cancellations		$1,050
Employee Discounts		$850
Net Sales		$99,800

6. Opening inventory at retail for a lingerie department is $113,000. Purchases at retail for the 6-month period beginning February 1 were $141,000 and net sales for the same period totaled $107,000. Find the closing book inventory at retail if

markdowns were $7,500, transfers in were $300, transfers out were $450, and employee discounts were $680.

7. Determine the gross margin percentage given the following figures:

	Cost	Retail
Opening Physical Inventory	$19,000	$42,000
Net Purchases	$28,000	$64,000
Freight	$830	
Net Sales		$51,200
Markdowns		$2,010
Additional Markup		$200
Employee Discounts		$520
Cash Discounts	$450	
Alterations		$110

8. For the figures in Problem 7, calculate the cumulative markup percentage on total merchandise handled and the maintained markup percentage.

Chapter 7 Review Exercise C

1. Find the shortage or overage percentage for the department reporting the following figures:

Gross Sales	$87,000
Customer Returns	$3,500
Opening Physical Inventory (retail)	$101,000
Markdowns	$11,000
Markdown Cancellations	$2,500
Employee Discounts	$ 1,000
Gross Purchases	$107,000
RTVs	$2,000
Closing Physical Inventory (retail)	$111,450

2. The pottery buyer showed a planned sales figure of $34,000 with an estimated shortage of 2.2%. Calculate the planned shortage dollars.

3. Find the closing inventory at (a) retail and (b) cost given the following figures:

	Cost	Retail
Net Sales		$335,000
Opening Physical Inventory	$151,000	$291,000
Markdowns		$62,000
Net Purchases	$261,000	$469,000
Employee Discounts		$11,000
Freight		$5,000

4. If cash discounts totaled $1,200 and alterations costs were $400 for the department in Problem 3, calculate the (a) cumulative markup percentage on total merchandise handled, (b) the maintained markup percentage, and (c) the gross margin percentage.

5. Net sales in the men's furnishings department were $35,650. The book inventory at the end of the period was $89,700 at retail and the physical count at retail totaled $91,200. Did the department experience a shortage or overage? What was the percentage of shortage or overage?

6. Calculate the closing book inventory at retail given the following:

Opening Physical Inventory	$55,000
Gross Purchases	$84,000
RTVs	$3,500
Markdowns	$6,200
Markdown Cancellations	$350
Employee Discounts	$750
Transfers In	$1,020
Transfers Out	$840
Gross Sales	$61,310
Customer Returns	$1,260

7. Opening inventory at retail for an accessories department is $112,000. Purchases at retail for the 6-month period beginning February 1 were $120,000 and net sales for the same period totaled $97,000. Find the closing book inventory at retail if markdowns were $6,900, and employee discounts were $800.

8. If the cumulative markup percentage on total merchandise handled was 52%, what would the closing book inventory be at cost for the accessories department in Problem 7?

Retail Method of Inventory Valuation
Excel Tutorial

Opening the File

1. Open Excel (usually located on your desktop as an icon or can be accessed from the Start menu in the bottom left-hand corner of your screen).

2. Choose **File>Open**, and then locate the file entitled **Lesson7.1.xls**. You can open this file by double-clicking on the filename. Your screen should resemble **Figure 7.1**.

Fig. 7.1:

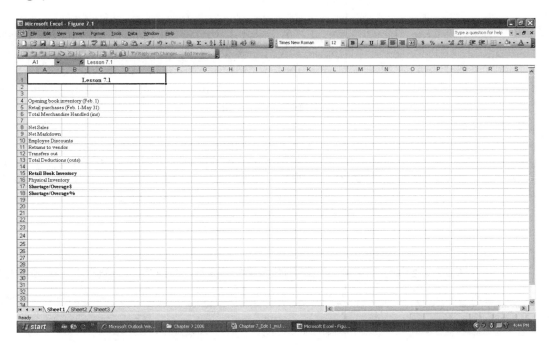

Completing the Spreadsheet

Given the following scenario, calculate the retail book inventory and shortage/overage for the period:

3. On January 31, the physical inventory count in the men's shirt department at the Greenhill location totaled $45,000. On February 1, the opening retail inventory of this department was $45,000. From February 1 to May 31 retail purchases amounted to $79,000 and were received into stock. Net sales during this period were $51,000 and markdowns of $4,700 were taken. Employee discounts amounted to $1,200 and $350 in merchandise was returned to the vendor. Another

$500 in merchandise was sent to the Shorthill location during the period at the request of the divisional merchandise manager. A physical count of the inventory in the store on May 31 revealed merchandise valued at $65,500 at retail.

4. Enter the data given for additions to retail value into the spreadsheet. Place the figure for opening inventory at retail in cell **D4**. Enter the number as **45,000**. You will format these figures as currency in a later step. Complete the data entry for additions to retail inventory by placing **79,000** in cell **D5** to represent retail purchases.

5. Total the additions to retail inventory by placing your cursor in cell **D6** and pressing the autosum (Σ) button in the toolbar. A formula will appear at your cursor: **=SUM(D9:D10)**. Since this formula is correct, press **Enter** or click on the green check mark ($\checkmark$) in the formula bar.

6. Enter the data given for deductions from retail value (outs) into the spreadsheet. Place the figure for net sales into cell **D8**. Again, enter the number as **51,000**; you will be asked to format these figures as currency in a later step. Complete the data entry for deductions from retail inventory (outs) by entering in the remaining variables in column D of the appropriate rows.

7. Total the deductions to retail inventory by placing your cursor in cell **D13**, and press the autosum (Σ) button in the toolbar. A flashing dotted line should appear around cells **D8 through D12**. Press Enter or click on the green check mark ($\checkmark$) in the formula bar. At this point, your screen should resemble Figure 7.2.

Fig. 7.2:

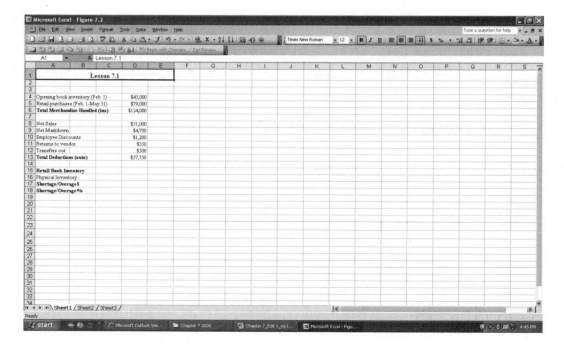

8. Enter the formula in cell **D15** that will allow you to calculate the retail book inventory. The formula will read **=D6-D13**.

9. Enter the physical inventory figure in cell **D16**.

10. Enter the formula in cell **D17** that will calculate the shortage or overage for the men's shirt department. The shortage or overage is calculated by subtracting the physical inventory from the book inventory figure: **=D15-D16**.

11. Enter the formula in cell **D18** that will calculate the percentage of net sales that the shortage/overage found in step 10 represents: **=D17/D8**. At this point your work should resemble **Figure 7.3**.

Fig. 7.3:

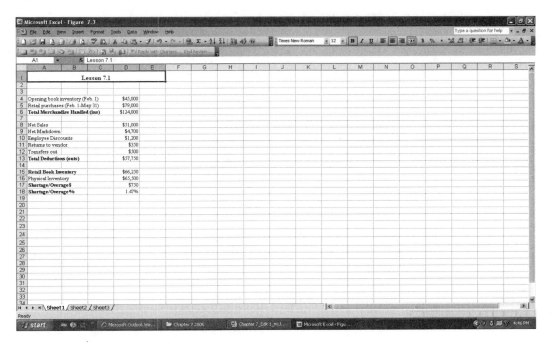

Setting a Print Area and Formatting the Page

12. Now you are almost ready to complete the assignment and print. First you need to set the area of the spreadsheet that you would like to print. Click on cell **A1** and highlight down to cell **E18**. Then select **File>Print Area>Select Print Area**.

13. Next, select **File>Page setup**. Select the tab labeled **Sheet**. You will see that the gridlines and row/column headings have a check mark (✓) beside them. Click on these to eliminate the (✓) and turn off the gridlines and row/column headings.

You can select **File>Print Preview** to see how your spreadsheet will look when printed.

14. When you are through previewing the page, choose **Close,** which will take you back to your working spreadsheet.

Saving Your Work and Printing

15. Before you print and turn in your assignment, save your work. (In fact, you should save **often** during your work session to be sure that you have saved changes made to the worksheet). Save your work on your travel drive and label it **Lesson7.1(your initials here with no spaces).**

Printing Formulas

16. Your instructor may request that you also print out your spreadsheet assignment showing all the formulas you have written.

Retail Method of Inventory Valuation Review Problems Using Excel

Review Problem 7.1

Open a blank Excel spreadsheet.

1. Save the blank spreadsheet to your own travel drive and give it an appropriate filename. To be consistent, this file should be named **Review7.1(your initials here with no spaces).** Now you are ready to begin working.

2. Determine the closing book inventory at retail and shortage/overage in dollars and percentage given the following:

   - Physical Inventory (July 31) $165,000
   - Opening Physical Inventory (February 1) $198,000
   - Gross Sales $236,000
   - Employee Discounts $950
   - Purchases $226,500
   - Markup Cancellations $800
   - Additional Markup $2,100
   - Markdown Cancellation $1,800
   - Returns to Vendor $3,500
   - Customer Returns $8,500
   - Markdowns $17,500

3. Be sure to save your work and print out the final results as directed by your instructor.

Review Problem 7.2

Open a blank Excel spreadsheet.

1. Save the blank spreadsheet to your own travel drive and give it an appropriate filename. To be consistent, this file should be named **Review 7.2(your initials here with no spaces)**. Now you are ready to begin working.

2. The following figures are from a juniors' sportswear department:

   - Markdowns $12,000
   - Purchases $205,000
   - Returns to Vendor (RTVs) $15,500
   - Transfers In $3,500
   - Transfers Out $1,950
   - Net Sales $172,000
   - Opening physical inventory $135,000

3. Determine the closing book inventory for the period.

4. Be sure to save your work and print out the final results as directed by your instructor.

Review Problem 7.3

Open a blank Excel spreadsheet.

1. Save the blank spreadsheet to your own travel drive and give it an appropriate filename. To be consistent, this file should be named **Review 7.3(your initials here with no spaces)**. Now you are ready to begin working.

2. A costume jewelry department had the following figures for a four-month period:

   - Net Sales $410,000
   - Purchases $595,000
   - Opening Inventory $260,000
   - Markdowns $89,000
   - Employee Discounts $8,300
   - Closing Physical Count $281,000
   - 51.5% Markup on Total Merchandise Handled

3. Create a spreadsheet that includes all the data listed above and allows you to calculate

- Book Inventory at retail
- Book Inventory at cost [*HINT:* Cost = Retail × (100% − MU%)]
- Shortage/Overage dollars and percentage

4. Be sure to save your work and print out the final results as directed by your instructor.

Review Problem 7.4

Open a blank Excel spreadsheet.

1. Save the blank spreadsheet to your own travel drive and give it an appropriate filename. To be consistent, this file should be named **Review 7.4(your initials here with no spaces)**. Now you are ready to begin working.

2. The furniture department at Parkinson's Department Store recorded the following figures:

	Cost	Retail
Net Sales		$350,000
Opening Inventory	$175,000	$340,000
Markdowns		$38,000
RTVs	$14,000	$19,000
Employee Discounts		$ 8,000
Gross purchases	$180,000	$325,000

You have been assigned to complete a spreadsheet that determines the closing inventory at cost.

3. Be sure to give your charts appropriate titles, column headings, and other appropriate formatting. Make sure your work is formatted professionally and is easy to read.

4. Be sure to save your work and print out the final results as directed by your instructor.

HINT: You can use your text and/or previous lessons if you need to refresh your memory of formulas or formatting techniques.

Review Problem 7.5

Open a blank Excel spreadsheet.

1. Save the blank spreadsheet to your own travel drive and give it an appropriate filename. To be consistent, this file should be named **Review 7.5(your initials here with no spaces)**. Now you are ready to begin working.

2. Create a chart that determines the book inventory and shortage/overage in dollars and percentage given the following information for a lingerie department:

   - Physical Inventory (Jan. 31) $304,900
   - Opening Inventory (Aug. 1) $317,200
   - Gross Sales $420,300
   - Employee Discounts $2,980
   - Purchases $360,450
   - Additional Markup $3,100
   - Markdown Cancellation $7,800
   - Returns to Vendor $20,500
   - Customer Returns $11,320
   - Markdowns $49,500

3. If the markup percentage for the lingerie department is 49.5%, calculate the closing book inventory at cost and add it to the chart created in step 2.

4. Be sure to save your work and print out the final results as directed by your instructor.

Review Problem 7.6

Open a blank Excel spreadsheet.

1. Save the blank spreadsheet to your own travel drive and give it an appropriate filename. To be consistent, this file should be named **Review 7.6(your initials here with no spaces)**. Now you are ready to begin working.

2. A men's outerwear department had an opening inventory of $132,000. The net purchases were $105,000, gross sales were $115,500, customer returns were $3,500, and markdowns were $5,250. Shortages were estimated at 1.5%. Create a chart that depicts the information given and calculates the following:

   a. Closing retail book inventory
   b. Estimated physical inventory

3. Be sure to give your charts appropriate titles, column headings, and other appropriate formatting.

4. Make sure your work is formatted professionally and is easy to read.

5. Be sure to save your work and print out the final results as directed by your instructor.

CHAPTER 8

Six-Month Plans

The six-month merchandise plan represents retailers' efforts to maintain proper proportion between sales, inventories, and prices in order to turn a profit. The inventory levels should reflect customer demand while remaining consistent with the financial limits set by management. In this chapter you will learn to plan sales, stock, markdowns, and purchases as well as to determine gross margin, stock turn, and gross-margin-return-appropriate inventory levels to achieve sales and profit goals. This chapter also contains some useful tools that will allow us to evaluate the success of our merchandising strategy and inventory acquisitions.

The first tool is the **turnover** (a.k.a. *stock turn* or *inventory turn*) figure, which helps the buyer to determine if the right merchandise was purchased in the right quantities at the right time and placed in the right locations (or doors). Stock turn is the number of times the average stock or inventory is sold during a given time period. If the stock turn is too high, the buyer may spend inordinate amounts of time and money attaining new merchandise while losing sales due to inadequate stock or assortment. If the stock turn is too low, the buyer may have priced the merchandise too high, purchased merchandise that is not desirable to the customer, or planned poorly. Low stock turn often results in overbuying, heavy markdowns, and lowers gross margin and profit levels.

The second important tool is the ability to calculate the **gross margin return on inventory investment (GMROII)**. GMROII looks at the relationship of stock turn to profitability rather than net sales. While looking at stock turn allows us to determine if the inventory is moving at an appropriate rate, the calculation of GMROII allows us to determine if the turn is profitable. Sometimes inventory is turning well but the gross margin is too low. The activity is desirable but the profit results are not.

You will find the following concepts and definitions useful:

Average stock (a.k.a. *Average inventory*) The average level of inventory in stock across a given time period. Average stock can be calculated by adding the beginning of the month (BOM) stock levels for each month under consideration plus the end of the month (EOM) figure for the final month (a.k.a. end of period or end of season inventory) and then dividing by the number of months under consideration plus one.

Basic stock A determination of the level of merchandise that should be maintained at all times in addition to the planned sales for the month given an estimated rate of stock turn.

BOM or *Beginning of the month stock* The total stock on hand in dollars at the beginning of the month. (The BOM stock level for a given month is the equivalent of the end of the month stock level from the previous month.)

EOM or *End of the month stock* The total stock on hand in dollars at the end of the month. (The EOM stock level for a given month is the equivalent of the beginning of the month stock level for the coming month.)

Gross margin return on inventory investment (GMROII) The number of times that average stock turns into gross margin; utilized by many retailers to help evaluate the success of merchandising strategies.

Stock-Sales ratio The relationship of the BOM stock (i.e., stock on hand at the beginning of the month) to the planned sales for the month.

Turnover (a.k.a. *Stock turn*) The number of times that the average stock turns into net sales. Commonly calculated on a six-month basis to provide an assessment of the success or efficiency of the merchandising strategy.

You will find the following formulas useful in completing the six-month plan:

- **%sales increase = (TY planned sales – LY planned sales) ÷ LY planned sales**
- **seasonal planned sales = LY sales × planned % increase**
- **gross margin = expenses + profit**
- **gross margin return on inventory investment = gross margin $ ÷ average stock**

OR

- gross margin return on inventory investment = (gross margin % × stock turn) ÷ (100% – MU%)
- **turnover = net sales ÷ average stock**
- **average stock = net sales ÷ turnover**

OR

- average stock = (beg. inventories + ending inventory for the period) ÷ # of inventories
- stock-sales ratio = BOM stock ÷ sales (usually calculated for each month)
- BOM stock = planned monthly sales × stock-sales ratio
- basic stock = average stock – average monthly sales
- average stock = sales ÷ stock turn
- average monthly sales = sales for the period ÷ number of months (usually 6)
- planned purchases (receipts) = sales + markdowns + EOM – BOM
- planned purchases at cost =
  planned purchases at retail × (100% – planned markup%)

Six-Month Merchandise Plan Example

Planning Sales

The process of completing a six-month merchandise plan begins with planning net sales for the time period. (*See 1 on the Six-Month Merchandise Plan Example on your student CD.*) The process includes estimating total sales for the six-month period and allocating the total sales by month for each of the six months. The estimate of total sales as well as the expected sales for each month is influenced by a variety of factors including:

- Total and monthly sales for last year during the same time period.
- External factors that may influence sales including the economy, fashion trends, (e.g., the "casual Fridays" trend might impact sales of men's suits), consumer confidence and/or inflation, new competition or changes in competitor strategy, weather, etc.
- Internal factors within the control of the store or company may also influence sales, including changes in pricing or promotional strategies, changes in merchandising mix, store renovations, physical changes to departmental space or visual merchandising, etc.

It is important to remember that planned sales, indeed *all* planned figures in the six-month plan, represent goals that the buyer is striving to achieve, *but* these plans must also be realistic and based on the best possible estimates considering the factors listed above.

Calculating Total Planned Sales (a.k.a. Seasonal Sales)

The first step in planning sales for the period is to determine whether, based on a consideration of all the external and internal factors currently being experienced, total sales for this period can be expected to increase or decrease this year over the levels experienced last year during the same period. This can be done by subtracting last year's sales from this year's planned sales and dividing by last year's sales:

%Increase or Decrease in Sales =
   (This Year's Planned Sales – Last Year's Actual Sales) ÷ Last Year's Actual Sales

HINT: The figure you wish to compare to is always the denominator or divisor. For example, if you are comparing **this year** to **last year**, then last year's figure goes in the denominator.

Application

Last year's sales in the children's shoe department were $52,000 and the buyer plans a sales figure this year of $60,000. What is the planned percentage increase for this year?

%Increase in Sales = ($60,000 – $52,000) ÷ $52,000
%Increase in Sales = $8,000 ÷ $52,000
%Increase in Sales = 0.1538 or 15.38%

However, when external and/or internal forces indicate that sales may actually fall compared to the level experienced last year, the buyer would indicate a decrease:

Application

A local jewelry store is planning sales for this year during an economic downturn that has caused a significant drop in consumer spending. The buyer feels that sales for this year can be expected to fall significantly. If sales are expected to fall by $50,000 from last year's level of $250,000 to $200,000 this year, what will be the percentage decrease?

%Decrease in Sales = ($200,000 – $250,000) ÷ $250,000
%Decrease in Sales = – $50,000 ÷ $250,000
%Decrease in Sales = – 0.2 or 2% *

*When you label the finding "%Decrease," you do not need to retain the "–" sign

In the six-month merchandise planning process, the most common planning technique for the total sales figure is to determine last year's total sales and estimate a percentage increase or decrease based on the current external and internal factors the retailer is experiencing.

Application

If last year's actual sales in the juniors' sportswear department totaled $175,000 and the buyer plans a 6% increase for this year, calculate the planned total sales for this year.

Then the previous formula becomes:

This Year's Planned Sales=
    Last Year's Actual Sales + %Increase(Last Year's Actual Sales)

Then:

This Year's Planned Sales = $175,000 + 6%($175,000)
This Year's Planned Sales = $175,000 + $10,500
This Year's Planned Sales = $185,500

Now that you have calculated this year's planned sales, you can double-check your work using the original formula:

%Increase in Sales =
    (This Year's Planned Sales – Last Year's Actual Sales) ÷ Last Year's Actual Sales
%Increase in Sales = ($185,500 – $175,000) ÷ $175,000
%Increase in Sales = $10,500 ÷ $175,000
%Increase in Sales = 0.06 or 6%

Practicing What You Have Learned

For each problem, round currency to the nearest whole dollar and percentages to the nearest tenth.

1. If last year's actual sales in the toy department totaled $110,000 and the buyer plans this year's sales at $116,000, what is the planned percentage increase?

2. Actual sales for the leather goods department last year totaled $235,000 and the buyer plans a 4% increase this year. Calculate the planned sales dollars for this year.

3. A major manufacturer in the tri-city area recently relocated to China, significantly impacting the unemployment rate and economic conditions in the area. For this reason, the buyer for home goods expects sales to drop from $145,800 last year to $129,000 this year. Calculate the planned percentage decrease in sales.

4. Calculate the percentage increase/decrease in sales given the following:

    Last Year's Actual Sales = $420,000
    This Year's Planned Sales = $430,000

5. Calculate this year's planned sales given the following:

    Last Year's Actual Sales = $157,200
    Planned Percentage Increase in Sales = 8%

Calculating Planned Sales by Month

After calculating the total planned sales figure for this year, the amount of sales to be experienced during each of the months of the plan must be determined. As with total planned sales, if last year's sales for each month are available, sales for the same month this year will be based on last year and any environmental changes that may impact the sales. (*See 2 on the Six-Month Merchandise Plan Example on your student CD.*)

To determine what percentage of sales occurred in each month last year, divide the sales figure for the month by the total sales figure for the season.

Given the following:

	FEBRUARY	MARCH	APRIL	MAY	JUNE	JULY	TOTAL SALES
Last Year	$10,000	$20,000	$25,000	$20,000	$15,000	$10,000	$100,000
% to Total							

Then:

February Sales % = February Sales ÷ Total Sales
February Sales % = $10,000 ÷ $100,000
February Sales % = 0.1 or 10%

March Sales % = March Sales ÷ Total Sales
March Sales % = $20,000 ÷ $100,000
March Sales % = 0.2 or 20%

April Sales % = April Sales ÷ Total Sales
April Sales % = $25,000 ÷ $100,000
April Sales % = 0.25 or 25%

Complete the calculations for each of the months to find the following results:

	FEBRUARY	MARCH	APRIL	MAY	JUNE	JULY	TOTAL SALES
Last Year	$10,000	$20,000	$25,000	$20,000	$15,000	$10,000	$100,000
% to Total	10%	20% ←→25%	20%	15%	10%	

Now that percentages by month for last year have been determined, any adjustments can be made (determined by changing conditions) if necessary and then the sales for this year can be allocated.

Application

The buyer experiencing the sales figures in the example above last year plans a 5% increase for this year. He also realizes that the Easter holiday will fall in March this year instead of April as it did last year. Allocate the sales for each month this year, switching the percentages for March and April to account for the changing holiday.

First you must plan the 5% increase in total sales:

This Year's Planned Sales=
　　Last Year's Actual Sales + %Increase(Last Year's Actual Sales)

This Year's Planned Sales = $100,000 + 5%($100,000)
This Year's Planned Sales = $100,000 + $5,000
This Year's Planned Sales = $105,000

Then you will want to switch the percentages for March and April as indicated in bold below:

	FEBRUARY	MARCH	APRIL	MAY	JUNE	JULY	TOTAL SALES
Last Year	$ 10,000	$ 20,000	$25,000	$20,000	$15,000	$10,000	$100,000
% to Total	10%	20% ⟷ 25%		20%	15%	10%	
This Year							$105,000

Finally, you can allocate the sales for each month based on the total planned sales for this year:

February Sales = February Sales% × Total Sales
February Sales = 10% × $105,000
February Sales = $10,500

March Sales = March Sales% × Total Sales
March Sales = 25% ÷ $105,000
March Sales = $26,250

April Sales = April Sales% × Total Sales
April Sales = 20% ÷ $105,000
April Sales = $21,000

Complete the calculations for each month to find the following:

	FEBRUARY	MARCH	APRIL	MAY	JUNE	JULY	TOTAL SALES
Last Year	$10,000	$20,000	$25,000	$20,000	$15,000	$10,000	$100,000
% to Total	10%	20% ←—→ 25%		20%	15%	10%	
This Year	$10,500	$26,250	$21,000	$26,250	$15,750	$10,500	**$105,000**

HINT: It is also possible that you would be given the monthly percentages rather than having to calculate them based on last year. In this case, you would simply multiply the percentage by the total sales figure as you did in the last step of the example above.

Practicing What You Have Learned

For each problem, round currency to the nearest whole dollar and percentages to the nearest tenth.

6. If the planned total sales for a six-month season beginning in August are $280,000, find the planned sales for each month given the following percentages:

August	14%
September	20%
October	15%
November	18%
December	23%
January	10%

7. Calculate the planned monthly sales for this year given the following figures and utilizing the same percentage allocation as last year:

   Total Sales Last Year = $111,000
   This Year's Planned Sales = $130,000

	MONTHLY SALES LAST YEAR	% TO TOTAL LAST YEAR	PLANNED MONTHLY SALES THIS YEAR
February	$ 14,000		
March	$ 16,000		
April	$ 18,000		
May	$ 25,000		
June	$ 22,000		
July	$ 16,000		

8. Actual sales in the stationery department totaled $48,000 last year. If the buyer plans a sales increase this year of 6%, calculate the sales for each month given these figures from last year:

August	10%
September	12%
October	18%
November	22%
December	25%
January	13%

9. A luxury goods retailer has noticed a downturn in luxury spending and wishes to plan a sales decrease from last year's figures in order to avoid overbuying. Last year's actual sales were $240,000 and the retailer plans a sales decrease to $210,000. Calculate the (a) percentage decrease and (b) sales for each month given the following figures and assuming no change in percentage allocation.

February	22%
March	12%
April	12%
May	15%
June	25%
July	14%

10. If planned total sales for the handbag department are $138,000, plan the sales for each month given the following expected monthly allocation percentages.

August	15%
September	18%
October	12%
November	20%
December	25%
January	10%

Planning Stocks

After determining the planned sales for the six-month period, it is now time to plan inventory levels that will sufficiently cover the sales and any reductions to inventory that might be experienced such as markdowns and shortages. Retailers utilize a variety of methods to determine the dollar value of inventory necessary. In this section, we will cover three types of planning methods including stock-sales ratio, the basic stock method, and the weeks' supply method. The stock turn figure discussed earlier in the chapter is an important component for planning inventory levels; we will cover that concept before outlining the three planning methods.

> *HINT:* Remember that in the six-month planning process, it is only the dollar value of the inventory that is planned. What assortment of merchandise including colors, styles, sizes, and quantities of each item will be determined later?

Calculating Stock Turn

The stock turn figure is an important tool for evaluating the success of your merchandising strategy and inventory acquisitions. Stock turn (a.k.a. inventory turn or turnover) can be defined as the number of times that average stock *turns* into net sales (i.e., is sold) during a given period of time. **Average stock** is the average level of inventory in stock across a given time period. Average stock can be calculated by adding the beginning of the month (**BOM**) stock levels for each month under consideration plus the end of the month (**EOM**) figure for the final month (a.k.a. end of period or end of season inventory) and then dividing by the number of months under consideration plus one. (*See 3 on the Six-Month Merchandise Plan Example on your student CD.*)

$$\text{Average Stock} = \frac{\text{BOM stock for each month} + \text{EOM stock for final month}}{\text{Number of Months} + 1}$$

(or total number of figures in the numerator)

Application

An accessories department had net sales of $7,000 for the month of April. If the beginning of the month stock for April totaled $25,000 and at the end of April the inventory figure was $32,000, find the average stock for the month and the stock turn.

$$\text{Average Stock} = \frac{\$25,000 + \$32,000}{2}$$

Average Stock = $57,000 ÷ 2

Average Stock = $28,500

Then:

Stock turn = Net Sales ÷ Average Stock

Stock turn = $7,000 ÷ $28,500

Stock turn = 0.25 for the month

HINT: Stock turn is a ratio, *not* a percentage, so you do not shift the decimal to the right. Stock turn is usually calculated at six-month intervals or even yearly. Although it varies greatly by merchandise category and type of retailer, stock turn figures in the range of 2 to 4 are typical in the retail industry.

If stock turn is known, then the average stock figure can also be attained by dividing net sales for the period by the stock turn for the period:

Average Stock = Net Sales for Period ÷ Stock Turn for Period

Practicing What You Have Learned

For each problem, round currency to the nearest whole dollar and percentages or turnover to the nearest tenth.

11. The electronics department at a small retailer had net sales for the three month period of June–August of $12,000. Given the beginning of the month inventories listed below, calculate the average stock and stock turn for the department.

	BOM Stock
June	$ 9,500
July	$12,000
August	$14,000
September	$10,000*

> *HINT:* The end of the month stock level for August is the beginning of the month stock level for September. So in this example, EOM stock for the final month is $10,000.

---

12. Determine the turnover figure for a department with net sales of $1,240,000 and an average stock for the same time period of $785,000.

13. If net sales for a six month period were $90,000, calculate the turnover figure for the period given the following beginning of the month stock levels:

	BOM Stock
August	$33,000
September	$38,000
October	$29,000
November	$35,000
December	$42,000
January	$36,000
February	$32,000

14. If net sales for the period were $310,600 and the stock turn figure was 2.2, what was the average stock for the period?

15. Determine the average stock for a department experiencing net sales of $540,000 for a six month period and a stock turn of 3.9.

Basic Stock Method of Inventory Planning

Basic stock should be maintained at all times in addition to the planned sales for the month, based on an estimated rate of stock turn. The basic stock method of inventory planning provides BOM stock levels large enough to cover planned sales for the month plus some level of basic stock that remains constant during the planning period. Predicated on the average stock figure, the basic stock is calculated by subtracting the average monthly sales for the time period from the average stock for the time period.

Basic stock is meant to ensure that some basic level of inventory remains each month to guard against empty shelves and delays in new merchandise shipments. The basic stock method of inventory planning is best used in those environments where the stock turn is low (less than six times per year), which often means that it is utilized in less fashion-oriented departments. Fashion- oriented departments, by definition, try to buy slim and turn quick to keep fresh, new trends on the floor. (*See **4a** on the Six-Month Merchandise Plan Example on your student CD.*)

Basic Stock = Average Stock – Average Monthly Sales
       Where:

$$\text{Average Stock} = \frac{\text{BOM stock for each month} + \text{EOM stock for final month}}{\text{Number of Months} + 1}$$
(or total number of figures in the numerator)

And:

$$\text{Average Monthly Sales} = \frac{\text{Total of Planned Sales for each month in a given period}}{\text{Number of Months}}$$

Application

If a fine china department plans a stock turn of 2.1 and sales of $250,000 for the six month planning period, plan the BOM stock level for November if planned sales for November are $45,000.

First calculate the average stock figure for the period in question:

Average Stock = Net Sales for the Period ÷ Stock Turn for the Period
Average Stock = $250,000 ÷ 2.1
Average Stock = $119,048

Next calculate the average monthly sales figure:

Average Monthly Sales = Total Sales ÷ Number of months
Average Monthly Sales = $250,000 ÷ 6
Average Monthly Sales = $41,667

Now you can calculate the basic stock figure:

Basic Stock = Average Stock – Average Monthly Sales
Basic Stock = $119,048 – $41,667
Basic Stock = $77,381

Finally, calculate the BOM stock level for November:

BOM Stock for November = Planned Sales for November + Basic Stock
BOM Stock for November = $45,000 + $77,381
BOM Stock for November = $122,381

Practicing What You Have Learned

For each problem, round currency to the nearest whole dollar and percentages or turnover to the nearest tenth.

1. Calculate the basic stock figure for a luggage department that has annual sales of $450,000 and a stock turn annually of 5.0.

2. Calculate the January BOM stock figure using the basic stock method for a department with the following figures:

Planned sales for six-month period	$320,000
Planned stock turn for the period	4.5
Planned sales for January	$ 89,200

Calculate the BOM stock levels for each of the months below for a department with planned sales of $148,000 and an expected stock turn of 2.2.

February	$15,000
March	$22,000
April	$39,000
May	$30,000
June	$24,000
July	$18,000

Stock-Sales Ratio Method of Inventory Planning

A common method of inventory planning, the **stock-sales** ratio calculates the amount or level of stock that should be on hand each month based on the expected sales for that month. The most efficient ratios vary greatly by month, by product category, by store, etc. As with planning sales, most retailers begin with last year's ratio of stock to sales and then adjust accordingly after considering current conditions in the marketplace and last year's performance. (*See 4b on the Six-Month Merchandise Plan Example on your student CD.*)

Stock-sales ratios are usually presented with two decimal places and calculated for a one- month time frame in the following manner:

Stock-Sales Ratio = BOM stock ÷ Net Sales <u>for the month</u>

Application

Calculate the stock-sales ratio for February when the BOM stock for the month is $24,000 and net sales for the month are $14,800.

Stock-Sales Ratio = $24,000 ÷ $14,800
Stock-Sales Ratio = 1.62

It is also possible to calculate the beginning of the month stock level given the stock-sales ratio figure and the net sales for the month:

BOM Stock = Planned Net Sales for the month × Stock-Sales Ratio

Application

Calculate the desired BOM stock level if planned net sales for the month are $33,500 and the stock-sales ratio for the month is 2.7.

BOM Stock = $33,500 × 2.7
BOM Stock = $90,450

For the purposes of the six-month merchandise plan, if last year's stock-sales ratios for each month are available, ratios for the same month this year will be based on last year and any environmental changes that may impact the sales. You can also calculate the stock-sales ratio for each month given the BOM stocks and actual sales for each month.

To determine what stock-sales ratio was utilized in each month last year, simply divide the BOM stock figure for the month by the net sales figure for the month.

Given the following:

	FEBRUARY	MARCH	APRIL	MAY	JUNE	JULY	TOTAL SALES
Last Year	$10,000	$20,000	$25,000	$20,000	$15,000	$10,000	$100,000
BOM Stock	$27,000	$46,000	$49,000	$37,000	$28,000	$22,000	
Stock-Sales Ratio							

Then:

February Stock-Sales Ratio = BOM February Stock ÷ February Sales
February Stock-Sales Ratio = $27,000 ÷ $10,000
February Stock-Sales Ratio = 2.7

March Stock-Sales Ratio = BOM March Stock ÷ March Sales
March Stock-Sales Ratio = $46,000 ÷ $20,000
March Stock-Sales = 2.3

April Stock-Sales Ratio = BOM April Stock ÷ April Sales
April Sales % = $49,000 ÷ $25,000
April Sales % = 1.96

You would complete the calculations for each of the months to find the following results:

	FEBRUARY	MARCH	APRIL	MAY	JUNE	JULY	TOTAL SALES
Last Year	$ 10,000	$ 20,000	$25,000	$20,000	$15,000	$10,000	$100,000
BOM Stock	$27,000	$46,000	$49,000	$37,000	$28,000	$22,000	
Stock-Sales Ratio	2.70	2.30	1.96	1.85	1.87	2.20	

Now that ratios by month for last year have been determined, any adjustments can be made (determined by changing conditions) if necessary and then the BOM stock levels for this year can be calculated.

Application

Using the sales figures and ratios in the previous example, plan the BOM stock levels using the stock-sales ratio method and planning for a 5% increase in total sales for this year.

Remember that the 5% increase gave us total sales for the period of $105,000 and a breakdown by month as indicated in the chart. If you utilize the stock-sales ratios from last year and transfer them into the chart as well, you are now prepared to calculate the BOM stock levels for each month:

	FEBRUARY	MARCH	APRIL	MAY	JUNE	JULY	TOTAL SALES
This Year Planned Sales	$10,500	$26,250	$21,000	$20,000	$15,750	$10,500	$105,000
Stock-Sales Ratio	2.70	2.30	1.96	1.85	1.87	2.20	
BOM Stock							

Then:

BOM Stock for February = Net Sales for February × February Stock-Sales Ratio
BOM Stock for February = $10,500 × 2.7
BOM Stock for February = $28,350

BOM stock for March = Net Sales for March × March Stock-Sales Ratio
BOM Stock for March = $26,250 × 2.3
BOM Stock for March = $60,375

BOM Stock for April = Net Sales for April × April Stock-Sales Ratio
BOM Stock for April = $21,000 × 1.96
BOM Stock for April = $41,160

You would complete the calculations for each month to find the following:

	FEBRUARY	MARCH	APRIL	MAY	JUNE	JULY	TOTAL SALES
This Year Planned Sales	$10,500	$26,250	$21,000	$20,000	$15,750	$10,500	**$105,000**
Stock-Sales Ratio	2.70	2.30	1.96	1.85	1.87	2.20	
BOM Stock	$28,350	$60,375	$41,160	$48,563	$29,453	$23,100	

Practicing What You Have Learned

For each problem, round currency to the nearest whole dollar and ratios to the nearest tenth.

19. If planned sales for the month of October are $17,500 and the planned stock-sales ratio is 2.3, calculate the BOM stock level for the month of October.

20. Calculate the stock-sales ratio for June when BOM stock is $58,200 and sales for the month total $30,000.

21. Calculate the BOM inventory levels for the following months given the planned sales and stock-sales ratios below:

	Planned Sales	**Stock-Sales Ratio**
August	$102,400	3.1
September	$114,000	2.5
October	$ 98,500	2.2
November	$100,600	2.1
December	$104,000	2.0
January	$ 91,200	2.5

Given the following figures from last year, calculate the stock-sales ratio for each month:

	Last Year's Sales	BOM Stock
February	$18,000	$39,000
March	$14,500	$42,000
April	$16,200	$40,000
May	$17,300	$35,000
June	$15,000	$32,000
July	$12,000	$34,000

Weeks Supply Method of Inventory Planning

Because the weeks supply method, by definition, calculates stock on a weekly basis, it is not utilized in the six-month merchandise plan. This method sets the necessary stock level to some predetermined number of weeks of supply of goods. It is most often used with categories that do not experience much fluctuation in sales volume and semi-perishable items where delivery must occur on a very regular basis.

Utilizing this inventory management method requires determining the annual stock turn and then dividing by 52 (weeks in a year) to determine the weeks supply that need to be on hand at any given time.

Application

If the annual stock turn for athletic socks is 13, determine the weeks of supply that should be planned.

Then:

Weeks' Supply = 52 weeks per year ÷ Stock Turn
Weeks' Supply = 52 ÷ 15
Weeks' Supply = 4

Planning Markdowns

Even the most experienced and best retailers have to take markdowns. Whether it is to stimulate sales during uncooperative weather patterns or to move merchandise that turned out to be less than desirable to the customers, retailers plan a markup high enough to cover these types of circumstances. Markdowns, like sales and inventory levels, are based heavily on last year's figures with adjustments for changing internal and external environmental factors (e.g., weather, economic downturn, new stores, new competition, etc.).

For the six-month plan, just as with planning total sales, the starting point is planning the total markdowns for the season based on last year. Generally the buyer looks at the total actual markdown percentage and dollar amount experienced last year and decides whether to alter that percentage up or down based on environmental conditions and the success level of last year's strategies. (*See 5 on the Six-Month Merchandise Plan Example on your student CD.*)

If a buyer plans an increase in sales of 5% (as in the "Calculating Planned Sales by Month" application example above) with a total planned sales of $105,000 and experienced a 12% actual markdown figure last year, then the buyer must decide whether the 12% is a reasonable figure given conditions this year or if it should be adjusted. If the buyer feels that, for a variety of reasons, the markdowns this year should be calculated at 14%, then the total markdown dollars could be determined by multiplying the new total planned sales figure by 14% to get the markdown dollars.

For example:

Markdown\$ = Total Planned Sales for Season × Planned Markdown% for Season
Markdown\$ = $105,000 × 14%
Markdown\$ = $14,700

	FEBRUARY	MARCH	APRIL	MAY	JUNE	JULY	TOTAL SALES
Last Year Actual Sales	$10,000	$20,000	$25,000	$20,000	$15,000	$10,000	$100,000
This Year Planned Sales	$10,500	$26,250	$21,000	$26,250	$15,750	$10,500	$105,000
Last Year Actual Markdowns							12% 12,000
This Year Planned Markdowns							14% $14,700

Calculating Planned Monthly Markdowns

After calculating the total planned markdown figure for this year, the amount of markdown to be experienced during each month of the plan must be determined. As with total planned sales, if last year's markdowns for each month are available, markdowns for the same month this year will be based on last year and any environmental changes that may impact the markdowns. (*See 6 on the Six-Month Merchandise Plan Example on your student CD.*)

To determine what percentage of markdowns occurred in each month last year, divide the markdown figure for the month by the total markdown figure for the season.

Given the following example:

	FEBRUARY	MARCH	APRIL	MAY	JUNE	JULY	TOTAL SALES
Last Year Actual Sales	$10,000	$20,000	$25,000	$20,000	$15,000	$10,000	$100,000
This Year Planned Sales	$10,500	$26,250	$21,000	$26,250	$15,750	$10,500	$105,000
Last Year Actual Markdowns	$1,200	$1,800	$2,400	$2,640	$2,160	$1,800	12% 12,000
Last Year Markdown%							
This Year Planned Markdowns							14% $14,700

Then:

February Markdown% Last Year = February Markdown$ ÷ Total Markdown$
February Markdown% Last Year = $1,200 ÷ $12,000
February Markdown% Last Year = 10%

March Markdown% Last Year = March Markdown$ ÷ Total Markdown$
March Markdown% Last Year = $1,800 ÷ $12,000
March Markdown% Last Year = 15%

April Markdown% Last Year = April Markdown$ ÷ Total Markdown$
April Markdown% Last Year = $2,400 ÷ $12,000
April Markdown% Last Year = 20%

You would complete the calculations for each of the months to find the following results:

	FEBRUARY	MARCH	APRIL	MAY	JUNE	JULY	TOTAL SALES
Last Year Actual Sales	$10,000	$20,000	$25,000	$20,000	$15,000	$10,000	$100,000
This Year Planned Sales	$10,500	$26,250	$21,000	$26,250	$15,750	$10,500	$105,000
Last Year Actual Markdowns	$1,200	$1,800	$2,400	$2,640	$2,160	$1,800	12% 12,000
Last Year Markdown%	10%	15%	20%	22%	18%	15%	
This Year Planned Markdowns							14% $14,700

Now that percentages by month for last year have been determined, any adjustments can be made (determined by changing conditions) if necessary and then the sales for this year can be allocated.

Application

The buyer experiencing the sales figures and markdown figures in the previous example plans a total markdown of 14% but plans to distribute markdowns across the six months in accordance with last year's percentages.

Since you have already calculated the 14% total planned markdowns of $14,700 based on the increased sales figures for this year of $105,000, you can allocate the markdowns for each month as follows:

February Planned Markdown$ = February Markdown% × This Year's Total Markdown$
February Planned Markdown$ = 10% × $14,700
February Planned Markdown$ = $1,470

March Planned Markdown$ = March Markdown% × This Year's Total Markdown$
March Planned Markdown$ = 15% × $14,700
March Planned Markdown$ = $2,205

April Planned Markdown\$ = April Markdown% × This Year's Total Markdown\$
April Planned Markdown\$ = 20% × \$14,700
April Planned Markdown\$ = \$2,940

You would complete the calculations for each month to find the following:

	FEBRUARY	MARCH	APRIL	MAY	JUNE	JULY	TOTAL SALES
Last Year Actual Sales	\$10,000	\$20,000	\$25,000	\$20,000	\$15,000	\$10,000	\$100,000
This Year Planned Sales	\$10,500	\$26,250	\$21,000	\$26,250	\$15,750	\$10,500	\$105,000
Last Year Actual Markdowns	\$1,200	\$1,800	\$2,400	\$2,640	\$2,160	\$1,800	12% 12,000
Last Year Markdown%	10%	15%	20%	22%	18%	15%	
This Year Planned Markdowns	\$1,470	\$2.205	\$2,940	\$3,234	\$2,646	\$2,205	**14% \$14,700**

HINT: It is also possible that you would be given the monthly percentages rather than having to calculate them based on last year. In this case, multiply the percentage by the total sales figure as you did in the last step of the previous example.

Practicing What You Have Learned

For each problem, round currency to the nearest whole dollar and percentages to the nearest tenth.

23. If markdowns for the active wear department at a local store were \$3,080 and net sales were \$27,900, calculate the markdown percentage for the month.

24. If markdowns last year were 15% on sales of \$204,500 and the plans this year are for an overall increase in sales of 4%, what would the total markdown dollars be if markdowns are planned at 17% this year?

25. If the total markdown figure for the ladies' shoe department is $32,600, calculate the markdown dollars for each month given the following percentages:

February	20%
March	15%
April	18%
May	15%
June	18%
July	14%

Planning Purchases

The planned purchases for each month represent the retail value of goods that can be added to the inventory levels each month. The purchases planned are calculated by month and are meant to cover the sales for the month and the markdowns (reductions) that need to be taken, and leave the department or store with some level of ending inventory each month to start of the next month until more merchandise arrives. (Remember that the EOM stock of one month is equal to the BOM stock of the next month. Similarly, the BOM stock of the coming month is equal to the EOM stock of the month before.) (*See 7 on the Six-Month Merchandise Plan Example on your student CD.*)

Now that most of the components of the six-month merchandise plan have been covered, arriving at a planned purchase figure for each month is a simple calculation:

Planned Purchases at Retail = Sales + Markdowns + EOM Stock* – BOM Stock

HINT: The EOM stock figure will be the BOM stock figure of the next month.

The formula not only totals all the sales, markdowns, and ending inventory needed to cover the plans for the month, but also subtracts any merchandise you had at the beginning of the month. You will not need to buy that amount since it is already on hand.

Application

Given the following information, plan purchases for the month of August.

Planned BOM Stock – August 1	$64,000
Planned Sales for August	$63,000
Planned Markdowns for August	$ 7,500
Planned BOM Stock – September 1	$58,000

Then:

Planned Purchases for August = Planned Sales + Planned Markdowns + Planned EOM − Planned BOM
Planned Purchases for August = $63,000 + $7,500 + $58,000 − $64,000
Planned Purchases for August = $64,500

In a six-month plan, this calculation will be completed for each of the six months.

Planning Purchases at Cost

The calculations above plan for the retail value of merchandise that can be added to inventory each month. It is important, however, for the buyer to understand the amount at cost (or that can be spent). For this calculation, we refer back to Chapter 5 where we learned the formula for converting retail value to cost.

Remember:

Cost Value = Retail Value × (100% − MU%)

Application

If the planned purchases for August were $64,500 and the planned markup percentage was 48.5%, calculate the planned purchases at cost.

Planned Purchases at Cost = $64,500 × (100% − 48.5%)
Planned Purchases at Cost = $64,500 × 51.5%
Planned Purchases at Cost = $33,217.50

Practicing What You Have Learned

For each problem, round currency to the nearest whole dollar and percentages to the nearest tenth.

26. Calculate the planned purchases at (a) retail and (b) cost given the following data:

December Sales	$18,000
Markdowns	$ 2,550
BOM Stock for December	$32,000
BOM Stock for January	$41,000
Planned Markup	52%

27. Calculate the planned purchases at retail given the following data:

	Sales	Markdowns	EOM	BOM
August	$17,000	$1,050	$31,000	$36,000
September	$13,000	$ 890	$28,000	$30,500
October	$16,000	$1,200	$40,000	$38,000
November	$21,000	$3,000	$38,000	$45,000
December	$23,000	$2,400	$40,000	$42,000

28. The infants' department planned the following figures for July:

Sales	$38,420
Stock-Sales Ratio	2.3
Markdowns	8%
EOM stock for July	$55,000

Calculate the planned purchases for July.

29. If the planned markup for the infants' department in Problem 28 is 50.5%, calculate the planned purchases at cost.

Calculating Gross Margin Return on Inventory Investment

Now that we have learned to calculate the dollar value of the inventory needed (and thus the amount of money to be spent on inventory), it is important to determine if the dollars are well spent. The gross margin return on inventory investment (GMROII) looks at the relationship of stock turn to profitability rather than net sales. It is possible for the inventory to be turning well but the gross margin might be quite low. In this case, the retailer may prefer to have merchandise in that space that will yield a better margin for the dollar investment. (*See 8 on the Six-Month Merchandise Plan Example on your student CD.*)

Application

If the average inventory value at cost is $25,000 and the gross margin is $89,000, calculate the gross margin return on inventory investment.

GMROII = Gross Margin $ ÷ Average Stock (at Cost)
GMROII = $89,000 ÷ $25,000
GMROII = 3.56

We can also utilize many of the concepts learned previously to help determine the dollar values of the factors necessary for the calculation. GMROII can also be calculated by multiplying the gross margin percentage by the inventory turn and dividing by the cost complement (100% − MU%).

Application

If the gross margin percentage for the electronics department is 43% and the stock turn figure is 3.0, calculate the GMROII that is achieved with a markup of 49.5%

GMROII = (Gross Margin % × Stock Turn) ÷ (100% − Markup%)
GMROII = (43% × 3.0) ÷ (100% − 49.5%)
GMROII = (0.43 × 3.0) ÷ (1.00 − 0.495)
GMROII = 1.29 ÷ 0.505
GMROII = 2.55

Practicing What You Have Learned

For each problem, round currency to the nearest whole dollar and percentages to the nearest tenth.

30. Calculate the gross margin return on inventory investment given the following figures:

Gross Margin	38%
Stock turn	2.8
Markup%	52.5%

31. If the lingerie department had net sales of $45,000 and a gross margin of 41%, calculate the GMROII if the average stock at cost for the department was $39,000.

32. If a department has the following figures, calculate the GMROII:

Net Sales	$38,500
Stock Turn	2.5
Gross Margin	43%
Markup	50%

Chapter 8 Review Exercise A

Complete the blank six-month plan form using the following data:

Sales for the six-month period beginning in August are planned at $350,000 and total markdowns during the period are planned at 18%. The department utilizes the basic stock method for planning BOM stock levels and the average stock figure will be used as the ending inventory figure and expects a turnover rate of 3.0.

MONTH	% SALES BY MONTH	% MARKDOWNS BY MONTH
August	14%	18%
September	20%	20%
October	15%	12%
November	17%	15%
December	23%	19%
January	11%	16%

a. Calculate planned sales by month
b. Calculate total planned markdown dollars
c. Calculate planned markdowns by month
d. Calculate planned BOM stock levels
e. Calculate average stock
f. Calculate planned purchases by month (at retail)
g. Calculate the initial markup percentage and gross margin percentage given the following:

   Operating Expenses = 30%   Planned Profit = 5%   Cash Discounts = 2%

h. Calculate planned GMROII

Six-Month Plan Worksheet

Planning and Authorization

Buyer_____

Merchandise
Manager_____

Date Authorized_____

Six-Month Merchandise Plan

Six Month Merchandise Plan	Spring	February	March	April	May	June	July	Total	EOS Inv.
Department Name _____	Fall	August	September	October	November	December	January		Avg. Stock
From: February 1	LY **Sales $**								
To: July 31	TY Plan								
Department Financial Data	Actual								
LY TY Plan	LY **BOM $**								
	Stock/Sales Ratio								
	TY Plan								
Initial MU%	Actual								
Markdown %	LY **Receipts $**								
Shrinkage %	TY Plan								
(Workroom Cost)	Actual								
(Cash Discount)	LY **Markdown $**								
(Gross Margin)	Monthly MD%								
Average Stock	TY Plan								
Turnover Rate	Actual								

Chapter 8 Review Exercise B

Complete the blank six-month plan form on the next page using the following data:

Sales for the six-month period beginning in February are planned at $245,000 and total markdowns during the period are planned at 15%. Turnover is anticipated at 5.0. The department utilizes the stock-sales ratio method for planning BOM stock levels and the average stock figure will be used as the ending inventory figure.

MONTH	%SALES BY MONTH	%MARKDOWNS BY MONTH	STOCK SALES RATIO
February	15%	13%	2.2
March	18%	18%	1.9
April	15%	14%	2.5
May	19%	16%	2.5
June	21%	20%	2.0
July	12%	19%	1.7

a. Calculate planned sales by month
b. Calculate total planned markdown dollars
c. Calculate planned markdowns by month
d. Calculate planned BOM stock levels
e. Calculate average stock
f. Calculate planned purchases by month (at retail)
g. Calculate the initial markup percentage and gross margin percentage given the following:

Operating Expenses = 25%   Planned Profit = 6%   Cash Discounts = 4%

h. Calculate planned GMROII

Six-Month Plan Worksheet

Planning and Authorization

Buyer _____
Merchandise Manager _____
Date Authorized _____

Six-Month Merchandise Plan

Six Month Merchandise Plan		
Department Name _____		
From: February 1		
To: July 31		
Department Financial Data	LY	TY Plan
Initial MU%		
Markdown %		
Shrinkage %		
(Workroom Cost)		
(Cash Discount)		
(Gross Margin)		
Average Stock		
Turnover Rate		

	Spring / Fall	February / August	March / September	April / October	May / November	June / December	July / January	Total	EOS Inv. / Avg. Stock
LY Sales $									
TY Plan									
Actual									
LY BOM $									
Stock/Sales Ratio									
TY Plan									
Actual									
LY Receipts $									
TY Plan									
Actual									
LY Markdown $									
Monthly MD%									
TY Plan									
Actual									

Chapter 8 Review Exercise C

Complete a six-month plan given the following:

1. Last year's sales totaled $625,000. This year, sales are expected to increase by 4%.

2. Last year's sales figures by month were as follows:

    August = $100,000   September = $112,500
    October = $81,250   November = $125,000
    December = $137,500   January = $68,750

3. Last year's markdown figures by month were as follows:

    August = $14,000   September = $12,000
    October = $11,500   November = $18,000
    December = $19,500   January = $25,000

4. The buyer plans to utilize the basic stock method for planning BOM stock levels.

5. The turnover is planned at 3.0.

6. The average stock figure will be used as the ending inventory for the season.

Six-Month Plan Worksheet

Planning and Authorization

Buyer _____
Merchandise Manager _____
Date Authorized _____

Six-Month Merchandise Plan

Six Month Merchandise Plan		
Department Name _____		
From: February 1		
To: July 31		
Department Financial Data	LY	TY Plan
Initial MU%		
Markdown %		
Shrinkage %		
(Workroom Cost)		
(Cash Discount)		
(Gross Margin)		
Average Stock		
Turnover Rate		

	Spring	February	March	April	May	June	July	Total	EOS Inv.
	Fall	August	September	October	November	December	January		Avg. Stock
LY Sales $									
TY Plan									
Actual									
LY BOM $									
Stock/Sales Ratio									
TY Plan									
Actual									
LY Receipts $									
TY Plan									
Actual									
LY Markdown $									
Monthly MD%									
TY Plan									
Actual									

Six-Month Merchandise Plan
Excel Tutorial

Opening the File

1. Open Excel (usually located on your desktop as an icon or can be accessed from the Start menu in the bottom left-hand corner of your screen).

2. Choose **File>Open** and then locate the file entitled **Lesson8.1.xls**. You can open this file by double-clicking on the filename. Your screen should resemble **Figure 8.1**.

Fig. 8.1:

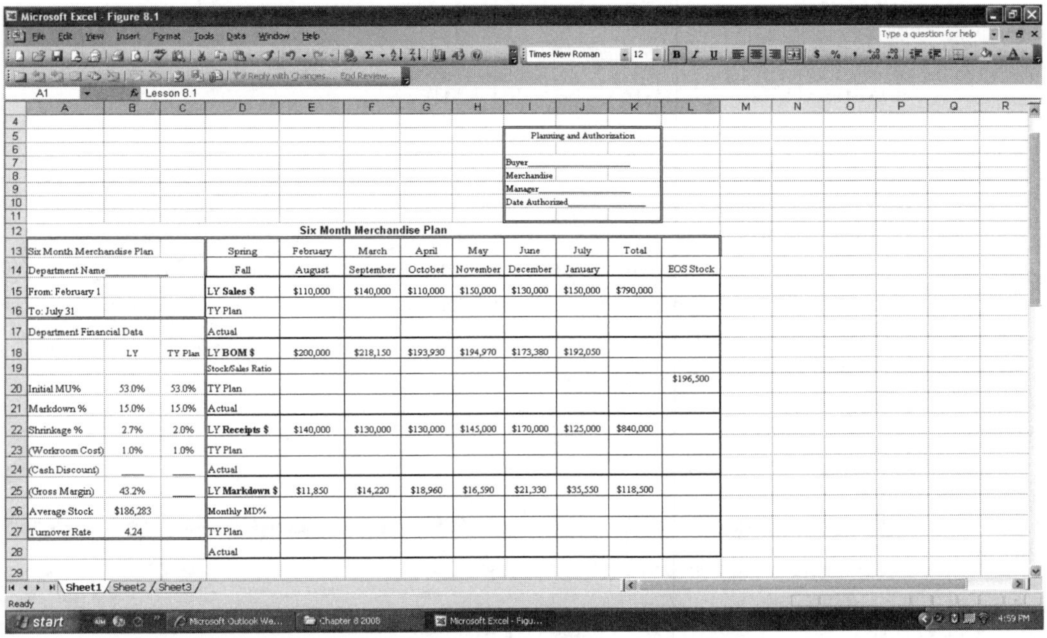

Completing the Spreadsheet

Given the information for last year, plan a 6% increase and complete the six month plan.

3. Enter the formula in Cell **K16** that will allow you to calculate a 6% increase in total sales for TY (this year). Your formula should read = **K15*1.06**. This formula allows you to encompass all of last year's sales (100%) plus 6% more. When you have finished typing the formula, press **Enter** or click on the green check mark (✓) in the formula bar.

HINT: Do not worry about the format of the numbers at this point. You will be asked to format these cells in a later step.

4. Enter the formula in cell **E16** that will allow you to calculate the monthly planned sales for February, taking into account last year's sales for the month and this year's planned increase in total sales. You will need to calculate the percentage of last year's total that occurred in February and then multiply that by this year's total planned sales. Your formula should read = **(E15/$K$15)*$K$16**. (The dollar signs in the formula let the spreadsheet know that those cells are absolute. The reference will not change when the formula is copied.) When you have finished typing the formula press **Enter**.

5. Copy the formula in cell **E16** to cells **F16** through **J16** to complete this year's monthly sales distribution.

Formatting Planned Sales Figures

6. Place your cursor on cell **E16** and hold down the left mouse button. Drag your cursor to cell **K16** to highlight these cells. Once the cells are highlighted, release the left mouse button. First click on Center ≡. Then make sure that your text is **8 pt. Times New Roman**. Then choose **Format>Cells** from the pull-down menu. Select **Currency** and make sure that the decimal places are set at **0**. Your screen should resemble **Figure 8.2**.

Fig. 8.2:

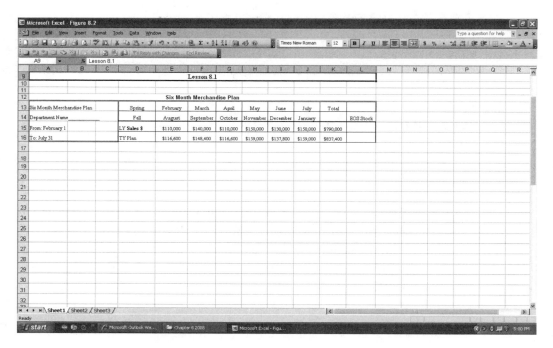

7. Enter the formula in cell **E19** that will allow you to calculate the stock to sales ratio for the month of February last year. Your formula will read = **E18/E15**.

> *HINT:* Once again, we will format these cells in a later step.

8. Copy the formula in cell **E19** to cells **F19 through J19** to complete the stock-sales ratios for the remaining months of the plan.

Formatting the Stock-Sales Ratio Figures

9. Place your cursor on cell **E19** and hold down the left mouse button. Drag your cursor to cell J19 to highlight these cells. Once the cells are highlighted, release the left mouse button. First click on Center ▤. Then make sure that your text is **8 pt. Times New Roman**. Then choose **Format>Cells** from the pull-down menu. Select Number and make sure that the decimal places are set at **2**.

10. Enter the formula in cell **E20** that will calculate TY Plan BOM for February using the stock-sales ratio. Your formula will read = **E19*E16**. (This formula assumes that the stock-to-sales ratios will remain the same as last year. Market intelligence may give the buyer reason to believe that these ratios should be adjusted, but for our purposes here we can assume that the ratios will remain unchanged.)

11. Copy the formula in cell **E20** to cells **F20 through J20** to complete the BOM stock calculations for the remaining months of the plan.

Formatting the BOM Stock Figures

12. **If the cells are not formatted in a similar manner to those above**, highlight cells **E20 through J20**. Once the cells are highlighted, release the left mouse button. First click on Center ▤. Then make sure that your text is **8 pt. Times New Roman**. Then choose **Format>Cells** from the pull-down menu. Select **Currency** and make sure that the decimal places are set at **0**.

13. Calculate total markdown by placing your cursor in cell **K27**. You will note that markdowns are planned at 15% just as they were last year. You can calculate the total dollar markdown amount much as you did the sales increase for this year in step 1. Your formula should read (= **K25*1.15**) to indicate that you need 100% of last year's sales plus an increase of 15%.

Determining the Percentage of Markdowns Monthly

14. When the percentage of markdowns for each month is not specified, we have to base this year's monthly markdowns on last year's allocation. First you need to determine each monthly markdown amount as a percent of last year's total markdowns. Place your cursor in cell **E26**. Then type the formula that divides last year's February markdowns by last year's total markdown amount (= **E25/$K$25**). Again we hold the cell in which the total markdowns are entered constant so that it remains the same when we copy the formula for the other months.

15. Placing your cursor on cell **E26**, copy the formula in cell **E26** to cells **F26 through J26**. These cells should be formatted as percentages. If not, hold down the left mouse button and drag the cursor from **E26** to **J26** to highlight the row. Once the cells are highlighted, release the left mouse button. First click on Center ≡. Then make sure that your text is **8 pt. Times New Roman**. Then choose **Format>Cells** from the pull-down menu. Select Percentage and make sure that the decimal places are set at **0**. Again make sure your text is not bold.

16. Enter the formula in cell **E27** that will calculate this year's monthly markdowns for February based on last year's percentage to total. The formula should read [= **E26*$K$27**]. This formula can then be copied into cells **F27 through J27**. Make sure the cells are formatted in the proper manner following the instructions in step 12. At this point, your screen should resemble **Figure 8.3**.

Fig. 8.3:

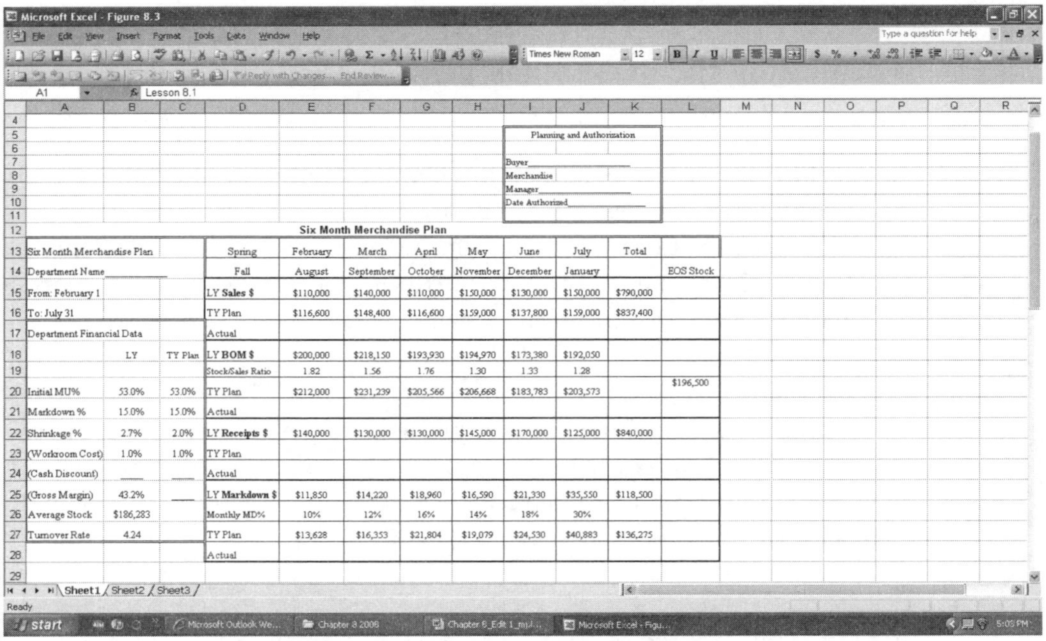

17. Calculate the monthly receipts (OTB) by writing a formula in cell **E23** (= **E15+E27+F20-E20**). This formula can now be copied to cells **F23 through I23**. (You will be asked to enter a formula for July (**J23**) in step 19. If the formatting is not consistent, you will need to complete the formatting process for cells **E23 through I23** just as you did in step 12.)

> *HINT:* Sometimes when you insert a formula in a cell the result will be ######. This usually happens when the cell is not formatted yet (e.g., formatted as a percentage with two decimal places). If the cell is formatted properly, then you will simply need to widen the column using the **Format** menu and then selecting **Column** and then **Width**. You should widen only as much as necessary to reveal the results and remove the ###### symbol. You can also widen by placing your cursor on the dividing line to the right side of the column you wish to widen in the column headings (e.g., the line between A and B). When placed above the line, your cursor will become a two-way arrow pointing left and right with a thick center line. You simply hold down the left mouse button and drag the column to the width of your choice.

18. Enter the formula that will calculate average stock (a.k.a. average inventory) in cell **C26**. This can be done by averaging all the BOM stock figures and the end of season stock figure (E.O.S.). Your formula should read =**(E20+F20+G20+H20+I20+J20+L20)/7**. You will need to format the cell as currency for consistency as above.

19. Calculate July receipts (OTB) for the spreadsheet. The EOM stock figure necessary to complete the Open-To-Buy Formula (OTB) is equal to the BOM stock figure for the next month. Your formula in cell **J23** should read (= **J16+J27+L20-J20**).

20. Enter the formula in cell **C27** that will calculate the turnover for this year. This can be done by placing your cursor in cell **C27** and then enter (= **K16/C26**).

> *HINT:* Remember that **turnover** (a.k.a. stock turn) is defined as the number of times that average stock turns into net sales. Your screen should now resemble **Figure 8.4**.

Fig. 8.4:

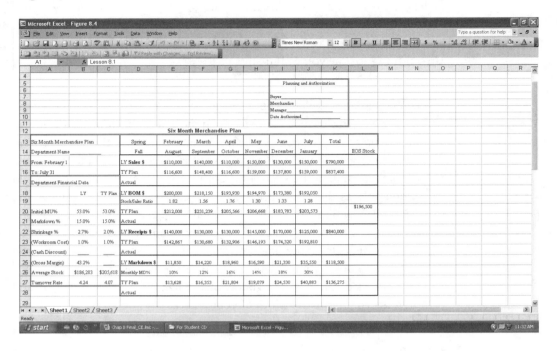

Setting a Print Area and Formatting the Page

21. Now you are almost ready to complete the assignment. First you need to set the area of the spreadsheet that you would like to print. Simply click on cell **A1** and highlight down to cell **L28**. Then select **File>Print Area>Set Print Area**.

22. Next, select **File>Page Setup>Sheet**. You will see that the gridlines and row/column headings have a check mark (✓) beside them. Click on these to eliminate the (✓) and turn off the gridlines and row/column headings. You can select **Print Preview** to see how your spreadsheet will look when printed.

23. When you are through previewing the page, choose **Close**, which will take you back to your working spreadsheet.

Saving Your Work and Printing

24. Before you print and turn in your assignment, save your work. (In fact, you should save **often** during your work session to be sure that you have saved changes made to the worksheet). Save your work on your travel drive and label it **Lesson8.1(your initials here with no spaces)**.

25. Print out the final results as directed by your instructor. Refer to Chapter 1 for instructions if necessary.

Six-Month Merchandise Plan Review Problems Using Excel

Review Problem 8.1

Open the Excel spreadsheet titled **Lesson8.2.xls**. Your screen should resemble **Figure 8.5**.

Fig. 8.5:

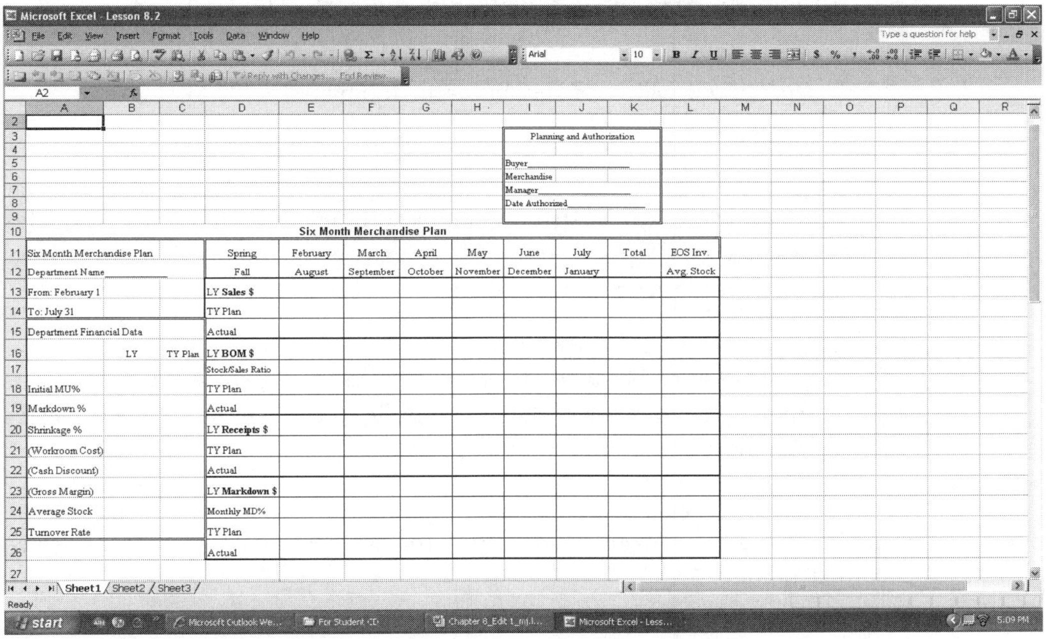

1. Save the blank spreadsheet to your own travel drive and give it an appropriate filename. To be consistent, this file should be named **Review8.1(your initials here with no spaces)**.

In Lesson 8.1, you completed a six-month merchandise plan using the stock-sales ratio to plan BOM stock levels. Use the following data to complete the blank spreadsheet using the basic stock method for planning BOM stock levels.

2. The men's sportswear department has planned sales for this year of $227,000. Monthly sales are planned as follows:

   • February 12%
   • March 18%
   • April 21%

- May 21%
- June 16%
- July 12%

3. Markdowns are planned for 14% for the season and are allocated as follows:

- February 21%
- March 18%
- April 21%
- May 12%
- June 15%
- July 13%

4. Turnover is expected to remain similar to last year at 3.2.

> *HINT:* You will need this figure to complete the BOM stocks using the basic stock method.

5. Make sure your spreadsheet includes completed planned monthly sales, planned BOM stock levels, planned monthly markdowns, planned monthly receipts, average stock, and turnover rate when complete.

> *HINT:* Remember that you will first need to determine average stock for the season in order to determine basic stock. Use the formulas listed at the front of this chapter.

6. Be sure to save your work and print out the final results as directed by your instructor.

Review Problem 8.2

Open the Excel spreadsheet you completed in **Lesson8.1**. Your screen should resemble **Figure 8.4**.

Fig. 8.4:

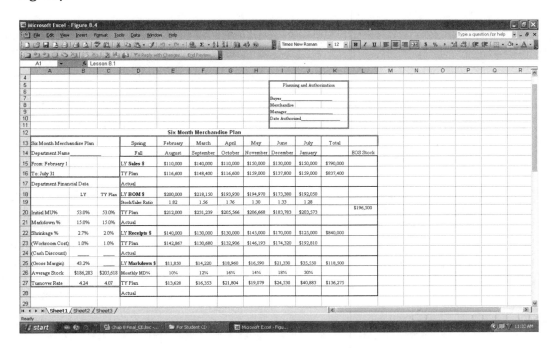

1. Save the spreadsheet to your own travel drive and give it an appropriate filename. This file should be renamed **Review8.2(your initials here with no spaces)**. **Choose File>Save As...** to rename your file.

2. You recently completed this six-month seasonal merchandise plan. When you presented your plan to the divisional merchandise manager, she indicated that with the recent downturn in the economy, she felt the following changes should be made:

   • Instead of a 6% increase, you and she agree that a 4% increase may be a more realistic goal.
   • She also expects the overall markdown percentages to increase by 2%.
   • You also realize during your discussion that Easter will fall at the end of March this year rather than in April as it did last year. Because your department runs a big Easter sale every year two weeks prior to the holiday, you will need to change the markdown percentage for March to the percentage you had allocated to April last year (and then the percentage for March will be allocated to April).

3. Be sure to save your work and print out the final results as directed by your instructor.

4. Your instructor may want you to complete Review Problem 8.6 along with this assignment. Be sure to ask before shutting down your computer and turning in your work.

Review Problem 8.3

Open the Excel spreadsheet **Review8.1(your initials)**.

1. Save the spreadsheet to your own travel drive and give it an appropriate filename. To be consistent, this file should be named **Review8.3(your initials here with no spaces)**. Now you are ready to begin working. Choose **File>Save As...** to rename your file.

For this exercise, you are going to be able to compare the BOM stock levels using the basic stock method to those obtained using the stock-sales ratio method.

2. Given the following stock-sales ratios for each month, calculate the BOM stock levels in the example using the stock-sales ratio method (replacing those figures obtained using the basic stock method).

   - February 2.0
   - March 2.3
   - April 2.8
   - May 3.0
   - June 2.5
   - July 2.0

3. Be sure to save your work and print out the final results.

4. Now, print out the file **Review8.1(your initials)** as well.

5. Comparing the two files, write a brief summary of the significant differences. This information should be typed and the differences can be presented as bullet points.

6. Staple all three printouts together for submission to the instructor.

Review Problem 8.4

Open a blank Excel spreadsheet.

1. Save the blank spreadsheet to your own travel drive and give it an appropriate filename. To be consistent, this file should be named **Review8.4(your initials here with no spaces)**.

2. Using the figures given below for Chad's Card Shop, create a spreadsheet that lists the given figures, yearly average stock figure, turnover for the year, turnover for September, and the stock-sales ratio for December.

	BOM stocks	Net Sales
January	$125,000	$58,000
February	94,000	37,000
March	105,000	47,950
April	102,000	66,500
May	103,300	48,200
June	99,680	37,500
July	92,000	26,700
August	122,000	56,100
September	137,000	60,730
October	104,000	45,800
November	115,000	40,650
December	120,000	78,300
January	89,420	

3. Be sure to give your charts appropriate titles, column headings, and other appropriate formatting.

4. Make sure your work is formatted professionally and is easy to read.

5. Be sure to save your work and print out the final results as directed by your instructor.

> *HINT:* You can use your text and/or previous lessons if you should need to refresh your memory of formulas or formatting techniques.

Review Problem 8.5

Open the Excel spreadsheet **Lesson8.1.xls**.

1. It is probably best that you start by saving the blank spreadsheet to your own travel drive and give it an appropriate filename. This file should be renamed

Review8.5(your initials here with no spaces). Choose **File>Save as** to rename your file.

2. Complete a six-month merchandise plan using the stock-sales ratio to plan BOM stock levels.

   - February 2.0
   - March 2.3
   - April 2.8
   - May 2.5
   - June 2.5
   - July 2.0

3. Sales estimates total an increase of 6% and monthly sales are planned as follows:

   - February 12%
   - March 14%
   - April 22%
   - May 22%
   - June 16%
   - July 14%

4. Markdowns are planned for 18% for the season and are allocated as follows:

   - February 16%
   - March 17%
   - April 18%
   - May 17%
   - June 15%
   - July 17%

5. Turnover is expected to remain similar to last year at 4.2.

6. Make sure your spreadsheet includes completed planned monthly sales, planned BOM stock levels, planned monthly markdowns, planned monthly receipts, average stock, and turnover rate when complete.

7. Be sure to save your work and print out the final results as directed by your instructor.

Review Problem 8.6

For this assignment you will want to open the Excel spreadsheet containing your answers for **Review8.2**.

1. It is probably best that you start by saving the blank spreadsheet to your own travel drive and giving it an appropriate filename. This file should be renamed **Review8.6(your initials here with no spaces)**. Choose **File>Save As...** to rename your file.

2. Your divisional merchandise manager (DMM) has just pointed out that you forgot to calculate gross margin for this seasonal merchandise plan. Calculate the gross margin for this year given the figures for initial markup, markdown, shrinkage, and workroom costs. This year the DMM plans to take advantage of a 3% cash discount.

   HINT: You may want to refer to the formulas in your textbook or at the beginning of this chapter in order to complete this calculation. In addition, remember that to convert a retail figure to cost you simply need to find the cost complement.

3. Be sure to **save** your work and print out the final results as directed by your instructor.

CHAPTER 9

Purchase Performance and Profitability

The six-month merchandise plan represents the retailers' efforts to maintain proper proportion between sales, inventories, and prices in order to turn a profit. In this chapter, we will examine the methods for selecting the assortment of merchandise and analyzing the performance of those selections. The first consideration is the **open-to-buy** figure, which helps to guide the buyer's purchases to meet the needs of the six-month plan without accumulating excess inventory (i.e., over-buying). Open-to-buy is calculated regularly throughout the six-month time period to determine the amount of merchandise needed without exceeding the planned end of the period inventory levels.

Once the dollar open-to-buy figure is calculated, the buyer must decide which merchandise to purchase including the classifications (e.g., men's shoes, women's wear, etc.), subclassifications (e.g., athletic shoes, knit tops, etc.), quantities, colors, and sizes. This process, known as **assortment planning**, can then be analyzed by vendor or classification to determine the success of the buy.

You will find the following concepts and definitions useful.

Assortment plan The planned unit breakdown of purchases into the styles, sizes, and colors that will best meet customer demand.

Model Stock The assortment of brands, styles, sizes, colors, etc. that is determined by the buyer to best suit the needs of the target customers for the business.

Open-to-buy The purchase dollar or unit amount of merchandise remaining to meet planned beginning of the period inventory levels. Remember that the inventory levels at the end of one period are equal to the inventory levels at the beginning of the next period.

You will find the following formulas useful in your calculations:

- **Open-to-Buy = Merchandise Needed − (Merchandise On Hand + On Order)**
- **Open-to-Buy = Planned Sales + Markdowns + Planned EOM Stock − (On Hand + On Order)**

Calculating Dollar Open-To-Buy at the Beginning of the Month

The dollar amount of open-to-buy (OTB) can be calculated by subtracting the merchandise already in stock from the total amount of merchandise needed to fulfill the inventory levels in the six-month plan:

Open-To-Buy = Total Merchandise Needed − Total Merchandise In Stock

The OTB figure differs from the planned purchases figure in Chapter 8 because it takes into account any merchandise that is on order (purchased) but has not yet been received in stock. The planned purchases calculated in the six-month plan provide a guideline for monthly dollar amounts available for merchandise receipt during the month. However, buyers often place purchase orders throughout the month, not just at the beginning. A buyer may make purchases to replace goods that are turning (i.e., selling) well, take advantage of a special buy on desirable goods, or to replenish sizes and colors needed to fill in a broken assortment.

Although it is important to make the most accurate projections possible, consumer behavior is often not easily predicted and the buyer must continually monitor inventory levels and sales. Sales have a direct impact on the open-to-buy figure (i.e., the dollar amount available for new purchases). If inventory levels are lower than planned, it will be much more difficult to sell the remaining merchandise. If inventory levels are higher than planned (i.e., sales are lower than planned), the overstocked levels will leave the buyer with little or no money for new purchases.

Application

Open-To-Buy =   Planned Sales
                         + Planned Markdowns
                         + Planned EOM Stock
                         −Planned BOM stock (Stock On Hand)
                         −Stock on Order

If the actual stock on May 1 is $89,000 and another $13,500 has been ordered but has not been received into stock yet, what would be the OTB for the month given the following plans:

Planned Sales	$72,000
Planned Markdowns	$4,000
Planned EOM for May	$68,000

Then:

OTB = Planned Sales + Planned Markdowns + Planned EOM − BOM − Stock on Order
OTB = $72,000 + $4,000 + $68,000 − $89,000 − $13,500
OTB = $41,500

In the case above, the merchandise needed is equivalent to the planned sales, planned markdowns, and planned end of the month inventory. The merchandise available, or merchandise in inventory and on order, is the beginning of the month inventory and the stock on order.

Calculating Open-To-Buy in the Middle of the Month

The OTB figure can be calculated at any point during a month to determine the balance of purchases necessary to fulfill the buyer's plans for the month. The basic formula is the same as when planning OTB for the beginning of the month, but the figures must be adjusted to take into account that sales and inventory activity that has occurred up to that point.

Application

Determine the OTB figure for October 15 given the following:

BOM Stock for October 1	$16,000
Orders received as of October 15	$2,000
Stock on Order October 15	$2,500
Planned BOM Stock for November 1	$22,000
Planned sales for October	$11,200
Actual Sales as of October 15	$5,500
Planned Markdowns for October	$1,600
Actual Markdowns as of October 15	$900

Then you must first determine the remainder of the merchandise needed and merchandise available, taking into account the activity (e.g., sales, markdowns, and merchandise receipts) that has occurred to date.

The remainder of merchandise needed:

Planned EOM stock for October		$22,000
Planned Sales for October	$11,200	
Actual Sales as of October 15	+$5,500	
Balance of Sales Remaining		+$5,700
Planned Markdowns for October	$1,600	
Actual Markdowns as of October 15	$900	
Balance of Markdowns Remaining		+$700

Remainder of Merchandise Needed as of October 15 $28,400

And the merchandise available as of October 15:

BOM stock for October	$16,000	
Orders Received	+$2,000	
Total Merchandise Handled		$18,000
Actual Sales as of October 15	$ 5,500	
Actual Markdowns as of October 15	+ $900	
Total Reductions to Inventory		−$6,400
Total Merchandise On Hand		$11,600
Merchandise On Order as of October 15		+2,500

Merchandise Available as of October 15 $14,100

Then:

$$\text{OTB for Remainder of the Month} = \underline{\text{Remainder of Merchandise Needed} - \text{Merchandise Available}}$$

OTB for Remainder of the Month = $28,400
                        −$14,100

OTB for Remainder of the Month = $14,300

If the OTB figure is negative (i.e., the merchandise available is higher in dollar value than the merchandise needed to meet plan needs), the buyer has no money remaining for the purchase of goods and she is thought to be "overbought." The only solution is to correct the overbought situation. The buyer might consider canceling any orders that are overdue, taking markdowns on slow moving merchandise, returning goods to vendor where possible, or negotiating the postponement of outstanding orders where possible.

Practicing What You Have Learned

1. A buyer plans sales for the month of April in the women's accessories department at $12,500. The BOM stock for the department on April 1 is $23,000 and there is $4,500 of merchandise on order but not yet received. If markdowns are planned at $850 for the month and the EOM stock is planned at $19,500, what is the OTB figure on April 1?

2. On June 14, the stock on hand is $8,500 with planned sales for the remainder of the month totaling $6,500 and planned markdowns totaling $300 for the remainder of the month. Another $1,700 in merchandise has been ordered but not yet received and the planned EOM stock for June is $6,900. Find the OTB figure for the remainder of June.

    HINT: For this problem, you will not need to calculate the total merchandise on hand because it is given.

3. The women's shoe department reported the following plans for November:

Planned Sales	$15,000
Planned Markdowns	12%
Planned BOM stock for November	$23,000
Planned EOM stock for November	$21,000
Planned Markup	52%

Calculate the OTB at (a) retail and (b) cost. (.)

    HINT: Remember that a retail figure can be converted to cost using the cost complement of the markup percentage.

4. Determine the OTB figure for September 12 given the following information:

Planned sales for September	$102,000
Actual sales as of September 12	$48,000
Planned markdowns for September	$8,500
Actual markdowns as of September 12	$3,800
Planned EOM stock for September	$289,000
Planned BOM stock for September	$256,000
Orders received as of September 12	$14,000
Stock on order as of September 12	$10,000

5. If the total amount of merchandise available exceeds the total amount of merchandise needed, what is the buyer's OTB situation?

Planning the Assortment

Now that the six-month plan is complete and the dollar amount of purchases (OTB) has been determined, the buyer must determine on which merchandise to spend those dollars. The buyer must prepare a detailed plan for spending in each merchandise category for which he is responsible.

Perhaps one of the most important factors impacting whether a six-month plan and OTB figure are successful and adequate is the proper planning of the assortment. The buyer must have the right merchandise, at the right place, at the right time. The "right merchandise" can be translated into the "the right vendors" (i.e., brands) and styles in the right colors, quantities, and sizes. If not, sales may be weak and markdowns may be extensive, leading to a less than adequate open-to-buy or overbought situation. None of these options are appealing to a buyer.

Merchandise assortments must be planned in conjunction with the goals, objectives, and strategies of the retail firm. For instance, is the retailer known for carrying trendy, fashionable merchandise? Is the retailer using a promotional strategy (e.g., offering merchandise at "sale" prices regularly)? Is the retail store known for a wide and shallow product offering with many brands and/or product categories in few colors and/or styles? Alternatively, is the retail store known for a narrow and deep product offering with fewer brands and/or product categories in many colors and/or styles?

Most buyers are responsible for buying specific classifications of merchandise (e.g., men's shoes, misses' dresses, juniors' tops, etc.). The buyers will then break those classifications down into subclassifications (e.g., dress sandals, sweaters, blouses, etc.). Finally, each subclass can be broken down into selection factors consistent with the policies of the retailer (e.g., brands, price points, colors, sizes, etc.). Is the policy driven by branded goods or private label? Does the department utilize several price points in each subclassification? Is the retailer fashion-driven or a basics provider? If a mix of fashion and basics are desirable, in what percentages?

The process of planning the assortment will lead to the determination of a **model stock**. Model stock is that assortment of brands, styles, sizes, colors, etc. that is judged to be best to suit the needs of a target market. If the assortment is planned properly, sales and profits can be maximized. As with the six-month plan, figures from last year and consideration of current market conditions and trends will help to determine the proper assortment.

Application

A juniors' tops buyer is preparing an assortment plan for summer private label tank tops. She plans to carry 100% cotton tanks in two styles, rib knit scoop and racerback. The tanks come in sizes S, M, L, and XL and the buyer's research indicates that jade, amethyst, and bronze will be fashion colors this season. The buyer will also carry basic colors of white, black, and seashell. Last year's distributions are listed below and the buyer expects no significant changes.

Size Distribution			Color Distribution	
Small	10%		Fashion Colors	40%
Medium	25%		Basic Colors	60%
Large	45%			
X-Large	20%		Style Distribution	
			Rib Knit Scoop	70%
			Racerback	30%

If the buyer has an OTB of $5,000 and the tanks cost $5.00 each, create an assortment plan.

First, determine the total number (units) of tanks that can be purchased given the OTB figure and unit cost.

Total Units = $5,000 ÷ $5.00
Total Units = 1000

Next calculate the total units in each style (assuming that both styles will have an assortment of fashion and basic colors).

Rib Knit Scoop Units = 1,000 Total Units × 70%
Rib Knit Scoop Units = 700

Racerback Units = 1,000 Total Units × 30%
Racerback Units = 300

Next the styles must be broken into the proper size distribution:

700 Rib Knit Scoop Tanks × 10% = 70 Small
700 Rib Knit Scoop Tanks × 25% = 175 Medium

700 Rib Knit Scoop Tanks × 45% = 315 Large
700 Rib Knit Scoop Tanks × 20% = 140 X-Large

300 Racerback Tanks × 10% = 30 Small
300 Racerback Tanks × 25% = 75 Medium
300 Racerback Tanks × 45% = 120 Large
300 Racerback Tanks × 20% = 60 X-Large

And then finally, a color breakdown must be determined. This will be heavily based on the buyer perceptions of which colors are likely to be most popular and in which styles. For ease here, we are assuming that the color breakdown will be the same for each style of tank. However, in a real life situation the buyer might reason that since racerback tanks are more often used for exercise, they are more likely to sell in black and white rather than fashion colors.

70 Small Rib Knit Scoop Tanks × 40% = 28 in fashion colors
70 Small Rib Knit Scoop Tanks × 60% = 42 in basic colors

175 Medium Rib Knit Scoop Tanks × 40% = 70 in fashion colors
175 Medium Rib Knit Scoop Tanks × 60% = 105 in basic colors

315 Large Rib Knit Scoop Tanks × 40% = 126 in fashion colors
315 Large Rib Knit Scoop Tanks × 60% = 189 in basic colors

140 X-Large Rib Knit Scoop Tanks × 40% = 56 in fashion colors
140 X-Large Rib Knit Scoop Tanks × 60% = 84 in basic colors

Then the racerback tanks could be assorted in the same manner and the colors would be distributed across the sizes as the buyer sees fit according to trend forecasts.

HINT: You will find this particular task much easier to perform using a spreadsheet rather than by hand.

Vendor Analysis

Once the open-to-buy has been determined, the assortment received, and the merchandise sold, the buyer must analyze the results. This analysis can then be used to assist the buyer in future buying plans and assortment plans. One type of analysis the buyer may find useful is a vendor analysis. Although many factors are relevant in determining which vendors to carry, it is important to determine how each of the vendor's products performed and what steps to take next.

In many cases, a buyer will receive an operating statement, for example, for a hosiery department. The operating statement will compare many financial figures for two or more years for every hosiery department in the chain (if there is more than one store or door). Figures like net sales, gross margin, markup, markdowns, stock turn, sales per square foot, etc. are commonly included.

On such statements there is commonly a median figure calculated for each factor. The median represents the "mid-point" of a range of data. If three stores listed a gross margin of 58%, 55%, and 53%, respectively, then the 55% would be the median figure. For a basic assessment of the productivity of a vendor, a comparison can be made of the results produced by the particular vendor's merchandise and the median for the chain. Useful comparisons include markup, markdowns, and gross margin. If the vendor performed better than the median, the results can be considered successful. If the vendor did not meet or exceed the median, a remedy may be sought.

Remedies include but are not limited to:

Markdown Allowance   An arrangement whereby a vendor agrees to pay (at cost) for all markdowns taken on their merchandise over a stipulated percentage. In most cases, the buyer would desire at least enough to reach the median figure.

Markup Allowance   An arrangement whereby a vendor agrees to provide funding for an additional percentage of markup. In most cases, a buyer would desire at least enough additional markup to reach the median figure.

Application

If the departmental operating statement for the hosiery department reports a median gross margin of 49.3%, median markdowns of 31.9%, and median markup of 58%, analyze the hosiery vendors with the following results:

VENDOR	GROSS MARGIN	MD	MU
TSH	51.3%	56.5%	66.2%
FIT Hosiery	44.5%	26.7%	52.4%
Pearle	46.2%	44.4%	59.5%

For each vendor:

Start by analyzing the gross margin figure.

TSH Gross Margin = 51.3%   Median Gross Margin = 49.3%

If the gross margin is good (i.e., above the median), then although some analysis of the markdown and markup figures may occur, you may want to consider intensifying coverage (buying more) of this vendor. Remember the role that markup and markdowns play in calculating the gross margin. Generally, if the gross margin is higher than the median, as it is with TSH, the markup is high enough to offset any markdowns. In this case, the markdowns for TSH are quite high but the markup is high as well.

FIT Gross Margin = 44.5%   Median Gross Margin = 49.3%

In this case, the gross margin for FIT is significantly lower than the median gross margin. Because there seems to be a problem, analyze the markdowns and markup to see what remedies, if any, might possibly help.

FIT Markdowns = 26.7%   Median Markdowns = 31.9%
FIT Markup = 52.4%   Median Markup = 58%

In this case, the markdowns are low and indicate no problem. However, the markup is much lower than the median. The buyer may want to try to negotiate a markup allowance to correct the margin problems. The markup allowance should be enough to bring the markup at least back to the median of 58%.

For the final vendor, Pearle, start again by looking at the gross margin:

Pearle Gross Margin = 46.2%   Median Gross Margin = 49.3%

Because the gross margin is lower than the median, it is again necessary to investigate the markdown percentage and markup percentage.

Pearle Markdowns = 44.4%   Median Markdowns = 31.9%
Pearle Markup = 59.5%   Median Markup = 58%

For Pearle, the markup percentage is higher than the median and does not appear to be a problem. However, the markdown percentage is significantly higher than the median and therefore a remedy may be desirable. The buyer may wish to try to negotiate a markdown allowance to help bring the markdown percentage down to at least the median markdown figure of 31.9%. This action may help correct the deficient gross margin.

There are some cases where the gross margin will be significantly lower than the median, markdown percentage high, and markup percentage low. In the instance where all factors are not up to or exceeding the median, the buyer may want to consider eliminating the vendor. However, as stated earlier, many factors should be considered before eliminating a vendor. Is the vendor having a weak season but has been a solid performer in the past? Is the vendor a name that your customer expects to see (i.e., is important for maintaining your store image)?

Chapter 9 Review Exercise A

1. What is the OTB figure for the men's sportswear department if the planned purchases total $525,000 and outstanding orders not yet received into stock total $220,000?

2. The toy department has stock on hand October 15 totaling $88,500. If planned sales for the remainder of the month are estimated at $14,000 with planned markdowns for the remainder estimated at $750, what would be the OTB for October with a planned EOM stock of $92,000?

3. The following figures were recorded on July 13:

Planned sales for July	$95,000
Actual sales as of July 13	$48,000
Planned markdowns for July	$6,000
Actual markdowns as of July 13	$2,800
Planned EOM stock for July	$176,000
Planned BOM stock for July	$161,000
Orders received as of July 13	$1,400
Stock on order as of July 13	$3,000

4. You are the buyer for collegiate T-shirts at a local college bookstore. For the upcoming fall semester, you need to purchase an assortment of short-sleeve T-shirts with a budget of $10,000. If the shirts cost $8.00 each and you plan to retail them for $20.00 in an August promotion to new students and their parents, plan an assortment given the following:

Sizes: S (15%), M (30%). L (30%), and XL (25%)
Colors: Blue (35%), White (35%), Gray (30%)

5. If a departmental operating statement indicates a median gross margin of 51%, median markdowns of 28%, and a median markup figure of 55.3%, analyze the following vendors and make a recommendation for negotiations:

VENDOR	GROSS MARGIN	MD%	MU%
A	55%	30%	58%
B	46.8%	27%	52%

Chapter 9 Review Exercise B

1. What is the OTB figure for the juniors' swimwear department if the planned purchases total $125,800 and outstanding orders not yet received into stock total $37,000?

2. The toy department has stock on hand December 10 totaling $122,000. If planned sales for the remainder of the month are estimated at $35,000 with planned markdowns for the remainder estimated at $2,000, what would be the OTB for December with a planned EOM stock of $82,000?

3. The following figures were recorded on July 13:

Planned sales for July	$235,000
Actual sales as of July 13	$105,000
Planned markdowns for July	$16,000
Actual markdowns as of July 13	$9,750
Planned EOM stock for July	$195,000
Planned BOM stock for July	$201,000
Orders received as of July 13	$11,000
Stock on order as of July 13	$0

4. You are the buyer for water shoes at a local beach gift shop. For the upcoming season, you need to purchase an assortment of shoes with a budget of $7,500. If the shoes cost $6.00 each and you plan to retail them for $20.00, plan an assortment given the following:

   Sizes: S (10%), M (35%). L (30%), and XL (25%)
   Colors: Blue (30%), Black (40%), Pink (30%)

5. If a departmental operating statement indicates a median gross margin of 50.5%, median markdowns of 29% and median markup figure of 52.0%, analyze the following vendors and make a recommendation for negotiations:

VENDOR	GROSS MARGIN	MD%	MU%
A	45%	34%	54%
B	49.5%	27%	50%

Chapter 9 Review Exercise C

1. The women's shoe department reported the following plans for April:

Planned Sales	$23,000
Planned Markdowns	18.5%
Planned BOM stock for November	$43,000
Planned EOM stock for November	$41,000
Planned Markup	51.5%

   Calculate the OTB at (a) retail and (b) cost.

2. The buyer in the children's department needs to purchase an order of cardigan sweaters for an upcoming promotion. Her budget is $6,000 and she plans to purchase her assortment from two vendors. Plan the assortment given the following:

   Vendor A: Cost $10.00 will comprise 40% of stock
   Vendor B: Cost $12.00 will comprise 60% of stock

   Size Assortment Plan: S (20%), M (25%), L (25%), and XL (30%)

   Color Assortment Plan: Pink (35%), White (65%)

3. If a departmental operating statement indicates a median gross margin of 53%, median markdowns of 26.5%, and median markup figure of 58.0%, analyze the following vendors and make a recommendation for negotiations:

VENDOR	GROSS MARGIN	MD%	MU%
A	51%	34%	54%
B	54.5%	27%	58%

4. Give two actions that may help a buyer remedy an overbought situation.

Purchase Performance and Profitability
Excel Tutorial

Opening a File

1. Open Excel (usually located on your desktop as an icon or can be accessed from the Start menu in the bottom left-hand corner of your screen).

2. Choose **File>Open**, and then locate the file entitled **Lesson9.1.xls**. You can open this file by double-clicking on the filename. Your screen should resemble **Figure 9.1**.

Fig. 9.1:

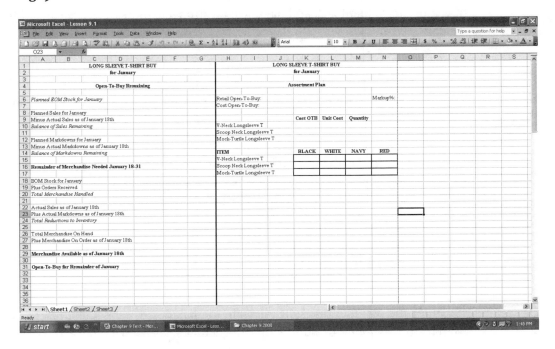

Completing the Spreadsheet

Given the following scenario, calculate the open-to-buy remaining for the month and complete an assortment plan for the merchandise:

3. On January 18, a buyer has an opportunity to purchase a grouping of long sleeve, athletic, T-shirts in V-neck, scoop neck, and mock turtleneck styles. The buyer received an update on sales and markdowns to date:

BOM Stock for January 1	$36,000
Orders received as of January 18th	$6,000
Stock on Order January 18th	$2,000

Planned BOM Stock for February 1	$42,000
Planned sales for January	$16,000
Actual Sales as of January 18th	$7,000
Planned Markdowns for January	$2,000
Actual Markdowns as of January 18th	$1,000

The buyer plans to determine the open-to-buy figure remaining for the month of January with a planned markup of 50% and then create an assortment plan for the merchandise he intends to purchase with the open-to-buy dollars.

The T-shirts will cost $8.00 each for the V-neck and scoop neck and $10.00 for the mock turtleneck. The buyer expects to allocate 30% of the stock to the mock turtle-necks and split the remaining 70% evenly between scoop neck and V-neck shirts. The buyer also feels that black and navy will be stronger colors at 35% each and the other 2 colors (red and white) should constitute about 15% each of the inventory.

4. Enter the sales, stock, and markdown figures in the appropriate cells. Begin by placing your cursor in **F6**, and enter the EOM figure given for January of $42,000. Enter **42,000** with no currency formatting. You will format the spreadsheet later in the exercise.

   HINT: In this example, the EOM figure for January is not given but the BOM figure for February is given. The stock available at the beginning of the month of February (BOM) is equal to the stock on hand at the end of the month of January (EOM).

5. Enter the planned sales figure of **16,000** in cell **E8** and the actual sales as of January 18 of **7,000** in cell **E9**.

6. Enter the formula that will calculate the balance of sales remaining in cell **F10**. This can be done by subtracting the actual sales as of January 18 (E9) from the planned sales for the month of January (E8). Place your cursor in cell **F10** and type =E8-E9.

7. Enter the planned markdowns figure of **2,000** in cell **E12** and the actual mark-downs as of January 18 of **1,000** in cell **E13**.

8. Enter the formula that will calculate the balance of markdowns remaining in cell **F14**. This can be done by subtracting the actual markdowns as of January 18 (**E13**) from the planned markdowns for the month of January (**E12**). Place your cursor in cell **F14** and type =E12-E13.

9. Enter the formula that will calculate the remainder of merchandise needed July 18-July 31 in cell **F16**. This can be done by adding the planned EOM stock for January, the balance of sales remaining (**F10**), and the balance of markdowns remaining (**F14**). Place your cursor in cell **F16** and type **=F6+F10+F14**. Your screen should resemble **Figure 9.2**.

Fig. 9.2:

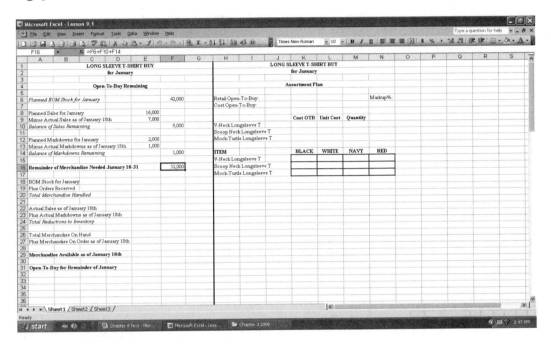

10. Format the data entries. Placing your cursor in cell **E6**, hold down the left mouse button and drag down to cell **F16** to highlight the quantity cells. After highlighting, choose **Center** ▤ to center the data in the cells. While the cells are still highlighted, choose **Format>Cells**. When the menu appears, select the tab labeled **Currency** and indicate on the right that there should be **0 Decimal Places** and a **$ symbol** for each number. You will also want to select **8 pt Times New** Roman font. Your screen should resemble **Figure 9.3**.

Fig. 9.3:

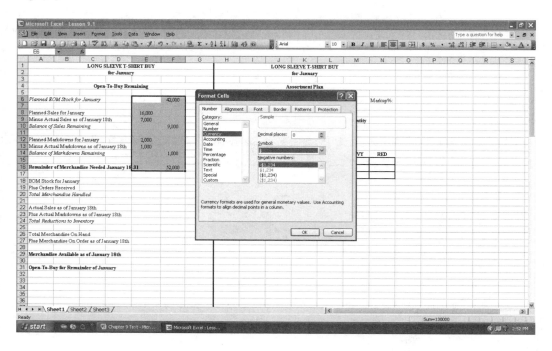

11. Select **OK** to complete the formatting process.

12. Enter the planned BOM stock figure for January of **36,000** in cell **E18** and the orders received as of January 18 of **6,000** in cell **E19**.

13. Enter the formula that will calculate the total merchandise handled in cell **F20**. This can be done by adding the orders received as of January 18 (**E19**) to the planned BOM stock for January (**E18**). Place your cursor in cell **F20** and enter **=E18+E19**.

14. Enter the actual sales as of January 18 of **7,000** in cell **E22** and the actual markdowns as of January 18 of **1,000** in cell **E23**.

15. Enter the formula that will calculate the total reductions to inventory in cell **F24**. This can be done by adding the actual sales as of January 18 (**E22**) to the actual markdowns as of January 18 (**E23**). In cell **F24** enter **=E22+E23**.

16. Enter the formula that will calculate the total merchandise on hand in cell **F26**. This can be done by subtracting the total reductions in inventory (**F24**) from the total merchandise handled (**F20**). Placing your cursor in cell **F26**, enter **=F20-F24**.

17. Enter the merchandise on order as of January 18 figure of $2,000 in cell **F27**.

18. Enter the formula that will calculate the merchandise available as of January 18 in cell **F29**. This can be done by adding the total merchandise on hand (**F26**) and the merchandise on order as of January 18 (**F27**). In cell **F29 type =F26+F27**.

19. Format the data entries. Placing your cursor in cell **E18**, hold down the left mouse button and drag down to cell **F29** to highlight the quantity cells. After highlighting, select **Center** . While the cells are still highlighted, choose **Format>Cells**. When the menu appears, select the tab labeled **Currency** and indicate on the right that there should be **0 Decimal Places** and a **$ symbol** for each number.

20. For effective communication the figures in **F16** and **F29** should be **Bold**. If these figures do not appear in bold, format properly by selecting the cell and touching the bold button **B**. Your screen should resemble **Figure 9.4**.

Fig. 9.4:

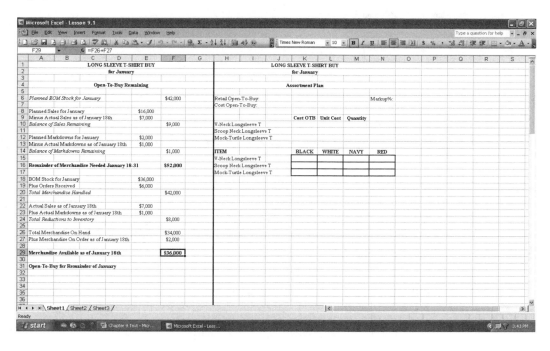

21. Enter the formula that will calculate the open-to-buy figure for the remainder of January in cell F31. This can be done by subtracting the merchandise available as of January 18 from the remainder of merchandise needed. Place your cursor in cell **F31** and enter **=F16-F29**.

22. Enter the retail open-to-buy figure from cell **F31** in cell **J6**. **Center** the figure in the cell.

23. Enter the markup percentage of 50% in cell **O6** and **center** the figure in the cell.

24. Enter the formula that will convert the retail open-to-buy figure from retail to cost. Place your cursor in cell **J7** and enter **=J6*(100%-O6)**. Press **Enter. Center** the data in the cell. Your screen should resemble **Figure 9.5**.

Fig. 9.5:

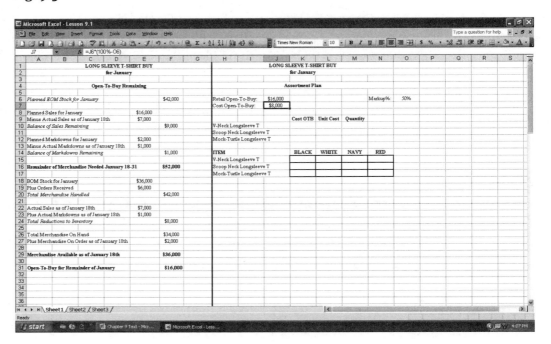

25. Enter the data for the unit cost of each shirt in the appropriate cells. Place your cursor in **L10** and enter the **$8.00** cost of the long sleeve V-neck shirts. Repeat the process in **L11** for scoop neck shirts and in **L12** for mock turtleneck shirts. Remember that the mock turtleneck is slightly higher at $10.00 per unit. **Center** the data in the cells if needed.

26. Enter the formula that will calculate the open-to-buy at cost for each type of long sleeve T-shirt. Placing your cursor in cell **K10, type =J7*.35**. This formula indicates that 35% of the open-to-buy is to be spent on V-neck shirts. Repeat the process for scoop neck (35%) and mock turtleneck shirts (30%) as well.

> *HINT:* If the cells are not centered and formatted as currency with no decimal places when you have completed the formulas, take time now to format them properly.

27. Enter the formula that will calculate quantities of each style that the buyer can carry given the open-to-buy dollars for each. Place your cursor in cell **M10** and enter **=K10/L10**. Copy this formula into cells **M11 and M12** to complete the calculations for each style. Your screen should resemble **Figure 9.6**.

Fig. 9.6:

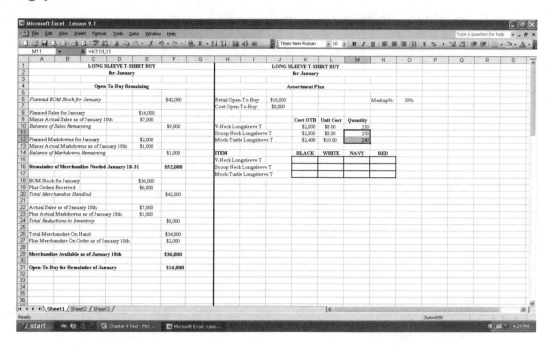

28. Enter the formula that will divide the total quantity of V-neck shirts into color assortments based on the buyer's plans. Remember that the buyer felt both black and blue should constitute 35% of the stock each, while red and white should run 15% each. In cell **K15** enter =M10*.35 to calculate the quantity of black V-neck shirts.

29. Repeat the process in cell **L15**. Enter = **M10*.15** to calculate the quantity of white V-neck shirts. In cell **M15** enter = **M10*.35** to calculate the quantity of blue V-neck shirts needed. In cell **N15** enter = **M10*.15** to calculate the quantity of red V-neck shirts needed.

> *HINT:* It is not possible to buy a fraction of a shirt. Many of the numbers you will calculate need to be converted to whole numbers. Complete the chart and you will format the numbers in a later step.

30. Repeat the process to calculate the quantities of each color for the scoop neck and mock turtleneck shirts just as you did with the V-neck in the previous steps. When the chart is complete it should resemble **Figure 9.7**.

Fig. 9.7:

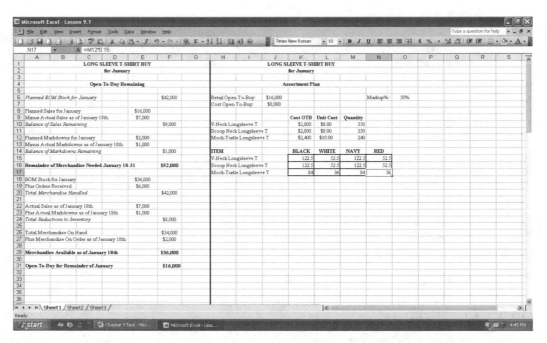

31. Now you are almost ready to complete the assignment and print. First you need to format the item numbers as whole numbers. Beginning in cell **K15** and highlighting through **N17**, select **Format>Cells>Number** and then select **0 decimal places**.

32. Finally, set the area of the spreadsheet that you would like to print. Click on cell **A1** and highlight down to cell **O31**. Then select **File>Print Area>Select Print Area**.

33. Next, select **File>Page setup**. Select the tab labeled **Sheet**. You will see that the gridlines and row/column headings have a check mark (✓) beside them. Click on these to eliminate the (✓) and turn off the gridlines and row/column headings. You can select **File>Print Preview** to see how your spreadsheet will look when printed.

34. When you are through previewing the page, choose **Close**, which will take you back to your working spreadsheet.

Saving Your Work and Printing

35. Before you print and turn in your assignment save your work. (In fact, you should save **often** during your work session to be sure that you have saved changes made to the worksheet.) Save your work on your travel drive and label it **Lesson9.1(your initials here with no spaces)**.

Printing Formulas

36. Your instructor may request that you also print out your spreadsheet assignment showing all the formulas you have written.

Purchase Performance and Profitability Review Problems Using Excel

Review Problem 9.1

1. Save the blank spreadsheet to your own travel drive and give it an appropriate filename. To be consistent, this file should be named **Review 9.1(your initials here with no spaces)**. Now you are ready to begin working.

2. Stacey Potts, the juniors' denim buyer, has just negotiated a special deal with one of her most popular vendors. Stacey returned to the office on July 10 to determine her current open-to-buy figure in order to maximize the volume of jeans that can be purchased at the special price. Stacey hopes to purchase the jeans from the vendor to boost her back-to-school jean inventory. Given the following figures, what is Stacey's current open-to-buy?

BOM Stock for July 1	$146,000
Orders received as of July 10	$17,000
Stock on Order July 10	$10,000
Planned BOM Stock for August 1	$182,000
Planned sales for July	$65,000
Actual Sales as of July 10	$28,000
Planned Markdowns for July	$8,000
Actual Markdowns as of July 10	$3,000

3. Be sure to give your chart appropriate title, column headings, etc.

4. When you have completed your spreadsheet, you will want to set the print area and choose a format for the page that you feel presents the information in a professional manner. You can then save your work one last time and print.

Review Problem 9.2

Open a blank Excel spreadsheet.

1. Save the blank spreadsheet to your own travel drive and give it an appropriate filename. To be consistent, this file should be named **Review 9.2(your initials here with no spaces)**. Now you are ready to begin working.

2. An accessories buyer has $30,000 open-to-buy for the month of September allocated to women's pashmina scarves and wraps. Markup is figured at 55%. Given the following information about last year's allocation and this year's plans, create an assortment plan for purchases that utilizes the entire $30,000.

Last Year's Allocation		This Year's Allocation		Cost
Cashmere Knit Scarf	40%	Cashmere Knit Scarf	50%	$16.00/each
Pure PashminaScarf	40%	Pure Pashmina Scarf	30%	$14.00/each
3-Ply Pashmina Wrap	20%	3-Ply Pashmina Wrap	20%	$22.00/each
Black	50%	Black	40%	
Beige	20%	Beige	20%	
Camel	15%	Camel	20%	
Cranberry	15%	Cranberry	20%	

HINT: Remember that the open-to-buy figure is stated at retail. It must be converted to cost in order for the buyer to determine how much can be spent on the scarves and wraps.

3. Although it is not necessary to include last year's figures in the chart, it is important to notice where the assortment percentages differ and consider the reasons that the buyer felt it necessary to make such changes. Perhaps pashmina scarves are beginning to wane in popularity and the buyer felt it necessary to lower the percentage of inventory that the pashmina scarves comprise. Perhaps fashion colors are strong sellers this year with less emphasis on black and the buyer felt it necessary to change the color allocations to better address consumer preferences.

4. It is not possible to have a fraction of a scarf or wrap. Remember to format all quantities in whole numbers. As a result, the quantities may not add up exactly to the total quantity the buyer intended but it is acceptable to be one or two items over or under the desired quantity.

5. Be sure to give your chart appropriate title, column headings, etc.

6. When you have completed your spreadsheet, you will want to set the print area and choose a format for the page that you feel presents the information in a professional manner. You can then save your work one last time and print.

Practicing What You Have Learned

1. 153.04
2. 222.72
3. 5,255.49
4. 713.12
5. 8.32
6. .66
7. $64.50
8. $979.18
9. 1.452
10. 303.03
11. 45
12. 45.24

13. a. .005
    b. .25
    c. 1.00
    d. .333
    e. 1.25
    f. .75
    g. .60

14. a. 25%
    b. 12,550%
    c. 634.5%
    d. 7.6%
    e. 990%
    f. 1,075%
    g. 10.8%

15. a. 50% (1 ÷ 2 = .5)
    b. 150% (3 ÷ 2 = 1.5)
    c. 75% (3 ÷ 4 = .75)
    d. 3,350% (67 ÷ 2 = 33.5)
    e. 10% (1 ÷ 10 = .1)

     f.   66.7% (2 ÷ 3 = .667)
     g.   80% (4 ÷ 5 = .8)

16. $2,304.00
17. 90/small
     180/medium
     240/large
     90/x-large
18. $165.00
19. $248,395.80

ANSWERS – CHAPTER 2

Practicing What You Have Learned

1.	Net Sales	$453,704	100.0%
	– COGS	245,000	54.0%
	GM	208,704	46.0%
	– OE	195,003	43.0%
	Profit	13,701	3.0%
2.	Net Sales	$575,000	100.0%
	– COGS	279,500	48.6%
	GM	295,500	51.4%
	OE	218,500	38.0%
	Profit	77,000	13.4%
3.	Gross Sales	$1,200,000	
	– CR&A	67,000	
	Net Sales	$1,133,000	100.0%
	– COGS	589,160	52.0%
	GM	543,840	48.0%
	– OE	396,550	35.0%
	Profit	147,290	13.0%
4.	Net Sales	$262,500	100.0%
	– COGS	144,375	55.0%
	GM	118,125	45.0%
	– OE	107,625	52.0%
	Profit	10,500	4.0%
5.	Net Sales	$75,000	100.0%
	– COGS	30,000	40.0%
	GM	45,000	60.0%
	– OE	37,000	49.3%
	Profit	8,000	10.7%

6.	Net Sales	$250,000	100.0%
	– COGS	122,500	49.0%
	GM	127,500	51.0%
	– OE	120,000	48.0%
	Profit	7,500	3.0%

7. Net Sales = $357,143
8. Loss = (–83,0000) or (–6.0%)
9. Profit = $6,273 or 7.0%
10. Loss = (–7,500) or (–3.0%)
11. Loss = (–2,500) or (–1.0%)

12.	Net Sales	$689,000	100.0%
	– COGS	357,000	51.8%
	GM	332,000	48.2%
	– OE	202,000	29.3%
	Profit	130,000	18.9%

13.	Gross Sales	$17,500	
	– CR&A	350	
	Net Sales	$17,150	100.0%
	– COGS	8,440	49.2%
	GM	8,710	50.8%
	– OE	5,660	33.0%
	Profit	3,050	17.8%

14.	Net Sales	$103,700	100.0%
	– COGS	60,700	58.5%
	GM	43,000	41.5%
	– OE	39,889	38.5%
	Profit	3,111	3.0%

15.	Net Sales	$1,750,890	100.0%
	– COGS	892,954	51.0%
	GM	857,936	49.0%
	– OE	875,445	50.0%
	Loss	(–17,509)	(–1.0%)

16. Gross Sales
    – CR&A

Net Sales	$425,000	100.0%
Opening Inv.	$232,000	
+Bill COG	189,000	
+Freight	20,500	
Merch. Handled	441,500	Gross Margin
– Closing Inv.	197,000	$189,500
Gross COGS	244,500	44.6%
– Cash Discounts	9,000	
Net COGS	235,500	
+Alterations	0	
Total COGS	$235,500	55.4%
Salaries (Buying & Selling)	$ 48,000	
Executive Salaries	22,000	
Rent	26,000	
Utilities	18,000	Net Profit
Insurance	8,500	$51,500
Selling Supplies	15,000	12.1%
General Office	8,500	
Operating Expenses	$138,000	32.5%

Net Sales – Total COGS = Gross Margin
100.0% – 55.4% = 44.6%

Gross Margin – Operating Expenses = Net Profit (Loss)
44.6% – 32.5% = 12.1%

17.

Gross Sales	$1,274,300	
– CR&A	89,700	
Net Sales	$1,184,600	100.0%
Opening Inv.	$ 393,100	
+Bill COG	698,000	
+Freight	68,000	
Merch. Handled	1,159,100	
– Closing Inv.	402,000	
Gross COGS	757,100	
– Cash Discounts	38,500	
Net COGS	718,600	
+Alterations	12,300	
Total COGS	$ 730,900	61.7%
Salaries (Buying & Selling)	$ 82,000	
Executive Salaries	69,000	
Rent	98,000	
Insurance	19,000	
Maintenance	15,000	
Utilities	14,900	
Office Supplies	3,500	
Advertising	102,000	
Wrapping & Selling	22,000	
Operating Expenses	$425,400	35.9%

Gross Margin
$453,700
38.3%

Net Profit
$28,300
2.4%

Net Sales – Total COGS = Gross Margin
100.0% – 61.7% = 38.3%

Gross Margin – Operating Expenses = Net Profit (Loss)
38.3% – 35.9% = 2.4%

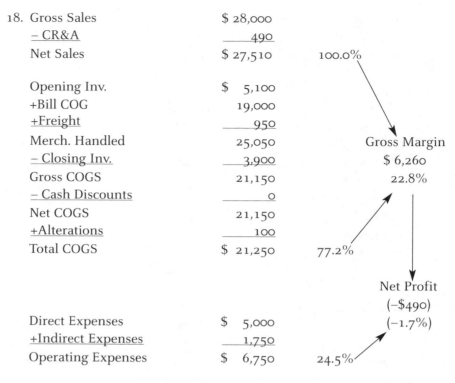

18.

Gross Sales	$ 28,000	
– CR&A	490	
Net Sales	$ 27,510	100.0%
Opening Inv.	$ 5,100	
+Bill COG	19,000	
+Freight	950	
Merch. Handled	25,050	Gross Margin
– Closing Inv.	3,900	$ 6,260
Gross COGS	21,150	22.8%
– Cash Discounts	0	
Net COGS	21,150	
+Alterations	100	
Total COGS	$ 21,250	77.2%
		Net Profit
		(–$490)
Direct Expenses	$ 5,000	(–1.7%)
+Indirect Expenses	1,750	
Operating Expenses	$ 6,750	24.5%

Net Sales – Total COGS = Gross Margin
100.0% – 77.2% = 22.8%

Gross Margin – Operating Expenses = Net Profit (Loss)
22.8% – 24.5% = –1.7% (Rounding may cause students to calculate –1.8%.)

19. Gross Margin = $62,200 or 36.1%

20. Operating Expenses = 46.5%

ANSWERS – CHAPTER 3

Practicing What You Have Learned

1. $189.00
2. $638.40
3. $332.50
4. $13,387.50
5. $2,266.89
6. 56.53%
7. $1,200.00 – $300.00 = $900.00
   $900.00 – $90.00 = $810.00
8. .75 × .90 = .675 or 67.5%
   $1,200.00 × 67.5% = $810.00

9. $4,050.00
10. $11,154.46
11. $637.50 (Buying more and taking cash discount results in lower billed cost.)
12. $1538.90
13. .75 × .85 ×.95 = .6056 or 60.6%
    .60 × .90 = .54 = 54%
    40% and 10% is the preferred discount
14. $1,430.75
15. $404.98
16. $2,232.50
17. $424.86
18. No, the invoice must be paid by November 20.
19. $1,823.04
20. $3,961.65

	Cash Discount	Net Payment
21.	April 11	May 1
22.	May 10	May 30
23.	July 20	August 9
24.	November 25	December 15
25.	August 9	August 29
26.	October 11	October 31
27.	May 10	May 30
28.	January 11	January 31
29.	March 27	April 16

30. The cash discount period ended before the merchandise was received in this case. The buyer should negotiate *at least* ROG terms but preferably extra dating or advanced dating.

31. $953.37
32. $2,238.72
33. $825.00
34. $617.30
35. $6,116.70
36. $815.21
37. $4,173.91
38. $260.22
39. $11,688.54
40. $232.18
41 a. the vendor
    b. the vendor
42. a. the buyer must reimburse the vendor
     b. the buyer

ANSWERS – CHAPTER 4

Practicing What You Have Learned

1. 21.1%
2. $1,184.40
3. $93,125.00
4. $23,100
5. 9.1%
6. $8,500.00
7. $2,075
8. Net MD = $375.00, Total MD = $1,000.00, MD Cancellations = $625.00
9. Net MD = $1,137.50, Total MD = $1,750.00, MD Cancellations = $612.50
10. Net MD = $947.00, Total MD = $1,200.00, MD Cancellations = $253.00
11. Net MD = $1,122.00, Total MD = $1,530.00, MD Cancellations = $408.00
12. $87.20
13. Sheila pays $212.50; Amy pays $187.50.
14. $306.74
15. $747.151

ANSWERS – CHAPTER 5

Practicing What You Have Learned

1. $25.00
2. $80.00
3. $84.00
4. $135.00
5. $63.00
6. $609.00
7. $19.99
8. $55.00
9. $3.00
10. a. 66.7%
    b. 200%
11. a. 45%
    b. 81.8%
12. a. 56%
    b. 127.3%
13. $437.50
14. $48.00
15. $38.75
16. $15.75
17. $559.65
18. $119.60

ANSWERS – CHAPTER 6

Practicing What You Have Learned

1. 50.8%
2. 64.4%
3. 51.5%
4. 41.2%
5. 50.8%
6. 46.6%
7. 56.1%
8. 53.8%
9. 51.9%
10. 52.8%
11. 49.9%
12. MMU = 24.4% GM = 26.5%
13. MMU = 43.8%
14. MMU = 31.2%
15. GM = 35.4%
16. $9.84 per pair
17. 62.9%
18. $5.25 each
19. $21.00 each
20. 60.2%

ANSWERS – CHAPTER 7

Practicing What You Have Learned

1. $49,000
2. $168,450
3. $36,300
4. $56,700
5. $130,800
6. –$1,400 (overage)
7. $2,000 (shortage)
8. –$950 (overage)
9. $1,200 (shortage)
10. – $3,500 (overage)
11. $1,200
12. 3.1%
13. $2,280
14. $= –$1,400 (overage)% = 3.6%
15. $2,190

16. $56.052
17. TMH at retail = $331,500; Closing Book Inventory at cost = $143,800
18. $134,400
19. a. Closing Book Inv. At Retail = $125,850; Closing Book Inv. At Cost = $56,255
    b. Gross Margin = 54.5%
    c. $1,650 shortage
20. a. Cumulative MU% = 54.5%
    b. Maintained MU% = 51.3%
    c. Gross Margin% = 53.0%

ANSWERS – CHAPTER 8

Practicing What You Have Learned

1. 5.5%
2. $244,400
3. 11.5%
4. 2.4%
5. $169,776
6. August = $39,200   September = $56,000
   October = $42,000   November = $50,400
   December = $64,400   January = $28,000
7. February = $16,380   March = $18,720
   April = $21,060   May = $29,250
   June = $25,740   July = $18,720
8. August = $5,088   September = $6,106
   October = $9,158   November = $11,194
   December = $12,720   January = $6,614

9. a. 12.5%
   b. February = $46,200   March = $25,200
      April = $25,200   May = $31,500
      June = $52,500   July = $29,400
10. August = $20,700   September = $24,840
    October = $16,560   November = $27,600
    December = $34,500   January = $13,800

11. $11,375
12. 1.6
13. 2.6
14. $141,182
15. $138,462
16. $15,000
17. $106,978

18. February = $57,606   March = $64,606
    April = $81,606   May = $72,606
    June = $66,606   July = $60,606
19. $40,250
20. 1.9
21. August = $317,440   September = $285,000
    October = $216,700   November = $211,260
    December = $208,000   January = $228,000
22. February = 2.2   March = 2.9
    April = 2.5   May = 2.0
    June = 2.1   July = 2.8
23 11.0%
24. $36,156
25. February = $6,520   March = $4,890
    April = $5,868   May = $4,890
    June = $4,868   July = $4,564
26. $93,550 at retail, $44,904 at cost
27. August = $13,050   September = $11,390
    October = $19,200   November = $17,000
    December = $23,400
28. $8,128 at retail
29. $4,023 at cost
30. 2.2
31. 0.5
32. 2.2

ANSWERS – CHAPTER 9

Practicing What You Have Learned

1. $5,350
2. $3,500
3. a. $14,800 at retail
   b. $7,104 at cost
4. $41,800
5. The buyer is overbought with no OTB available.

Glossary

Advanced dating or **Postdating**   A situation where the vendor places a future date on the invoice and then offers regular dating terms.

Anticipation   An extra discount sometimes offered as an incentive for the retailer to pay as early as possible in an extended cash discount period. When offered and received, this discount is added to the cash discount and deducted from the billed cost. This is the only time discounts will be added together.

Assortment plan   The planned unit breakdown of purchases into the styles, sizes, and colors that will best meet customer demand.

Average inventory or **Average stock**   The average level of inventory in stock across a given time period. Average stock can be calculated by adding the beginning of the month (BOM) stock levels for each month under consideration plus the end of the month (EOM) figure for the final month (a.k.a. End of Period or End of Season Inventory) and then dividing by the number of months under consideration plus one.

Average markup   The average or mean markup taken on a group of merchandise where portions of the merchandise carry different or varying markups.

Average stock or **Average inventory**   The average level of inventory in stock across a given time period. Average stock can be calculated by adding the beginning of the month (BOM) stock levels for each month under consideration plus the end of the month (EOM) figure for the final month (a.k.a. end of period or end of season inventory) and then dividing by the number of months under consideration plus one.

Basic stock   A determination of the level of merchandise that should be maintained at all times in addition to the planned sales for the month given an estimated rate of stock turn.

Beginning of the month (BOM) stock   The total stock on hand in dollars at the beginning of the month. (The BOM stock level for a given month is the equivalent of the end of the month stock level from the previous month.)

Billed cost   Purchase price as it appears on the invoice.

BOM stock   *See* Beginning of the month

Billed percent   *See* On Percent

BOOK INVENTORY or **PERPETUAL INVENTORY**   A running total and record of the retail value of merchandise in the department or store including all movement of merchandise in and out of the department or store.

CASH DISCOUNT   The most common type of discount. Cash discounts are offered as an incentive for the buyer to pay the amount due early. The time frame for taking the cash discount is often dependent on the dating terms agreed upon during the negotiation process.

CASH ON DELIVERY (COD) DATING   Payment must be rendered in full when the goods are delivered.

CHARGES REVERSED   Used in conjunction with one of the negotiated FOB terms, the term indicates that the vendor will maintain ownership of the goods and incur the risks of transportation to the negotiated destination, but the buyer will pay the transportation charges from the factory.

CLOSING INVENTORY AT COST   The cost value of the merchandise remaining in stock at the end of the period.

COD DATING   *See* Cash on delivery

COST or **COST PRICE**   The amount a retailer pays a vendor for merchandise purchased.

COST COMPLEMENT   The difference between 100% and the markup percent. (100% is often referred to as the retail percent.)

COST OF GOODS SOLD (A.K.A. COST OF MERCHANDISE SOLD)   Billed cost of the merchandise, plus freight or transportation costs, plus alteration/workroom costs, minus any cash discounts earned.

COST PRICE or **COST**   The amount a retailer pays a vendor for merchandise purchased.

CUMULATIVE MARKUP   The markup percentage achieved on a group of goods over a period of time. Usually all goods available plus any new purchases received for an extended period of time. Does not include markdowns.

CUSTOMER RETURNS AND ALLOWANCES (CUSTOMER R&A)   Returns are goods returned to the store after initial purchase. Allowances are price adjustments made for customers when goods are found to be slightly damaged or soiled to allow customers to have the damage repaired (e.g. have a garment cleaned to remove a makeup stain or replace a button). These are the only percentages in a skeletal profit and loss statement that are based on gross sales.

DATING   The negotiated length of time the retailer has to pay the invoice with or without the cash discount.

DELIVERED COST   The purchase price as it appears on the invoice plus any transportation costs incurred.

DIRECT EXPENSES   Department expenses that are directly related to that department's business. These expenses would cease to exist if the department ceased to exist. Usually includes such expenses as sales personnel salaries, selling supplies, travel for buying staff, and advertising expenditures for department.

EMPLOYEE DISCOUNT   A percentage reduction off the retail price of merchandise often extended as a fringe benefit to personnel.

END OF MONTH (EOM) DATING   The cash discount period is offered 10 days from the end of the month in which the merchandise is invoiced. Traditionally, invoices dated after the 25th of the month allow 10 days from the end of the following month.

End of the month (EOM) stock   The total stock on hand in dollars at the end of the month. (The EOM stock level for a given month is the equivalent of the beginning of the month stock level for the coming month.)

EOM dating   *See* End of month dating

EOM stock   *See* End of month stock

Extra dating   The cash discount is calculated from the date of invoice but a specific number of extra days are added to the cash discount period. Otherwise the net (full amount) of the bill is due within 20 days after the last day to take the cash discount.

Final selling price   The price at which merchandise is sold. The price obtained could be equal to the initial retail price but often reflects a reduction from the initial retail price.

FOB Destination   Term commonly used to indicate that the vendor is responsible for all transportation costs and owns the merchandise until it reaches a point designated by the retailer. This specified destination is commonly the store or a warehouse utilized by the retailer but could also be a port of entry into the country. This term can also be written as *FOB Store, FOB Warehouse, FOB City,* or *FOB Port.* All are destination points that the buyer may negotiate. The terminology indicates that the vendor pays for transportation up to the destination selected and then the buyer must pay to transport the merchandise from that point to the final point of sale (usually the store).

FOB Factory   Term commonly used to indicate that the buyer is responsible for all transportation costs and owns the merchandise from the moment it leaves the factory.

Free on Board (FOB)   The term used to express the terms of transportation. Generally followed by a location or destination, the term indicates that transportation is "free" to the buyer to the location or destination stated.

Freight Prepaid   Most commonly used in conjunction with one of the negotiated FOB terms (e.g., FOB Factory, Freight Prepaid). If, under the negotiated terms, the buyer is responsible for transportation costs, the vendor must be reimbursed when the costs for the merchandise are paid.

Gross cost of merchandise sold   The total merchandise handled at cost (which includes opening inventory, purchases, freight, etc.) minus the ending inventory at cost (which takes into account sales, reductions, customer returns, etc.)

Gross margin   Sometimes referred to as *gross profit*, this figure is obtained by subtracting the cost of goods sold from net sales. Gross margin can also be calculated by adding profit and expenses if the two figures are given.

Gross margin return on inventory investment (GMROII)   The number of time that average stock turns into gross margin.

Gross profit   An alternative term used to describe gross margin.

Gross sales   The total sales for any given period *before* deducting the retail value of goods returned to the store and/or making price allowances.

Hot items   Highly desirable items experiencing a surge in sales for a given time period.

INDIRECT EXPENSES   Expenses that are incurred that are not directly related to a specific department. Examples might include store maintenance and security, senior executive salaries, and insurance. Such expenses are usually distributed among the individual departments on the basis of sales volume.

INITIAL MARKUP   The difference between the billed cost of merchandise as stated on the invoice and the initial retail price placed on the item. (Remember that the billed cost reflects any quantity and/or trade discounts but not any applicable cash discount.)

INITIAL RETAIL or **ORIGINAL RETAIL**   The original retail price at which merchandise is offered for sale.

LANDED COST   The purchase price as it appears on the invoice plus any transportation costs incurred and any import/duty costs incurred.

LOADING   An adjustment to the cost price of an item to allow for an additional cash discount. A retailer or store may prefer a standard cash discount that is greater than the cash discount being offered by the vendor. The price of the item is adjusted upward, or *loaded*, in order to accommodate the higher cash discount, while resulting in the same payment to the vendor. (Loaded Cost = Net Cost ÷ Complement of the Desired Cash Discount.)

MAINTAINED MARKUP   The difference between net sales and the cost of merchandise sold. Does not include cash discounts, alterations, etc. While maintained markup is related to gross margin, the latter is adjusted for cash discounts received and any alteration/workroom expenses encountered.

MARKDOWN   A reduction in the original or previous price of an item or a group of items.

MARKDOWN ALLOWANCE   An arrangement whereby a vendor agrees to pay (at cost) for all markdowns taken on merchandise over a stipulated percentage.

MARKDOWN CANCELLATION   An increase in the retail price of an item or group of items that offsets all or a portion of a previously taken markdown.

MARKUP   The difference between the amount the retailer pays a vendor and the price of merchandise sold to the end consumer. Can be stated in dollars or percentage format.

MARKUP ALLOWANCE   An arrangement whereby a vendor agrees to provide funding for an additional percentage of markup.

MARKUP DOLLARS   The dollar difference between the cost price and the retail price of merchandise sold to the end consumer.

MEDIAN   The middle figure or value in an ascending or descending list of figures or values.

MODEL STOCK   The assortment of brands, styles, sizes, colors, etc. that is determined by the buyer to best suit the needs of the target customers for the business.

NET (TERMS)   The full amount due to a vendor when the cash discount is not taken.

NET MARKDOWN   The difference between total markdowns and any markdown cancellations that occur.

NET SALES   The total sales for any given period *after* returns and/or price allowances are deducted. Always equal to 100% in a skeletal profit and loss statement.

On percent or **Billed percent**   The on percent or billed percent is the complement of a discount percentage given. For example, if a discount of discount of 40% is given, then the complement would be 100% − 40% or 60%. Therefore, the on percent or billed percent is equal to 60%.

Open-to-buy   The purchase dollar or unit amount of merchandise remaining to meet planned beginning of the period inventory levels. Remember that the inventory levels at the end of one period are equal to the inventory levels at the beginning of the next period.

Opening inventory   The retail value of the merchandise at the beginning of the period.

Opening inventory at cost   The cost value of the merchandise at the beginning of the period.

Operating expense   The expenses incurred by the retailer during any given period. Usually divided into direct and indirect expenses on a profit and loss statement.

Overage Retail dollar difference between the book inventory (numerical or statistical count) and the physical inventory (actual physical count) of merchandise where the physical inventory indicates that there is more merchandise on hand than the books indicate.

Perpetual inventory or **Book inventory**   A running total and record of the retail value of merchandise in the department or store including all movement of merchandise in and out of the department or store.

Physical inventory   The retail value of all goods physically counted in the store or department at a given point in time.

Prestige price zone   The highest price zone utilized by retailers, which adds to the "prestige" or standing of the merchandise.

Price lining   The practice of determining retail price points that may be attractive to the target customer.

Price zone   A group of price lines that may appeal to the target customer. Common price zones are promotional (low), volume (medium), and prestige (high).

Profit and loss statement (a.k.a income statement)   A summary financial statement prepared at the end of a specified period that indicates the relationship of the sales, cost of merchandise, and expenses to the profitability of an organization or business. These statements can also be prepared at the store or department level if desired.

Promotional price zone   Lowest price zone utilized by retailers to drive business to the store.

Purchases   Billed cost of new goods purchased during the period, minus any returns to, or allowances from, the vendor.

Quantity discount   Percentage of the billed cost that is deducted when a pre-arranged quantity of merchandise is purchased. Often used as an incentive to get the buyer to commit to a larger quantity of goods from one vendor.

Regular dating   The cash discount period is calculated from the date of invoice (which is usually the same date that the merchandise is shipped). Example 2/10, n/30 where a 2% cash discount can be taken if payment is made within 10 days of the date of invoice, otherwise the net amount (payment in full) is due within 30 days of the date of invoice.

Retail or **retail price**   The price of merchandise to the end consumer.

Retail method of inventory   An accounting method used by retailers that assesses the retail value of merchandise in stock and allows for determination of the cost value.

Retail price or **Retail**   The price of merchandise to the end consumer.

Reductions   Any factor that reduces the value of the inventory a retailer carries. Can include markdowns, shortages in stock, (e.g. shipping shortage, damaged goods, theft), employee discounts, etc.

Receipt of goods (ROG) dating   The cash discount period is offered for 10 days after the goods are received. In this case, the date of the invoice is not used in the calculation of the discount period.

ROG dating   *See* Receipt of goods

Series discount A series of trade discounts deducted from the list price. *See* Trade Discount

Shortages   Retail dollar difference between the book inventory (numerical or statistical count) and the physical inventory (actual physical count) of merchandise, where the book inventory indicates that there is more merchandise on hand than is actually found when the physical inventory count is completed.

Skeletal profit and loss statement   A shortened version of a profit and loss statement that allows quick calculation of profit and loss at any given time. The skeletal statement (a.k.a. skeletal P&L) utilizes net sales, cost of merchandise sold, and expenses to attain the gross margin, also known as gross profit, and profit figures.

Stock-Sales ratio   The relationship of the BOM stock (i.e., stock on hand at the beginning of the month) to the planned sales for the month.

Stock turn or **Turnover**   The number of times that the average stock turns into net sales. Commonly calculated on a six-month basis to provide an assessment of the success or efficiency of the merchandising strategy.

Total cost of merchandise sold   The gross cost of merchandise sold minus any cash discounts received plus any alteration costs incurred.

Trade discount   A percentage or series of percentages deducted from the list price. These discounts are not dependent on when the invoice is paid. If expressed as a series (for example, 40%, 15%, 10%), they must be taken individually and in order. You cannot add these discounts together (for example, a discount of 40%, 15%, 10% *is not* equivalent to a discount of 65%.)

Turnover (a.k.a. Stock turn)   The number of times that the average stock turns into net sales. Commonly calculated on a six-month basis to provide an assessment of the success or efficiency of the merchandising strategy.

Volume price zone   A moderate or medium price zone, which usually constitutes the majority of the business for a retailer.

Index